ROUGH
GUIDES

D0626859

POCKET **ROUGH GUIDE**
LONDON

Updated by
ALICE PARK

CONTENTS

LONDON

London is a very big city: stretching for more than thirty miles from east to west, it has a population of just over 8.5 million. Ethnically and linguistically, it's Europe's most diverse metropolis, offering cultural and culinary delights from right across the globe. The city dominates the national horizon, too. This is where most of the country's news and money are made, it's where central government resides and, as far as its inhabitants are concerned, provincial life begins beyond the circuit of the city's orbital motorway.

View from the Sky Garden

On the Regent's Canal, Little Venice

For the visitor, it's a thrilling destination. The biggest problem for newcomers is that the city can seem bewilderingly amorphous, with no single predominant focus of interest. Londoners tend to cope with all this by compartmentalizing their city, identifying strongly with the neighbourhoods in which they work or live, just making occasional forays into the West End, London's shopping and entertainment heartland. As a visitor, the key to enjoying London, then, is not to try and do everything in a single visit – concentrate on one or two areas and you'll get a lot more out of the place.

The capital's traditional sights – Big Ben, Westminster Abbey, Buckingham Palace, St Paul's Cathedral and the Tower of London – continue to draw in millions of tourists every year. Things change fast, though, and the regular emergence of new attractions ensures that there's plenty to do even for those who've visited before. London's world-class museums and galleries – of which there are dozens – are generally forward-looking places, often re-designing and re-imagining their spaces (see box below), while the tourist and transport infrastructure is generally pretty good, if crowded.

What's new

London's museums are masters of reinvention, with even the most established ones rolling out new exhibitions, refits and redesigns. Both an entertaining ride and fascinating insight into the workings of the city, the Mail Rail (see page 77) is one of London's most appealing new attractions. Older subterranean intrigue can be found at the re-created Roman Mithraeum (see page 82), while the new extension at the V&A (see page 125), remodelled galleries at the Science Museum (see page 124) and refurbished Hayward Gallery (see page 104) all provide reasons for return visits.

When to visit

Despite the temperateness of the English climate, it's impossible to say with any degree of certainty that the weather will be pleasant in any given month. While always unpredictable, English summer days tend to range from a comfortable 22°C up to 30°C, while the winters (average daily temperature 6–10°C) don't get very cold – though they're often wet. However, whenever you come, be prepared for all eventualities: it has been known to snow at Easter and rain all day on August bank holiday weekend. As far as crowds go, tourists stream into London pretty much all year round, with peak season from Easter to October and in the run-up to Christmas, when you'll need to book your accommodation well in advance.

Monuments from the capital's glorious past are everywhere, from medieval banqueting halls and the great churches of Christopher Wren to the eclectic Victorian architecture of the triumphalist British Empire. There's also much enjoyment to be had from the city's quiet Georgian squares, the narrow alleyways of the City of London, the riverside walks and the assorted quirks of what is still identifiably a collection of villages. And urban London is offset by surprisingly large expanses of greenery: Hyde Park, Green Park and St James's Park are all within a few minutes' walk of the West End, while, further afield, you can enjoy the more expansive parklands of Hampstead Heath and Richmond Park.

You could spend days just shopping in London, too, mixing with the upper classes in the "tiara triangle" around Harrods, or sampling the offbeat weekend markets of Portobello Road, Camden and Spitalfields. The music, clubbing and LGBTQ scenes are second to none, and mainstream arts are no less exciting, with regular opportunities to catch first-rate theatre companies, dance troupes, exhibitions and opera. The city's pubs have always had heaps of atmosphere, but food is a major attraction too, with over sixty Michelin-starred restaurants and the widest choice of cuisines on the planet.

Rope Walk, Maltby Street Market in Bermondsey

Where to...

Eat

With thousands of cafés, pubs and restaurants, you're never far from a good place to fill your stomach. For the widest choice, make for **Soho**, nearby **Covent Garden** or **East London**, where you'll find everything from Italian coffee houses to Japanese noodle stands. The city's food scene is global, exciting and ever-changing. Some districts retain distinct specialities, whether Portuguese in **Ladbroke Grove** or Bangladeshi in **Tower Hamlets**. London's also a great place for snacking, with a vibrant street-food culture: **Borough Market**, **Maltby Street**, **Camden Market**, **Spitalfields** and **Shoreditch** are all good hunting grounds.
OUR FAVOURITES: The Ivy Café see page 50, Dishoom see page 70, Duck and Waffle see page 84

Drink

Found on just about every street corner, the pub remains one of the nation's most enduring social institutions and its popularity in London shows no sign of waning. **The City** has probably the best choice of long-established drinking holes – though with the average pint costing over £5, it's worth knowing that you can pay much less at Sam Smith's pubs. **Soho** and the **East End** attract a clubbier crowd, so you'll find a wide choice of bars and clubs alongside good-old-fashioned pubs. For a riverside drink, head for the **South Bank** or **Docklands**, and for a lazy Sunday afternoon mosey on up to **Hampstead** or down to **Greenwich**.
OUR FAVOURITES: The Black Friar see page 85, George Inn see page 117, Cutty Sark see page 151

Shop

From the folie de grandeur of Harrods to the street markets of Camden and Spitalfields, London is a shopper's playground. In the West End, **Oxford Street** is Europe's busiest shopping street, followed closely by Regent Street – here you'll find pretty much every mainstream shop you could wish for. **Covent Garden** is an appealing focus for fashion and designer wear. **St James's** equips the English gentleman, **Bond Street** deals with the ladies, but for haute couture – and Harrods – head for **Knightsbridge** and Sloane Street. For something more offbeat, or vintage, head out to **Camden Market** or **Spitalfields** and **Brick Lane**.
OUR FAVOURITES: Hamley's see page 48, Beyond Retro see page 93, Harrods see page 129

Go out

As well as two top-class **opera** houses, London has many **theatres**, most of which are centrally located in the West End districts of Soho and Covent Garden, and boasts more **comedy venues** than any other city in the world. Although you'll find **clubs** and **live music venues** all across the capital, East London is the centre of the city's clubland. London is also the **LGBTQ** capital of Europe, with Soho, the East End and Vauxhall the go-to areas.
OUR FAVOURITES: Ronnie Scott's see page 65, XOYO see page 97, Royal Albert Hall see page 133

London at a glance

Bloomsbury p.66.
The area of leafy Georgian squares is dominated by the British Museum and the University of London, while to its north, the former warehouses along Regent's Canal are now home to some of central London's most enticing new developments.

Hampstead and Highgate p.140.
Elegant Georgian backstreets and the wild Heath appeal in Hampstead, while Highgate's gothic cemetery remains one of the city's most atmospheric spots.

Regent's Park and Camden p.134.
A pristine royal park and an enduringly popular street market are connected by a picturesque old canal.

Mayfair and Marylebone p.40.
Two aspirational West End suburbs harbouring some of the city's most exclusive shops and hotels. Mayfair is grander, while Marylebone retains a genteel village-like feel, and has some excellent restaurants.

Soho and Covent Garden p.52.
Bohemian Soho and cultural Covent Garden sit at the heart of the city's West End.

St James's p.34.
Exclusive enclave that's home to traditional menswear shops, upmarket galleries and auction houses – and Buckingham Palace.

Kensington and Chelsea p.118.
Stretching west from the centre, and encompassing the majestic Hyde Park, London's wealthiest borough includes South Kensington, with its trio of superb national museums.

Whitehall and Westminster p.24.
Centre of the British government, including the Houses of Parliament and Westminster Abbey.

◁ **Kew and Richmond** p.152.
Kew is home to world-renowned botanic gardens and Richmond boasts the perfect riverside setting.

◁ **Hampton Court** p.158.
Henry VIII's royal palace, accessible by train or boat.

The East End p.88.
You'll find some of London's best bars and clubs (and the Olympic Park) in a series of neighbourhoods to the east of the City: Spitalfields and Brick Lane, Shoreditch and Hoxton, Bethnal Green and Hackney.

The City p.72.
Established by the Romans, the City is London's financial heart and home to St Paul's Cathedral, while on its edges Clerkenwell appeals for its historic pubs, varied dining options and quieter ambience.

Bankside and Borough p.110.
Popular riverside neighbourhood, with Tate Modern as its centrepiece, the gourmet Borough Market to tempt you alongside some charming old pubs.

The Tower and Docklands p.98.
The mighty Tower of London is one of London's essential sights. Beyond here, explore the riverside St Katherine's Docks, and the old quays and docks to its east, culminating in London's second financial centre, Canary Wharf.

South Bank and around p.104.
The cultural powerhouse of the Southbank Centre and the lively riverside walk draws in the crowds.

▷ **Greenwich** p.146.
Take the boat along the Thames to Greenwich for a splendid day out, as you explore its colourful royal and maritime sights.

15

Things not to miss

It's not possible to see everything that London has to offer in one trip – and we don't suggest you try. What follows is a selective taste of London's highlights, from the city's famous museums to its coolest markets.

< East London's markets
See page 89
Start at Columbia Road on a
Sunday morning to enjoy the
famous flower market, then dig
out some vintage finds around
Spitalfields and Brick Lane.

> South Bank
See page 104
Stroll along the riverbank's
Thames Path from the London
Eye to the Tate Modern and
beyond.

∨ Greenwich
See page 146
Explore below deck at the Cutty
Sark, soak up naval history at the
National Maritime Museum and
climb up to the Royal Observatory
in Greenwich Park to enjoy the
view over the river.

< London pubs
See pages 71, 87, 96 and 117
Choose from one of London's classic drinking holes: Ye Olde Cheshire Cheese near Holborn, and Borough's Royal Oak, are charmingly unchanging; the Euston Tap or Mother Kelly's Tap Room offer large craft brew selections.

∨ Hampton Court Palace
See page 158
This sprawling red-brick Tudor edifice is without a doubt the finest of London's royal palaces.

< **Houses of Parliament**
See page 31
See the "mother of all parliaments" at work from the public gallery; visit for Question Time; or take a tour.

∨ **South Kensington's Museums**
See page 123
Three extraordinary museums – the Natural History Museum, Victoria and Albert and Science Museum – stand together, so whatever your interests, you'll find an exhibition to spark your imagination.

THINGS NOT TO MISS

∧ Tate Modern
See page 111
A wonderful hotchpotch of global contemporary art, from video works to gargantuan installations, and sublime views from its extension roof terrace.

< London's theatres
See page 58
If you crave the glitz and glamour of a West End musical, try your luck at the TCKTS booth on Leicester Square for discount tickets. For new writing, visit the Royal Court, the National Theatre (particularly the Dorfman space), the Donmar or Old Vic.

∧ Tower of London
See page 98
England's most perfectly preserved medieval fortress and safe-deposit box for the Crown Jewels.

∨ Borough Market
See page 116
London's upmarket larder, this historic market has an irresistible selection of British and international gourmet goods to sample, plus street food stalls, and some fine neighbourhood restaurants and pubs.

∧ **Hampstead Heath**
See page 140
North London's green lung and the city's most enjoyable public outdoor space.

< **National Gallery**
See page 25
A comprehensive overview of Western painting, from Renaissance classics to fin-de-siècle Parisian works.

< **British Museum**
See page 66
The oldest and greatest public museum on the planet, with objects from every corner of the globe.

∨ **The view from the Shard**
See page 114
Quite simply the most impressive view in London.

THINGS NOT TO MISS

Day One in London

Parliament Square. See page 31. Gaze at two of the capital's most remarkable buildings: the Houses of Parliament and Westminster Abbey.

Westminster Abbey. See page 29. Take time to explore the galleries and graves at this masterpiece of ecclesiastical architecture.

Churchill War Rooms. See page 29. Discover the subterranean rooms used by Churchill and his War Cabinet during World War II.

St James's Park. See page 34. One of London's smartest royal parks, with views across to Buckingham Palace, exotic ducks and even pelicans.

Lunch. See page 62. Picnic in St James's Park or head to Covent Garden's *Seven Dials* for lunch, grab a slice of gourmet pizza at *Homeslice* or opt for vegan fast food at *by CHLOE*.

Trafalgar Square. See page 24. London's finest set-piece square, overlooked by the National Gallery and famous for its fountains, fourth plinth and Nelson's Column.

British Museum. See page 66. One of the world's most amazing (and largest) museums, with everything from Egyptian mummies to Constructivist ceramics from the Russian Revolution.

Dinner. See page 70. Wander up to King's Cross's Granary Square and enjoy cocktails and delicious Indian dishes at *Dishoom* or inventive fresh flavours at *Caravan*.

St James's Park

Trafalgar Square

British Museum

Day Two in London

Harrods. See page 129. The queen of department stores, Harrods is a sight in itself, especially the Art Nouveau food hall.

Hyde Park. See page 119. Stroll along the Serpentine, go for a dip (if you're feeling brave) and check out the Diana Memorial Fountain.

Serpentine Gallery. See page 122. Sample some contemporary art for free and then have tea at the architecturally cutting-edge summer pavilion.

Albert Memorial. See page 122. Stop by this incredible, over-the-top neo-Gothic memorial to Queen Victoria's husband.

Albert Memorial

Lunch. See page 125. Housed in the museum's original refreshment rooms, the *V&A Café* is a visual treat, and serves everything from sandwiches to grilled fish and meat.

V&A. See page 125. South Kensington is home to a trio of fabulous museums, but the V&A's collection of applied arts is head and shoulders above the others.

Kensington Palace. See page 123. Princess Diana's former residence houses a display of her glamorous frocks, as well as some finely frescoed rooms.

Kensington Palace

Portobello Road Market. See page 127. Browse the antique shops or (if Saturday) the busy flea market.

Dinner. See page 131. Treat yourself to outstanding modern cuisine at *The Ledbury* or go for a drink and meal at *The Cow*.

Portobello Road Market

Riverside London

London grew up around the Thames, and a stroll (or a boat ride) along its banks is one of the city's real treats.

London Eye. See page 105. London's graceful millennial observation wheel has become one of the iconic symbols of the city despite its relative youth.

South Bank. See page 104. The views along the river from the South Bank's car-free promenade are some of London's best.

Tate Modern. See page 111. Feast your eyes on contemporary art from across the globe at the world's largest modern art gallery. Don't miss the sweeping vistas from the viewing platform.

Millennium Bridge. See page 110. London's only pedestrian-only river crossing offers great views of St Paul's Cathedral and the City.

Lunch. See page 116. Fill up at the food stalls in Borough Market (daily except Sun).

The Shard. See page 114. Scale London's most famous skyscraper and see the city spread out below you – and the hills and docks far beyond the edge of the city.

The Globe Theatre. See page 112. Loop back along the waterfront, and join the "groundlings" for an afternoon performance at Shakespeare's Globe.

Dinner. See page 116. Enjoy Middle Eastern flavours at *Bala Baya* or a Spanish feast at *Pizarro*, then settle in at one of Borough's fine historic pubs, like the *George Inn*.

London Eye

South Bank

The Globe Theatre

The City

From the Romans to rogue traders, the City has more history than the rest of London combined.

Sir John Soane's Museum. See page 76. The idiosyncratic home of the architect of the Bank of England is crammed with paintings and sculpture.

Temple Church. See page 72. Fascinating medieval round church, famed for its effigy tombs and appearance in *The Da Vinci Code*.

St Paul's Cathedral. See page 57. Climb up to the top of the dome of Wren's masterpiece for a fabulous view across the river.

 Lunch. See page 84. Tuck into fresh, seasonal food at *The Café Below*, in the atmospheric crypt of St Mary-le-Bow, or pub grub at the wonderful Art Nouveau *Black Friar*.

Museum of London. See page 79. From Roman mosaics to Wellington's boots, this museum encompasses the whole of London's history.

The London Mithraeum. See page 82. You can see the head of Mithras – dug up at this site – at the Museum of London, then make your way to the location of the original Roman temple in the heart of the city.

City skyscrapers. See page 81. Stand outside Richard Rogers' Lloyds Building for a panoramic view of the City's latest generation of skyscrapers, or visit the Sky Garden for a free eyeful of cityscape.

Old Spitalfields Market. See page 91. Though at its liveliest on Sundays, this old Victorian market hall has plenty of interest throughout the week.

St Paul's Cathedral

The Gherkin

Old Spitalfields Market

PLACES

Whitehall and Westminster

Whitehall is synonymous with the faceless, pinstriped bureaucracy who run the various governmental ministries located here, while Westminster remains home to the Houses of Parliament. Both are popular with visitors thanks to the Changing of the Guard, and familiar landmarks such as Nelson's Column, Big Ben and Westminster Abbey, London's most historic church. Political, religious and regal power has emanated from Whitehall and Westminster for almost a millennium. It was King Edward the Confessor who first established this spot as London's royal and ecclesiastical power base in the eleventh century. He built his palace and abbey some three miles upstream from the City of London, and it was in the abbey that the embryonic English parliament used to meet in the Middle Ages.

Trafalgar Square

MAP P.26, POCKET MAP G16
⊖ **Charing Cross.**

Nelson's Column, Trafalgar Square

As one of the few large public squares in London, Trafalgar Square has been a focus for political demonstrations since it was laid out in the 1820s. Along with its fountains, the square's central focal point is the deeply patriotic **Nelson's Column**, which stands 170ft high and is topped by a 17ft statue of the one-eyed, one-armed admiral who defeated the French (and died) at the 1805 Battle of Trafalgar. Nelson himself is actually quite hard to see – not so the giant bronze lions at the base of the column, which provide a popular photo opportunity. Stranded on a nearby traffic island is an equestrian statue of Charles I, while in the square's northeastern corner is one of George IV, which he himself originally commissioned for the top of Marble Arch. The **fourth plinth**, in the northwest corner, was built for an equestrian statue of William IV, but remained empty until 1999, since when it's been used to display alternating works of modern sculpture (Ⓦlondon.gov.uk/fourthplinth).

National Gallery

St Martin-in-the-Fields

MAP P.26, POCKET MAP G16
Duncannon St ⊖ Charing Cross ☎ 020
7766 1100, ⓦ www.stmartin-in-the-
fields.org. Mon–Fri 8am–6pm, Sat & Sun
9am–6pm. Free.
Something of a blueprint for
eighteenth-century churches across
the empire, St Martin-in-the-
Fields is fronted by a magnificent
Corinthian portico and topped
by an elaborate tower and steeple.
Designed by James Gibbs and
completed in 1726, the barrel-
vaulted interior features ornate,
sparkling white Italian plasterwork
and is best appreciated while
listening to one of the church's free
lunchtime concerts (Mon, Tues &
Fri) or ticketed, candle-lit evening
performances. Down in the large
crypt – accessible via an entrance
north of the church – there's a
licensed **café** (see page 33), shop,
gallery and **brass-rubbing centre**
(Mon–Wed 10am–6pm, Thurs–Sat
10am–7.45pm, Sun 11am–5pm).

National Gallery

MAP P.26, POCKET MAP G16
Trafalgar Square ⊖ Charing Cross ☎ 020
7747 2885, ⓦ nationalgallery.org.uk. Daily
10am–6pm, Fri till 9pm. Free.
Despite housing more than 2300
paintings, the main virtue of the
National Gallery is not so much
the collection's size, but its range,
depth and sheer quality. A quick
tally of the **Italian** masterpieces,
for example, includes works by
Uccello, Botticelli, Mantegna,
Piero della Francesca, Veronese,
Titian, Raphael, Michelangelo
and Caravaggio. From **Spain** there
are dazzling pieces by El Greco,
Velázquez and Goya; from the **Low
Countries**, van Eyck, Memling and
Rubens, and an array of Rembrandt
paintings that features some of his
most searching portraits. Poussin,
Claude, Watteau and the only
Jacques-Louis David paintings in
the country are the early highlights
of a **French** contingent, which also
has a particularly strong showing
of Cézanne and the Impressionists.
British art is also well represented,
with important works by Hogarth,
Gainsborough, Stubbs and Turner,
though for twentieth-century
British art – and many more
Turners – you'll need to move on
to Tate Britain on Millbank (see
page 32).

To view the collection chronologically, begin with the **Sainsbury Wing**, the softly-softly, postmodern 1980s adjunct which is linked to – and playfully imitates – the original Neoclassical building. However, with more than a thousand paintings on permanent display, you'll need stamina to see everything in one day, so if time is tight your best bet is to home in on your areas of special interest, having picked up a gallery plan at one of the information desks. Plans (£2) and audioguides (£5) are available – much better, though, are the gallery's **free guided tours** (daily 11.30am & 2.30pm), which set off from the Sainsbury Wing (Room 60), and focus on a representative sample of works.

National Portrait Gallery

MAP P.26, POCKET MAP G16
St Martin's Place ⊖ Charing Cross ☏ 020 7306 0055, ⓦ npg.org.uk. Daily 10am–6pm, Fri till 9pm. Free.

Founded in 1856 to house uplifting depictions of the good and the great, the National Portrait Gallery has some fine individual works. However, many of the studies are of less interest than their subjects, and the overall impression is of an overstuffed shrine to famous Brits rather than a museum offering any insight into the history of portraiture. Nevertheless, it is fascinating to trace who has been deemed worthy of admiration at any moment: aristocrats and artists in previous centuries, warmongers and imperialists in the early decades of the twentieth century, writers and poets in the 1930s and 1940s, and latterly, sportsmen and women, politicians and film and pop stars. The NPG's audiovisual guide (£3) gives useful biographical background information and the gallery's **special exhibitions** (for which

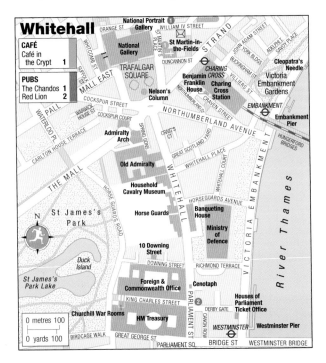

there's often an entrance charge) are well worth seeing – the photography shows, in particular, are usually excellent.

Whitehall

MAP P.26, POCKET MAP G17–G18
⊖ **Westminster or Charing Cross.**

Whitehall, the unusually broad avenue connecting Trafalgar Square to Parliament Square, is associated with the suited politicians charged with the day-to-day running of the country. Yet during the sixteenth and seventeenth centuries it served as the chief residence of England's kings and queens. Having started out as the London seat of the Archbishop of York, **Whitehall Palace** was confiscated and embellished by Henry VIII after a fire at Westminster made him homeless; it was here that he celebrated his marriage to Anne Boleyn in 1533, and where he died fourteen years later. Described by one contemporary chronicler as nothing but "a heap of houses erected at diverse times and of different models, made continuous", it boasted some two thousand rooms and stretched for half a mile along the Thames. Not much survived the fire of 1698, and subsequently, the royal residences shifted to St James's and Kensington. Since then, the key governmental ministries and offices have migrated here, rehousing themselves on an ever-increasing scale.

The statues dotted along Whitehall today recall the days when this street stood at the centre of an empire on which the sun never set, while just beyond the Downing Street gates, in the middle of the road, stands Edwin Lutyens' **Cenotaph**, commemorating the dead of both world wars. Eschewing any kind of Christian imagery, the plain monument is inscribed simply with the words "The Glorious

Cenotaph, Whitehall

Dead" and remains the focus of the country's Remembrance Sunday ceremony, held here in early November.

Banqueting House

MAP P.26, POCKET MAP G18
Whitehall ⊖ **Westminster** ☎ 020 3166 6000, ⊕ www.hrp.org.uk. Daily 10am–5pm; occasionally closes early, check ahead. £6.50 (£5.50 online in advance).

One of the few sections of Whitehall Palace to escape the 1698 fire, the Banqueting House was among the first Palladian buildings to be built in England. The one room open to the public has no original furnishings, but is well worth seeing for the superlative **Rubens ceiling paintings** commissioned by Charles I in the 1630s, depicting the union of England and Scotland, the peaceful reign of his father, James I, and finally his apotheosis (ask for an audioguide). Charles himself walked through the room for the last time in 1649, when he stepped onto the executioner's scaffold from one of its windows.

Daily inspection at Horse Guards

Horse Guards

MAP P.26, POCKET MAP G18

Whitehall ⊖ Charing Cross or Westminster.
Outside this modest building, built
in 1745 and once the old palace
guard house, two mounted sentries
of the **Queen's Household Cavalry**
and two horseless colleagues, all
in ceremonial uniform, are posted
daily from 10am to 4pm. With
nothing in particular to guard
nowadays, the sentries are basically
here for the tourists, though they
are under orders not to smile. Try
to coincide your visit with the
Changing of the Guard, when
a squad of mounted Household
Cavalry in full livery arrives to
relieve the guards (Mon–Sat 11am,
Sun 10am) – if you miss it, turn
up at 4pm for the elaborate **daily
inspection** by the Officer of the
Guard.

Household Cavalry Museum

MAP P.26, POCKET MAP G17

Whitehall ⊖ Westminster ☎ 020 7930
3070, ⊕ www.householdcavalrymuseum.
co.uk. Daily: April–Oct 10am–6pm; Nov–
March 10am–5pm. £8.

Round the back of Horse Guards,
you'll find the Household Cavalry
Museum, where you can try on
a trooper's elaborate uniform,
complete a horse quiz and learn
about the regiments' history.
With the stables immediately
adjacent, it's a sweet-smelling
place, and – horse-lovers will be
pleased to know – you can see
the beasts in their stalls through
a glass screen. Don't miss the
pocket Riot Act on display, which
ends with the wise warning:
"must read correctly: variance
fatal".

10 Downing Street

MAP P.26, POCKET MAP G18

⊖ Westminster.
Since the days of Margaret
Thatcher, London's most famous
address has been hidden behind
wrought-iron security gates. A
pretty plain, seventeenth-century
terraced house, no. 10 has been
the official home to every British
prime minister since it was
presented to Robert Walpole,
Britain's first PM, by George II
in 1732.

Churchill War Rooms

MAP P.26, POCKET MAP G18

King Charles St ⊖ Westminster
ⓘ 020 7416 5000, ⓦ iwm.org.uk. Daily
9.30am–6pm, July & Aug till 7pm. £21
(£18.90 online in advance).

In 1938, in anticipation of Nazi
air raids, the basement of the civil
service buildings on the south
side of King Charles Street was
converted into the **Cabinet War
Rooms**. It was here that Winston
Churchill directed operations
and held Cabinet meetings for
the duration of World War II.
The rooms have been left pretty
much as they were when they
were finally abandoned on VJ Day
1945, making for an atmospheric
underground trot through wartime
London. Also in the basement
is the self-contained **Churchill
Museum**, where you can hear
snippets of Churchill's most
famous speeches and check out his
trademark bowler, spotted bow tie

and half-chewed Havana, not to
mention his wonderful burgundy
zip-up "romper suit".

Westminster Abbey

MAP P.29, POCKET MAP G19

Parliament Square ⊖ Westminster ⓘ 020
7222 5152, ⓦ westminster-abbey.org.
Mon–Fri 9.30am–4.30pm, Wed until 6pm
(excluding some areas), Sat: May–Aug
9.30am–4.30pm, Sept–April 9.30am–
2.30pm, last entry 1hr before closing, Sun
for services. £22 (£20 online), including
multimedia guide, Queen's Diamond
Jubilee Galleries £5.

Venue for every coronation since
William the Conqueror, and
burial place of kings and queens,
Westminster Abbey embodies
much of England's history.

Entry is via the north transept,
cluttered with monuments to
politicians. From there you enter
the nave itself, narrow, light and,
at over 100ft in height, the tallest
in the country. The choir leads

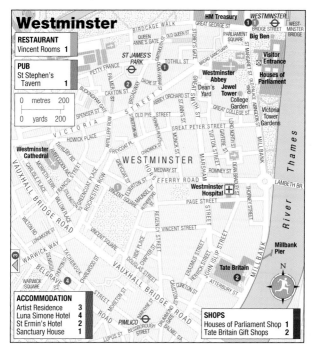

through to the central sanctuary, site of the coronations, and the wonderful **Cosmati floor mosaic**, constructed in the thirteenth century by Italian craftsmen. At the east end lies the abbey's most dazzling architectural set piece, the **Lady Chapel**, added by Henry VII in 1503 as his future resting place. With its intricately carved vaulting and fan-shaped gilded pendants, the chapel represents the final spectacular gasp of the English Perpendicular style. The public is no longer admitted to the **Shrine of Edward the Confessor**, the sacred heart of the building, except on a guided verger tour (£5), though you get to see Edward I's **Coronation Chair**, a decrepit oak throne from around 1300, and used at every coronation since.

Nowadays, the abbey's royal tombs are upstaged by **Poets' Corner**, in the south transept. The first occupant, Geoffrey Chaucer, was buried here in 1400, not because he was a poet but because he lived nearby. By the eighteenth century, however, this zone had become an artistic pantheon, and

since then has been filled with tributes to all shades of talent from William Blake to John Betjeman.

Accessed via a lift, the **Queen's Diamond Jubilee Galleries** inhabit a space 21m above the Abbey floor in the medieval triforium. The museum and viewing gallery displays altarpieces and treasures from the abbey's collections. You can see across to the Houses of Parliament from here and there are dizzying views down into the church.

Doors in the south choir aisle lead to the **Great Cloisters** (daily 9.30am–4.30pm), rebuilt after a fire in 1298. At the eastern end of the cloisters lies the octagonal **Chapter House** (Mon–Fri 10am–4.30pm, Sat 10am–2.30pm), where the House of Commons met from 1257. The thirteenth-century decorative paving tiles and apocalyptic wall-paintings have survived intact. From the cloisters you can make your way to the little-known **College Garden** (Tues–Thurs: April–Sept 10am–6pm; Oct–March 10am–4pm), a 900-year-old stretch of green which now provides a quiet retreat.

Westminster Abbey

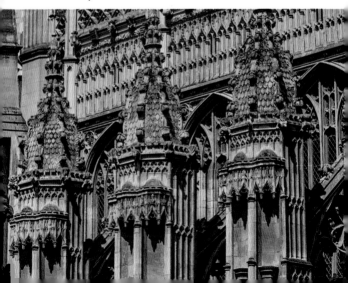

Houses of Parliament

MAP P.29, POCKET MAP H19
Parliament Square ⊖ Westminster ☏ 020 7219 4114, ⊕ parliament.uk.

Also known as the **Palace of Westminster**, the Houses of Parliament are one of London's best-known monuments and the ultimate symbol of a nation once confident of its place at the centre of the world. The city's finest example of Victorian Gothic Revival, the complex is distinguished above all by the ornate, gilded clock-tower popularly known as **Big Ben**, after the thirteen-ton main bell that strikes the hour (though it is currently silent and hidden under scaffolding while undergoing repairs, expected to last until 2021).

The original medieval palace burnt to the ground in 1834, but **Westminster Hall** survived, and its huge oak hammerbeam roof – and sheer scale – make it one of the most magnificent secular medieval halls in Europe; you get a glimpse of it en route to the public galleries. For centuries, the hall housed England's highest court of law and witnessed the trials of, among others, William Wallace, Guy Fawkes and Charles I.

To watch the proceedings in either the House of Commons or the Lords, simply join the queue for the **public galleries** (known as Strangers' Galleries) outside the Cromwell Green visitors' entrance. The public is let in slowly (House of Commons Mon from 2.30pm, Tues & Wed from 11.30am, Thurs & sitting Fri from 9.30am); security checks are tight, and the whole procedure can take an hour or more. To avoid the queues, turn up an hour or more later, when the crowds have usually thinned; check online to see the parliamentary schedule.

To see **Question Time** (Mon 2.30pm, Tues–Thurs 11.30am), when the House is at its most raucous and entertaining, UK citizens must book

Big Ben

a ticket several weeks in advance from their local MP.

Throughout the year there are audio and guided **tours** (every Sat all year, Mon–Sat during recess, including Easter & Aug, check and book online; audioguide £18.50, guided tour £25.50; or buy from ticket office, audioguide £20.50, guided tour £28, Victoria Embankment Mon–Fri 10am–4pm, Sat 8.45am–4.45pm), in which visitors get to walk through the two chambers, see some of the state rooms and admire Westminter Hall. All year round UK residents are entitled to a free tour of the palace; organize it through your local MP.

Jewel Tower

MAP P.29, POCKET MAP J9
Abingdon St ⊖ Westminster ☏ 020 7222 2219. April–Sept daily 10am–6pm; Oct daily 10am–5pm; Nov–March Sat & Sun 10am–4pm; £5.40.

The Jewel Tower is another remnant of the medieval palace. It once formed the corner of the original fortifications, and was constructed in around 1365 by Edward III as a giant strongbox for the crown jewels. These days, it houses a small exhibition on the history of the Jewel Tower, and a model of the old Palace of Westminster.

Westminster Cathedral

MAP P.29, POCKET MAP G9

Victoria St ⊖ Victoria ☏ 020 7798 9055, Ⓦ westminstercathedral.org.uk. Mon–Fri 7am–7pm, Sat & Sun 7.30am–8pm. Free.

Begun in 1895, the stripy neo-Byzantine, Roman Catholic Westminster Cathedral is one of London's most surprising churches, as well as one of the last – and the wildest – monuments to the Victorian era. Brick-built, and decorated with hoops of Portland stone, it culminates in a magnificent 274ft tapered **campanile**, served by a lift (Mon–Fri 9.30am–5pm, Sat & Sun 9.30am–6pm; £6). The interior is only half finished, so to get an idea of what the place should eventually look like, explore the side chapels whose rich, multicoloured decor uses over one hundred types of marble from around the world. Be sure, too, to check out the low-relief Stations of the Cross, sculpted by Eric Gill during World War I.

Tate Britain

MAP P.29, POCKET MAP J10

Millbank ⊖ Pimlico ☏ 020 7887 8888, Ⓦ tate.org.uk. Daily 10am–6pm. Free.

A purpose-built gallery founded in 1897 with money from sugar baron Henry Tate, Tate Britain is devoted almost exclusively to British art from 1500 to the present day. In addition, the gallery showcases contemporary British artists and sponsors the Turner Prize, the country's most prestigious modern-art award.

The pictures are displayed chronologically, with fairly regular re-hangs, but always include a fair selection of works by British artists such as Hogarth, Constable, Gainsborough, Reynolds and Blake, plus foreign artists like van Dyck who spent much of their career over here. The ever-popular **Pre-Raphaelites** are well represented, as are established twentieth-century greats including Stanley Spencer, Francis Bacon and Lucian Freud and living artists such as David Hockney. Lastly, don't miss the Tate's outstanding **Turner collection**, displayed in the Clore Gallery.

Inside Westminster Cathedral

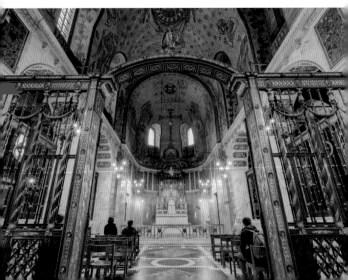

Shops

Houses of Parliament shop

MAP P.29, POCKET MAP G19

12 Bridge St ⊖ Westminster. Mon–Fri 9.30am–5.30pm, Sat 10am–5.30pm. Pick up copies of *Hansard* (the word-for-word account of parliament), the government's white and green papers and plenty of political literature.

Tate Britain gift shops

MAP P.29, POCKET MAP J10

Millbank ⊖ Pimlico. Daily 10am–5.50pm. Lots of art posters, from Constable to Turner Prize nonsense, plus books – covering history and culture, as well as art – and arty accessories.

Café and restaurant

Café in the Crypt

MAP P.26, POCKET MAP G16

St Martin-in-the-Fields, Duncannon St ⊖ Charing Cross. ☎ 020 7766 1158. Mon & Tues 10am–8pm, Wed 10am–10.30pm, Thurs–Sat 10am–9pm, Sun 11am–6pm. The tasty home-made comfort food and convenient, atmospheric location – below the church in the crypt – make this an ideal spot to fill up. Jazz nights Wed from 8pm (book in advance).

Vincent Rooms

MAP P.29, POCKET MAP H9

76 Vincent Square ⊖ Victoria or St James's Park ☎ 020 7802 8391, ⊛ thevincentrooms.co.uk. Reservations: Mon–Fri noon–1pm, plus Tues–Thurs 6–7pm (open till 9pm); term time only – closed Easter, summer and Xmas. Elegant brasserie serving up dishes cooked by the student chefs of Westminster Kingsway College, where Jamie Oliver learnt his trade. A real bargain (mains £10–12 in the brasserie; tasting menu for

Red Lion

£27.50 in the Escoffier Room dining room).

Pubs

The Chandos

MAP P.26, POCKET MAP G16

29 St Martin's Lane ⊖ Charing Cross. Mon–Sat 11am–11pm, Sun noon–10.30pm. If you can get one of the booths downstairs, or the leather sofas upstairs in the more relaxed Opera Room Bar, then you'll find it difficult to leave this Sam Smith's pub.

Red Lion

MAP P.26, POCKET MAP G18

48 Parliament St ⊖ Westminster. Mon–Fri 8am–11pm, Sat 8am–9pm, Sun 9am–9pm. Classic old pub with good pies, convenient for Westminster Abbey and Parliament. You may spot an MP or two enjoying a quiet pint.

St Stephen's Tavern

MAP P.29, POCKET MAP H19

10 Bridge St ⊖ Westminster. Mon–Sat 10am–11.30pm, Sun 10.30am–10.30pm. A beautifully restored and opulent Victorian pub, built in 1867, wall to wall with civil servants and MPs. Good real ales (including seasonal brews) and traditional pub food; they even offer breakfast.

St James's

An exclusive little enclave sandwiched between St James's Park and Piccadilly, St James's was laid out in the 1670s close to the royal seat of St James's Palace. Regal and aristocratic residences overlook nearby Green Park and the stately avenue of The Mall, while gentlemen's clubs cluster along Pall Mall and St James's Street, and jacket-and-tie restaurants and expense-account gentlemen's outfitters line Jermyn Street. Hardly surprising, then, that most Londoners rarely stray into this area. Plenty of folk, however, frequent St James's Park, with large numbers heading for the Queen's chief residence, Buckingham Palace, and the adjacent Queen's Gallery and Royal Mews.

The Mall

MAP P.35, POCKET MAP G17–E18
⊖ Charing Cross.

The tree-lined sweep of The Mall was laid out in the early twentieth century as a memorial to Queen Victoria. The bombastic **Admiralty Arch** was erected to mark the eastern entrance to The Mall, from Trafalgar Square, while at the other end, in front of Buckingham Palace, stands the ludicrously overblown **Victoria Memorial**, Edward VII's tribute to his mother. The Mall is best visited on a Sunday, when it's closed to traffic.

St James's Park

MAP P.35, POCKET MAP F18
⊖ St James's Park ⓦ royalparks.org.uk.
Daily 5am–midnight.

St James's Park

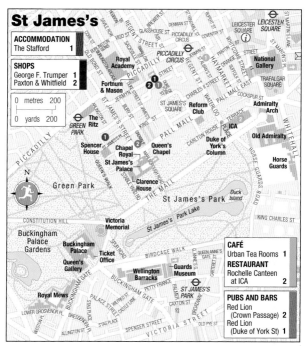

St James's

ACCOMMODATION	
The Stafford	1

SHOPS	
George F. Trumper	1
Paxton & Whitfield	2

0 metres 200
0 yards 200

CAFÉ	
Urban Tea Rooms	1
RESTAURANT	
Rochelle Canteen at ICA	2

PUBS AND BARS	
Red Lion (Crown Passage)	2
Red Lion (Duke of York St)	1

ST JAMES'S

St James's Park is the oldest of London's royal parks, having been enclosed for hunting purposes by Henry VIII and later opened to the public by Charles II. It was landscaped by Nash in the 1820s, and today its tree-lined lake is a favourite picnic spot for Whitehall's civil servants. Pelicans chill out at the eastern end, and there are exotic ducks, swans and geese aplenty. From the bridge across the lake there's also a fine view over to Westminster and the jumble of domes and pinnacles along Whitehall, with the London Eye peeking over it all – even dull Buckingham Palace looks majestic from here.

Guards Museum

MAP P.35, POCKET MAP E19
Birdcage Walk ⊖ St James's Park 📞 020 7414 3271, 🌐 theguardsmuseum.com. Daily 10am–4pm. £8.

The Neoclassical facade of the **Wellington Barracks**, built in 1833 and fronted by a parade ground, runs along the south side of St James's Park. In a bunker opposite the barracks' modern chapel, the Guards Museum endeavours to explain the complicated evolution of the Queen's Household Regiments, and provides a potted military history since the Civil War. Among the exhibits are the guards' glorious scarlet and blue uniforms, a lock of Wellington's hair and a whole load of war booty.

Buckingham Palace

MAP P.35, POCKET MAP D19
Buckingham Gate ⊖ Green Park 🌐 royalcollection.org.uk. Late July–Aug daily 9.30am–7pm; Sept daily 9.30am–6pm (last admission 90min before closing). £24. The graceless colossus of Buckingham Palace has served as the monarch's permanent

London residence only since Queen Victoria's reign. Bought by George III in 1762, the building was overhauled in the late 1820s, and again in time for George V's coronation in 1913, producing a Neoclassical monolith that's about as bland as it's possible to be.

For two months of the year, the hallowed portals are grudgingly nudged open to the public; timed tickets can be bought online in advance, or from the box office on the south side of the palace. The interior, however, is a bit of an anticlimax: of the palace's 775 rooms, you're permitted to see nineteen, and there's little sign of life as the Queen decamps to Scotland every summer. If the decor is disappointing, at least the art on display is top-notch, with several van Dycks, two Rembrandts, several Canalettos, a de Hooch and a wonderful Vermeer hanging in the Picture Gallery (though works are sometimes moved or loaned).

For the other ten months of the year, the palace is closed to visitors – not that this deters the loitering crowds who gather in some force to watch the Foot Guards' **Changing the Guard** ceremony (June & July daily 11am; Aug–May alternate days; check days in advance; no ceremony if it rains; ⓦ householddivision.org. uk). If the Queen is at home, the Royal Standard flies from the roof of the palace and four guards patrol; if not, the Union flag flutters aloft and just two guards stand out front.

Queen's Gallery

MAP P.35, POCKET MAP D19
Buckingham Gate ⊖ Victoria ☎ 020 7766 7300, ⓦ royalcollection.org.uk. Daily 10am–5.30pm, late July–early Sept opens 9.30am. £12.

The changing exhibitions here are drawn from the **Royal Collection**, the vast array of artworks snapped up by the royal family over the centuries, which is three times larger than that at the National Gallery. Among the thousands of works the curators have to choose from are some incredible masterpieces by Michelangelo, Reynolds, Gainsborough, Vermeer, van Dyck, Rubens, Rembrandt and Canaletto, as well as numerous Fabergé eggs and heaps of Sèvres porcelain.

Buckingham Palace

Royal Mews

MAP P.35, POCKET MAP D19
Buckingham Gate ⊖ Victoria
Ⓦ royalcollection.org.uk. April–Oct daily
10am–5pm; Nov, Feb & March Mon–Sat
10am–4pm. £11.

At the Nash-built Royal Mews,
you can view the **Queen's horses**
– or at least their backsides – in
their luxury stables, along with an
exhibition of equine accoutrements,
but it's the royal carriages, lined
up under a glass canopy in the
courtyard, that are the main
attraction. The most ornate is
the **Gold State Coach**, made for
George III in 1762, smothered in
22-carat gilding, panel paintings by
Cipriani and weighing four tons,
its axles supporting four life-size
Tritons blowing conches. Eight
horses are needed to pull it and the
whole experience apparently made
Queen Victoria feel quite sick;
since then it has only been used for
coronations and jubilees. The mews
also house the Royal Family's fleet
of Rolls-Royce Phantoms, Daimlers
and Bentleys, none of which is
obliged to carry number plates.

Gold State Coach

St James's Palace

MAP P.35, POCKET MAP E18
Marlborough Rd ⊖ Green Park Ⓦ www.
royal.gov.uk.

Built by Henry VIII for Anne
Boleyn, St James's Palace became
the principal royal residence
after Whitehall Palace burnt to
the ground in 1698, until the
court moved down the road to
Buckingham Palace under Queen
Victoria. The imposing red-brick
gate-tower that forms the main
entrance, and the **Chapel Royal**,
are all that remain of the original
Tudor palace. The rambling
complex is off-limits to the public,
though you can attend services at
the Chapel Royal (Oct to Good
Friday 8.30am & 11.15am), venue
for numerous royal weddings, and
at the Neoclassical **Queen's Chapel**
(Easter Sun to July Sun 8.30am &
11.15am).

The gentlemen's clubs

The **gentlemen's clubs** of St James's remain the final bastions of
the male chauvinism and public-school snobbery for which England
is famous. Their origins lie in the coffee- and chocolate-houses of
the eighteenth century, though the majority were founded in the
post-Napoleonic peace of the early nineteenth century by those who
yearned for the officers' mess; drinking, whoring and gambling were
the major features of early club life. The oldest clubs – like White's,
Brooks' and Boodle's – still boast a list of members that includes
royals, politicians and the military top brass. The Reform Club, on
Pall Mall, from which Phileas Fogg set off in Jules Verne's *Around
the World in Eighty Days*, is one of the more "progressive" – it was
one of the first to admit women as members.

Clarence House

MAP P.35, POCKET MAP E18
Stable Yard Rd ⊖ Green Park ☎ 0303
123 7321, ⊛ royalcollection.org.uk.
Aug Mon–Fri 10am–4.30pm, Sat & Sun
10am–5.30pm. £10.30.

Built in the 1820s by John Nash for the future William IV, and used as his principal residence, Clarence House was home to the **Queen Mother**, widow of George VI, until 2002, and is now the official London home of Charles and Camilla. A handful of rooms can be visited over the summer when the royals are in Scotland. Visits must be booked in advance and are by guided tour only, and the rooms are pretty unremarkable, so apart from a peek behind the scenes in a working royal palace, and a few mementoes of the Queen Mum, the main draw is a series of twentieth-century British paintings on display by the likes of Walter Sickert and Augustus John.

Spencer House

MAP P.35, POCKET MAP E18
St James's Place ⊖ Green Park ☎ 020
7514 1958, ⊛ www.spencerhouse.co.uk.
Jan–July & Sept–Dec Sun 10am–4.30pm.
No under 10s. £15.

Spencer House

Most of St James's palatial residences are closed to the public, with the exception of this superb Palladian mansion, built between 1756 and 1766. Ancestral home of the late Diana, Princess of Wales, it was last lived in by the family in 1926. Inside, guides take you on an hour-long tour through eight of the state rooms. The **Great Room** features a stunning coved and coffered ceiling in green, white and gold, while the **Painted Room** is a feast of Neoclassicism, decorated with murals in the "Pompeian manner". The most outrageous decor, though, is in **Lord Spencer's Room**, with its gilded palm-tree columns.

Green Park

MAP P.35, POCKET MAP D18
⊖ Green Park ⊛ royalparks.org.uk. Daily
24hr.

Laid out on the burial ground of the old lepers' hospital by Henry VIII, Green Park was left more or less flowerless – hence its name (officially "The Green Park") – and, apart from the springtime swathes of daffodils and crocuses, it remains mostly meadow, shaded by graceful London plane trees. In its time, however, it was a popular place for duels (banned from neighbouring St James's Park), ballooning and fireworks displays. One such display was immortalized by Handel's *Music for the Royal Fireworks*, performed here on April 27, 1749 to celebrate the Peace of Aix-la-Chapelle, which ended the eight-year War of the Austrian Succession – over ten thousand fireworks were let off, setting fire to the custom-built Temple of Peace and causing three fatalities. The music was a great success, however. Along the east side of the park runs the wide path of **Queen's Walk**, laid out for Queen Caroline, wife of George II, who had a little pavilion built nearby.

Shops

George F. Trumper
MAP P.35, POCKET MAP E16
1 Duke of York St ⊖ Piccadilly Circus.
Mon–Fri 9am–5.30pm, Sat 9am–5pm.
Founded in 1875, this impeccably
discreet "gentlemen's perfumer" is
the barber of choice, with a shaving
school that will teach you how to
execute the perfect wet shave.

Paxton & Whitfield
MAP P.35, POCKET MAP E16
93 Jermyn St ⊖ Piccadilly Circus. Mon–Sat
9am–6.30pm, Sun 11am–5pm.
Quintessentially English, this two
hundred-year-old cheese shop
offers a very traditional selection
of British and European varieties,
plus a good range of wine and
port.

Café and restaurant

Rochelle Canteen at ICA
MAP P.35, POCKET MAP F17
94 The Mall ⊖ Charing Cross. Tues–Sun
11am–11pm.
This minimal arts centre restaurant
and bar serves an inventive menu
(noon–3pm & 6–10pm) by Arnold
& Henderson, a team connected to
some of London's most respected
restaurants (the original *Rochelle* is
in east London); expect a mixture
of English dishes (rabbit pie) and
Mediterranean flavours on the
changing menu. Mains £15–20.

Urban tea rooms
MAP P.35, POCKET MAP F16
2A St James's Market ⊖ Piccadilly Circus.
Mon–Thurs 7am–5pm, Fri 7am–7pm, Sat
10am–5pm.
The St James's Market development
off Haymarket is a welcome
addition to an area full of tourist
traps, with a couple of classy dining
options. Nestled in among them
is this hip little tea shop and café

George F. Trumper

serving brunches, home-made
sandwiches, avocado toast, pastries
and a good range of teas, plus
drinks and cocktails.

Pubs and bars

Red Lion
MAP P.35, POCKET MAP E17
23 Crown Passage ⊖ Green Park. Mon–Sat
11am–11pm.
Hidden away in a passageway off
Pall Mall, this is a genuinely warm
and cosy local, with super-friendly
bar staff, well-kept Adnams beer
and good sandwiches.

Red Lion
MAP P.35, POCKET MAP E16
2 Duke of York St ⊖ Piccadilly Circus.
Mon–Sat 11.30am–11pm.
Glorious old Victorian gin palace
with elegant etched mirrors and
lots of polished wood. Offers a
commendable range of Fuller's ales,
with seasonal selections that change
every few weeks.

Mayfair and Marylebone

A whiff of exclusivity still pervades the streets of Mayfair, particularly Bond Street and its tributaries, where designer clothes emporia jostle for space with jewellers, bespoke tailors and fine art dealers. Most Londoners, however, stick to the more prosaic pleasures of Regent and Oxford streets, home to the flagship branches of the country's most popular chain stores. It's here that Londoners are referring to when they talk of the West End. Marylebone, to the north of Oxford Street, may not have quite the pedigree and snob value of Mayfair, but it's still a wealthy and aspirational area, and its mesh of smart Georgian streets and squares are a pleasure to wander, especially the chi-chi, village-like quarter around the High Street.

Piccadilly Circus

MAP P.41, POCKET MAP F16
⊖ Piccadilly Circus.

Characterless and congested, Piccadilly Circus is generally unloved by Londoners, who would rather detour through the backstreets of nearby Soho than face the maelstrom of this busy road junction.

Eros, Piccadilly Circus

Originally laid out in 1812 and now a major traffic bottleneck, it's by no means a picturesque place, and is probably best seen at night when the spread of vast illuminated signs (a feature since the Edwardian era) provide a touch of Las Vegas dazzle, and when the human traffic is at its most frenetic. Somewhat inexplicably, Piccadilly Circus attracts a steady flow of tourists, who come here to sit on the steps of the central fountain, which is topped by an aluminium statue popularly known as **Eros**, designed by Alfred Gilbert and first unveiled in 1893. Despite the bow and arrow, it depicts not the god of love but Anteros, the lesser-known god of requited love, and was erected to commemorate the Earl of Shaftesbury, a Bible-thumping social reformer who campaigned against child labour.

Regent Street

MAP P.41, POCKET MAP D14–E16
⊖ Piccadilly Circus or Oxford Circus.

Drawn up by John Nash in 1812 as both a luxury shopping street and a new, wide triumphal approach to Regent's Park, Regent Street was the city's first real attempt at dealing with traffic congestion.

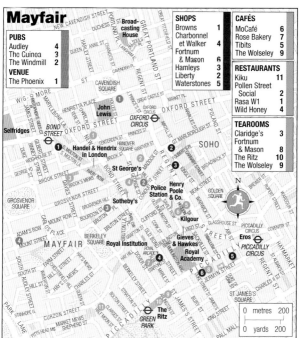

Mayfair

PUBS
Audley	4
The Guinea	3
The Windmill	2

VENUE
The Phoenix	1

SHOPS
Browns	1
Charbonnel et Walker	4
Fortnum & Mason	6
Hamleys	3
Liberty	2
Waterstones	5

CAFÉS
MoCafé	6
Rose Bakery	7
Tibits	8
The Wolseley	9

RESTAURANTS
Kiku	11
Pollen Street Social	2
Rasa W1	1
Wild Honey	4

TEAROOMS
Claridge's	3
Fortnum & Mason	8
The Ritz	10
The Wolseley	9

At the same time, it helped clear away a large area of slums and create a tangible borderline to shore up fashionable Mayfair against the chaotic maze of Soho. Even today, it's still possible to admire the stately intentions of Nash's plan, particularly evident in the **Quadrant**, the street's partially arcaded section which curves westwards from Piccadilly Circus. During the course of the nineteenth century, however, the increased purchasing power of the city's middle classes brought the tone of the street "down", and heavyweight stores catering for the masses now predominate.

Piccadilly

MAP P.41, POCKET MAP F16–C18
⊖ Piccadilly Circus or Green Park.
Piccadilly apparently got its name from the ruffs or "pickadills" worn by the dandies who promenaded along this wide boulevard in the late seventeenth century. Despite its fashionable pedigree, and the presence of **The Ritz** halfway along, it's no place for promenading in its current state, with traffic careering down it nose to tail day and night. Infinitely more pleasant places to window-shop are the various **nineteenth-century arcades** leading off the street, originally built to protect shoppers from the mud and horse-dung on the streets, but now equally useful for escaping exhaust fumes.

Burlington Arcade

MAP P.41, POCKET MAP D16–E16
Piccadilly ⊖ Green Park. Mon–Sat 9am–7.30pm, Sun 11am–6pm.
Lined with mahogany-fronted jewellers and gentlemen's outfitters, the Burlington Arcade is Piccadilly's longest and most expensive nineteenth-century arcade. It was built in 1819 for Lord Cavendish, then owner of neighbouring

Burlington House, to prevent commoners throwing rubbish into his garden. Upholding Regency decorum, it is still illegal to whistle, sing, hum, hurry, carry large packages or open umbrellas on this small stretch – the arcade's beadles (known as Burlington Berties), in their Edwardian frock-coats and gold-braided top hats, take the prevention of such criminality very seriously.

Royal Academy

MAP P.41, POCKET MAP E16
Burlington House, Piccadilly ⊖ Green Park ⓘ 020 7300 8000, ⓦ www.royalacademy. org.uk. Burlington House daily 10am–6pm, Fri till 10pm. Burlington Gardens Mon–Sat 8am–10pm, Sun 10am–6pm. Permanent gallery free; exhibitions from £16.

The Royal Academy of Arts (RA) occupies the enormous Burlington House, one of the few survivors of the aristocratic mansions that once lined Piccadilly. The country's first-ever formal art school, the Academy was founded in 1768 by a group of English painters including Thomas Gainsborough and Joshua Reynolds, the first president, whose statue now stands in the main courtyard, palette in hand.

The Academy has recently expanded into a second building – connected via a vaulted underpass, displaying sculpture and works by RA "Academicians" past, followed by a David Chipperfield-designed concrete stairway – with an entrance also on Burlington Gardens. The **Collection Gallery** in the Burlington Gardens building displays highlights from the RA's permanent collection, including a Rembrandtesque self-portrait by Reynolds, an appealing collection of London scenes by Constable and, as a magnificent centrepiece, a marble relief by Michelangelo, known as the *Taddei Tondo*.

The Academy is best known for its large special exhibitions, of which there are usually two or three at any one time, which could cover any genre or period from Old Masters to Ai Weiwei, and can attract large visitor numbers (book tickets in advance for major exhibitions). Its famous **Summer Exhibition** opens in June and runs until mid-August. Anyone can enter paintings in any style, and the lucky winners' works get exhibited and sold. In addition, RA Academicians are allowed to display six of their own works.

Royal Academy

Royal Institution

MAP P.41, POCKET MAP D16
21 Albemarle St ⊖ Green Park ☎ 020 7409 2992, ⊛ www.rigb.org. Mon–Fri 9am–6pm. Free.

Founded in 1799 "for teaching by courses of philosophical lectures and experiments the application of science to the common purposes of life", the Royal Institution is best known for its six Christmas Lectures, begun by **Michael Faraday** and designed to popularize science among schoolchildren. In the basement, there's an enjoyable interactive **museum** aimed at both kids and adults, where you can learn about the ten elements that have been discovered at the RI, and the famous experiments that have taken place here: Tyndall's blue sky tube, Humphry Davy's early lamps and Faraday's explorations into

Afternoon tea at The Ritz

Afternoon tea

The classic English **afternoon tea** – assorted sandwiches, scones and cream, cakes and tarts, and, of course, lashings of tea – is available all over London. The favoured venues for a treat are the capital's top hotels and most fashionable department stores; a selection of the best is given below. Expect to spend at least £50–60 a head (less at *The Wolseley*), and leave your jeans and trainers at home – most hotels will expect "smart casual attire", though only *The Ritz* insists on jacket and tie. It's essential to book ahead.

Claridge's

MAP P.41, POCKET MAP C15
49 Brook St ⊖ Bond Street ☎ 020 7629 8860, ⊛ claridges.co.uk. Daily every 15min 2.45–3.30pm & 4.45–5.30pm.

Fortnum & Mason

MAP P.41, POCKET MAP E16
181 Piccadilly ⊖ Green Park or Piccadilly Circus ☎ 020 7734 8040, ⊛ fortnumandmason.com. Mon–Sat 11.30am–7pm, Sun noon–6pm. M

The Ritz

MAP P.41, POCKET MAP D17
Palm Court, 150 Piccadilly ⊖ Green Park ☎ 020 7300 2345, ⊛ theritzlondon.com. Daily 11.30am, 1.30pm, 3.30pm, 5.30pm and 7.30pm.

The Wolseley

MAP P.41, POCKET MAP D13
160 Piccadilly ⊖ Green Park ☎ 020 7499 6996, ⊛ thewolseley.com. Mon–Fri 3–6.30pm, Sat & Sun 3.30–6.30pm.

Henry Poole & Co, Savile Row

electricity and electromagneticism – there's even a reconstruction of Faraday's lab from the 1850s.

Bond Street and around

MAP P.41, POCKET MAP C15–D16
⊖ Bond Street or Green Park.

While Oxford Street, Regent Street and Piccadilly are generally the home of mainstream brands, Bond Street maintains an air of exclusivity. It is, in fact, two streets rolled into one: the southern half, laid out in the 1680s, is known as Old Bond Street; its northern extension, which followed less than fifty years later, is New Bond Street. Both are pretty unassuming architecturally, but the shops that line them – and those of neighbouring Conduit Street and South Molton Street – are among the flashiest in London, dominated by **perfumeries**, **jewellers** and **designer clothing** emporia such as Versace, Gucci and Yves Saint-Laurent.

Auction houses

MAP P.41, POCKET MAP D15
⊖ Piccadilly Circus or Green Park.

In addition to fashion, Bond Street is renowned for its auction houses, which you can generally visit – and view their changing exhibits. The oldest is **Sotheby's**, at nos. 34–35, with a gallery at 31 George St. The exhibits (check website for viewing times;

ⓦsothebys.com) are free and open to the public, as are the auctions themselves.

Christie's, founded in 1766, and now the world's largest auction house, is over in St James's at 8 King St (ⓦchristies.com).

Savile Row

MAP P.41, POCKET MAP D15–E16
⊖ Green Park.

A classic address in sartorial matters, Savile Row has been *the* place to go for bespoke tailoring since the early nineteenth century. **Gieves & Hawkes**, at no. 1, were the first tailors to establish themselves here, back in 1785, with Nelson and Wellington among their first customers, while modernist **Kilgour**, at no. 8, famously made Fred Astaire's morning coat for *Top Hat*, helping to popularize Savile Row tailoring in the US. **Henry Poole & Co**, who moved to no. 15 in 1846, has cut suits for the likes of Napoleon III, Dickens and Churchill, and invented the short smoking jacket (originally designed for the future Edward VII), later popularized as the tuxedo.

Handel and Hendrix in London

MAP P.41, POCKET MAP C15
25 Brook St ⊖ Bond Street ☎ 020 7495 1685, ⓦ www.handelhendrix.org. Mon–Sat 11am–6pm. £10.

The German-born composer **George Frideric Handel** (1685–1759) spent the best part of his life in London, producing all his best-known works at what's now the Handel House Museum. The composer used the ground floor of the building as a sort of shop where subscribers could buy scores, while the first floor was employed as a rehearsal room. Although containing few original artefacts, the house has been painstakingly restored, and the exquisite harpsichords are used for rehearsals and regular concerts (check website). By a peculiar quirk of fate, the small third-floor flat of the neighbouring building, no. 23, was for a brief period in 1968–69 home to Jimi Hendrix and his girlfriend Kathy Etchingham. The flat has been re-created, complete with 1960s fabrics they bought from John Lewis and original guitars. There's also an exhibition on Hendrix's time in London.

St George's Church

MAP P.41, POCKET MAP D15
Hanover Square ⊖ Oxford Circus
☎ 020 7629 0874, Ⓦ www.
stgeorgeshanoversquare.org. Mon–Fri
8am–4pm, Wed till 6pm, Sun 8am–noon.
The much-copied Corinthian portico of St George's Church was the first of its kind in London when built in the 1720s. The church has long been Mayfair's most fashionable wedding venue, and those who tied the knot here have included the Shelleys, Benjamin Disraeli, George Eliot and Teddy Roosevelt. Handel, a confirmed bachelor, was a church warden for many years and even had his own pew.

Oxford Street

MAP P.41, POCKET MAP F14–15, E6–H6
⊖ Marble Arch, Bond Street, Oxford Circus
or Tottenham Court Road.
The old Roman road to Oxford has been London's main **shopping** destination for the last century.

Today, despite successive recessions and sky-high rents, this aesthetically unremarkable two-mile hotchpotch of shops is still one of the world's busiest streets. East of Oxford Circus, it forms the northern border of Soho; to the west, the one great landmark is **Selfridges**, a huge Edwardian pile fronted by giant Ionic columns, with the Queen of Time riding the ship of commerce and supporting an Art Deco clock above the main entrance. The store was opened in 1909 by Chicago millionaire Gordon Selfridge, who flaunted its 130 departments under the slogan, "Why not spend a day at Selfridges?"; he was later pensioned off after an altercation with the Inland Revenue.

Wallace Collection

MAP P.46, POCKET MAP B14
Hertford House, Manchester Square
⊖ Bond Street ☎ 020 7563 9500,
Ⓦ wallacecollection.org. Daily 10am–5pm.
Free.
Housed in a miniature eighteenth-century French-style chateau, the Wallace Collection is an old-fashioned place, with exhibits piled

Wallace Collection

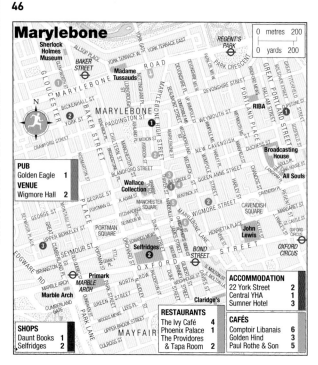

Marylebone

PUB	
Golden Eagle	1
VENUE	
Wigmore Hall	2

SHOPS	
Daunt Books	1
Selfridges	2

ACCOMMODATION	
22 York Street	2
Central YHA	1
Sumner Hotel	3

RESTAURANTS	
The Ivy Café	4
Phoenix Palace	1
The Providores & Tapa Room	2

CAFÉS	
Comptoir Libanais	6
Golden Hind	3
Paul Rothe & Son	5

high in glass cabinets, paintings covering every inch of wall space and a bloody great armoury. The collection is best known for its eighteenth-century French furniture and paintings (especially Watteau); look out, too, for Franz Hals' *Laughing Cavalier*, Titian's *Perseus and Andromeda*, Velázquez's *Lady with a Fan* and Rembrandt's portrait of his teenage son, Titus. Labelling can be pretty terse and paintings occasionally move about, so consider renting an audioguide (£4) or join a free tour (Mon–Thurs 2.30pm, Fri–Sun 11.30am & 2.30pm).

Staircase at RIBA

RIBA

MAP P.46, POCKET MAP C12

66 Portland Place ⊖ Regent's Park ☎ 020 7580 5533, ⓦ architecture.com. Building Mon–Fri 8am–5.30pm, Tues till 8pm, Sat 10am–5pm. Gallery Mon–Sat 10am–5pm, Tues till 8pm. Café Mon–Fri 8am–5pm, Sat 10am–5pm. Free.

With its sleek 1930s Portland-stone facade, the headquarters of the **Royal Institute of British Architects** is easily the finest building on Portland Place. Inside, the main staircase remains a wonderful period piece, with etched glass balustrades, walnut veneer and two large columns of black marble rising up on either side. You can view the interior en route to the institute's often thought-provoking first-floor architectural exhibitions (free) and to its café. The excellent bookshop is also worth a browse.

Madame Tussauds

MAP P.46, POCKET MAP A12
Marylebone Rd ⊖ Baker Street ☎ 0871 894 3000, ⓦ www.madametussauds.com. Times vary; usually Sept–June Mon–Fri 10am–4pm, Sat & Sun 9am–5pm; July & Aug Mon–Fri 9am–5pm, Sat & Sun 9am–6pm. Online tickets from £24.50.
Madame Tussaud's waxworks have been pulling in the crowds ever since the good lady arrived in London from France in 1802 bearing the sculpted heads of guillotined aristocrats. The entrance fee is extortionate, the likenesses occasionally dubious and the automated dummies inept, but you can still rely on finding London's biggest queues here – to avoid joining them, book your ticket online. There are photo opportunities galore throughout the first few sections, which are peppered with contemporary

celebrities from the BBC to Bollywood. A Sherlock Holmes-themed installation features costumed actors and theatrical sets that re-create Sherlock's London. The Tussauds finale is a manic five-minute "ride" through the history of London in a miniaturized taxi cab, followed by a thirty-minute, high-tech, Marvel-themed presentation, projected onto the dome of the adjoining Auditorium (formerly the Planetarium).

Sherlock Holmes Museum

MAP P.46, POCKET MAP A12
239 Baker St ⊖ Baker Street ☎ 020 7224 3688, ⓦ sherlock-holmes.co.uk. Daily 9.30am–6pm. £15.
Sherlock Holmes' fictional address was 221b Baker Street, hence the number on the door of the museum. Unashamedly touristy, the place is stuffed full of Victoriana and life-size models of characters from the books. It's an atmospheric and very competent exercise in period reconstruction – you can even don a deerstalker to have your picture taken by the fireside, looking like the great detective himself.

Sherlock Holmes Museum

MAYFAIR AND MARYLEBONE

Shops

Browns

MAP P.41, POCKET MAP C15
23–27 South Molton St ⊖ Bond Street.
Mon–Wed & Sat 10am–7pm, Thurs & Fri
10am–8pm, Sun noon–6pm.
Huge range of designer wear, with
big international names under the
same roof as the more cutting-edge,
up-and-coming designers. Browns
Menswear is at no. 23.

Charbonnel et Walker

MAP P.41, POCKET MAP D16
1 Royal Arcade, 28 Old Bond St ⊖ Green
Park. Mon–Sat 9.30am–6.30pm, Sun
noon–5pm.
Established in 1875, this is
where Her Majesty stocks up on
chocolate. The truffles and gift
sets are all presented in exquisite
packaging.

Daunt Books

MAP P.46, POCKET MAP B13
83 Marylebone High St ⊖ Baker Street.
Mon–Sat 9am–7.30pm, Sun 11am–6pm.
Wide and inspirational range of
travel literature and guidebooks,

Selfridges, Oxford Street

plus fiction and non-fiction,
presented by expert staff in the
beautiful, galleried interior of this
famous shop.

Fortnum & Mason

MAP P.41, POCKET MAP E16
181 Piccadilly ⊖ Green Park or Piccadilly
Circus. Mon–Sat 10am–9pm, Sun
11.30am–6pm.
Beautiful three hundred-year-old
department store with heavenly
murals, cherubs, chandeliers and
fountains as a backdrop to its
perfectly English offerings. Justly
famous for its fabulous, pricey
food, it also specializes in upmarket
designer clothes, furniture, luggage
and stationery.

Hamleys

MAP P.41, POCKET MAP D15
188–196 Regent St ⊖ Oxford Circus.
Mon–Fri 10am–9pm, Sat 9.30am–9pm, Sun
noon–6pm.
Possibly the world's largest toy
shop, and certainly a feast for the
eyes of most small children, with
lots of gadget demonstrations going
on throughout its seven floors of
mayhem.

Liberty

MAP P.41, POCKET MAP D15
210–220 Regent St ⊖ Oxford Circus. Mon–
Sat 10am–9pm, Sun 11.30am–6pm.
A fabulous, partly mock-Tudor
emporium of luxury. Best known
for its fabrics, though it is, in fact, a
full-blown department store.

Selfridges

MAP P.46, POCKET MAP B14
400 Oxford St ⊖ Bond Street. Hours vary;
usually Mon–Sat 9.30am–10pm, Sun
11.30am–6pm.
London's first great department
store, and still one of its best: a
huge, airy palace of luxury clothes,
food and furnishings.

Waterstones

MAP P.41, POCKET MAP E16
203–206 Piccadilly ⊖ Piccadilly Circus.
Mon–Sat 9am–10pm, Sun noon–6.30pm.

This flagship bookstore has six well-stocked floors of books and knowledgeable staff. It hosts plenty of bookish events, and the fifth-floor café-bar is pleasant with some intriguing views.

Cafés

Comptoir Libanais

MAP P.46, POCKET MAP B14
65 Wigmore St ⊖ Bond Street. Mon–Sat 8am–11pm, Sun 9am–10pm.
Bursting with atmosphere, this is one of a colourful, kitschy Middle Eastern deli/café chain; food is a simple and honest selection of mezze, wraps and tagines. Try the home-made lemonades.

Golden Hind

MAP P.46, POCKET MAP B13
73 Marylebone Lane ⊖ Bond Street. Mon–Fri noon–3pm & 6–10pm, Sat 6–10pm.
Marylebone's heritage fish-and-chip restaurant, founded in 1914, serves classic cod and chips from around £11.50, with salmon, skate and steamed fish options available.

MoCafé

MAP P.41, POCKET MAP E16
25 Heddon St ⊖ Piccadilly Circus. Mon–Sat noon–1am, Sun noon–5.30pm.
Serving reasonably priced, tasty snacks and afternoon tea in a wonderful Arabic tearoom – part of *Momo* restaurant – with a greenery-entangled terrace screened off from the restaurant-packed alleyway.

Paul Rothe & Son

MAP P.46, POCKET MAP B14
35 Marylebone Lane ⊖ Bond Street. Mon–Fri 8am–5pm, Sat 11.30am–5pm.
Traditional deli established in 1900, selling "English & Foreign Provisions", offering breakfasts, plus hot food and delicious sandwiches made to order. Friendly and wonderfully unchanging, with a few formica tables inside the shop, which is lined with jars

Paul Rothe & Son

upon jars of traditional jams and preserves.

Rose Bakery

MAP P.41, POCKET MAP D16
17–18 Dover St ⊖ Green Park. Mon–Sat 11am–6.30pm, Sun noon–5.30pm.
An offshoot of Paris's favourite English tearoom, serving simple home-made lunches and fabulous cakes in the high-fashion Dover Street Market designer store.

Tibits

MAP P.41, POCKET MAP E15
12–14 Heddon St ⊖ Piccadilly Circus. Mon–Wed 9am–10.30pm, Thurs & Fri 9am–midnight, Sat 11.30am–midnight, Sun 11.30am–10.30pm.
Spacious, rather glam veggie café serving more than forty salads and hot dishes from across the globe – help yourself from the buffet and pay by weight.

The Wolseley

MAP P.41, POCKET MAP D17
160 Piccadilly ⊖ Green Park ☏ 020 7409 6996. Mon–Fri 7am–midnight, Sat 8am–midnight, Sun 8am–11pm.
The European brasserie food is good if not that cheap, but the big

Pollen Street Social

draw is the lofty and opulent 1920s interior (built as the showroom for Wolseley cars). It's a great place for breakfast or a cream tea (see page 43) and very popular so book ahead.

Restaurants

Kiku

MAP P.41, POCKET MAP C17
17 Half Moon St ⊖ Green Park ☎ 020 7499 4208. Mon–Sat noon–2.30pm & 6–10.15pm, Sun 5.30–9.45pm.

This place has been serving top-quality sushi and sashimi for decades. "Kiku" means "pricey", and although prices do start from £4 for sushi, they rapidly rise. Take a seat at the counter and wonder at the dexterity of the knife man. Set lunch £28–38; mains start at around £14.

The Ivy Café

MAP P.46, POCKET MAP B13
96 Marylebone Lane ⊖ Bond Street ☎ 020 3301 0400. Mon–Fri 7.30am–1.30am, Sat 8am–1.30am, Sun 9am–12.30am.

A relaxed, but still glamorous, all-day brasserie offshoot of the famous *Ivy* restaurant, the *Ivy Café* serves

comfort-food classics – fishcakes or steak, egg and chips – plus an impressive selection of vegan and veggie choices. Mains £12–19.

Phoenix Palace

MAP P.46, POCKET MAP A12
5 Glentworth St ⊖ Baker Street ☎ 020 7486 3515. Mon–Sat noon–11.30pm, Sun 11am–10.30pm.

There's plenty to choose from in this huge, popular restaurant, with dishes from all over China. Good dim sum, too, served till 5pm. Mains £11–40.

Pollen Street Social

MAP P.41, POCKET MAP D15
8/10 Pollen St ⊖ Oxford Circus ☎ 020 7290 7600. Mon–Sat noon–2.30pm & 6–10.30pm.

Michelin-starred restaurant from wunderkind chef Jason Atherton, who produces delicate cuisine with wit and flair. Mains from £35; set lunches from £37.

The Providores & Tapa Room

MAP P.46, POCKET MAP B13
109 Marylebone High St ⊖ Baker Street ☎ 020 7935 6175. Tapa Room Mon–Fri 8am–11.30pm & noon–10.30pm, Sat 9am–3pm & 4–10.30pm, Sun 9am–3pm & 4–10pm. Restaurant Mon–Fri noon–3pm & 6–10.30pm, Sat 10am–3pm & 6–10.30pm, Sun 10am–3pm & 4–10pm; summer closed Sun eve.

Outstanding fusion restaurant split into two: the *Tapa Room* café and bar downstairs and an elegant restaurant upstairs. The food in both is inventive and beautiful. *Tapa Room* sharing plates from £6, brunch from £8; dinner £35 for two courses.

Rasa W1

MAP P.41, POCKET MAP C14
6 Dering St ⊖ Bond Street ☎ 020 7629 1346. Mon–Sat noon–3pm & 6–11pm, Sun 1–3pm & 6–9pm.

A superb South Indian restaurant dishing up tasty, subtle dishes from £7–8 – try the *bagar baingan* (aubergine in a creamy cashew sauce). Veggie options, including the *dosas*, are best.

Wild Honey

MAP P.41, POCKET MAP D15
12 St George St ⊖ Oxford Circus or Bond Street ⓣ 020 7758 9160. Mon–Sat noon–2.30pm & 6–10.30pm.
Very popular, high-end wood-panelled brasserie, serving up a daily-changing menu of slow-cooked, seasonal UK-sourced haute cuisine. Mains from £22; lunch menus £35.

Pubs and bars

Audley

MAP P.41, POCKET MAP B16
41 Mount St ⊖ Bond Street or Green Park. Mon–Sat 11am–11pm, Sun noon–10.30pm.
A grand Mayfair pub, with its original Victorian woodwork, chandeliers and clock.

Golden Eagle

MAP P.46, POCKET MAP B13
59 Marylebone Lane ⊖ Bond Street. Mon–Sat 11am–11pm, Sun noon–10.30pm.
Proper old neighbourhood pub, made up of one single room – they even have regular singalongs on the old "Joanna" (Tues, Thurs & Fri).

The Guinea

MAP P.41, POCKET MAP C16
30 Bruton Place ⊖ Bond Street or Oxford Circus. Mon–Sat 11am–11pm, Sun noon–5pm.
Pretty, old-fashioned, flower-strewn back-lane pub, serving good Young's bitter and tasty pies and steak sandwiches. There's a traditional steak restaurant (*The Guinea Grill*) attached.

The Windmill

MAP P.41, POCKET MAP D15
6–8 Mill St ⊖ Oxford Circus. Mon–Fri 11am–11pm, Sat noon–11pm, Sun noon–6pm.
Convivial, well-regarded pub just off Regent Street, a perfect retreat for exhausted shoppers with a summer roof terrace. The Young's beers are top-notch, as are the award-winning pies.

Venues

The Phoenix

MAP P.41, POCKET MAP D14
37 Cavendish Square ⊖ Oxford Circus ⓦ www.phoenixcavendishsquare.co.uk. Mon–Thurs noon–midnight, Fri 11am–2am, Sat noon–3am, Sun noon–midnight.
Friendly pub/club with a roster of enjoyable basement club nights from indie via disco to soul, plus good comedy nights.

Wigmore Hall

MAP P.46, POCKET MAP C14
36 Wigmore St ⊖ Bond Street ⓣ 020 7935 2141, ⓦ wigmore-hall.org.uk.
With its near-perfect acoustics, this intimate classical and chamber music venue – originally a piano showroom – is a favourite with artists and audiences alike. Book ahead.

Golden Eagle

Soho and Covent Garden

Soho is very much the heart of the West End, home to more theatres and cinemas than any other single area in London. As the city's premier red-light district for centuries, it retains an unorthodox and slightly raffish air that's unique in central London. Conventional sights are few and far between, yet it's a great area to wander through – whatever the hour there's always something going on. Soho has long been one of London's LGBTQ quarters, focused around Old Compton Street. More sanitized and brazenly commercial, Covent Garden is one of London's chief tourist attractions, thanks to its buskers, pedestrianized piazza and old Victorian market hall. Some three centuries ago the piazza was the great playground of eighteenth-century London. Nowadays, while the market is pretty, but touristy, the streets to the north boast some very fashionable boutiques.

Leicester Square

MAP P.54, POCKET MAP G16

⊖ Leicester Square.

By night, when the big cinemas and nightclubs are doing brisk

Leicester Square

business and the buskers are entertaining passers-by, Leicester Square is one of the most crowded places in London; on a Friday or Saturday night, it can seem as if half the youth of the city's suburbs have congregated here to get drunk, supplemented by a vast number of tourists. As a result, most Londoners avoid the place unless they're heading for one of the cinemas. It wasn't until the mid-nineteenth century that the square began to emerge as an entertainment zone, with accommodation houses (for prostitutes and their clients) and music halls. These included the grandiose **Empire**, now a cinema that's a favourite for big red-carpet premieres, and a couple of blocks east the **Hippodrome** – designed by Frank Matcham in 1900 – which is now the UK's biggest casino. Purpose-built movie houses moved in during the 1930s – a golden age evoked by the sleek black lines of the **Odeon** on the east side – and maintain their grip on the area.

Chinatown

Chinatown

MAP P.54, POCKET MAP F15–G15

⊖ Leicester Square.

A self-contained jumble of shops, cafés and restaurants, Chinatown is one of London's most distinct and popular ethnic enclaves. Centred around **Gerrard Street**, it's a tiny area of no more than three or four blocks, thick with the aromas of Chinese cooking and peppered with ersatz touches. Few of London's sixty thousand Chinese actually live in Chinatown, but it nonetheless remains a focus for the community: a place to do business or the weekly shopping, celebrate a wedding, or just meet up for meals – particularly on Sundays, when the restaurants overflow with Chinese families tucking into dim sum. Most Londoners come to Chinatown simply to eat – easy and inexpensive enough to do. Cantonese cuisine predominates, though the quality is variable.

Charing Cross Road

MAP P.54, POCKET MAP F14–G1

⊖ Leicester Square. 6

Charing Cross Road, which marks Soho's eastern border, boasts the highest concentration of bookshops anywhere in London. One of the first to open here, in 1906, was **Foyles** originally at no. 119 – Éamon de Valera, George Bernard Shaw, Walt Disney and Arthur Conan Doyle were all once regular customers. Now you'll find Foyles in vast premises at no. 107 (see page 60). You'll find more of Charing Cross Road's original character at the string of specialist and secondhand bookshops south of Cambridge Circus. One of the nicest places for specialist and antiquarian book-browsing is **Cecil Court**, the southernmost pedestrianized alleyway between Charing Cross Road and St Martin's Lane. These short, civilized, paved alleys boast specialist bookshops, plus various antiquarian dealers selling modern first editions, old theatre posters, coins and notes, cigarette cards, maps and children's books.

Old Compton Street

MAP P.54, POCKET MAP F15–G15

⊖ Leicester Square.

If Soho has a main drag, it has to be Old Compton Street, which

Soho and Covent Garden

ACCOMMODATION	
Dean Street Townhouse	5
The Fielding Hotel	4
Hazlitt's	3
Nadler Soho	2
Oxford Street YHA	1
Thistle Piccadilly	6

SHOPS	
Foyles	2
Japan Centre	7
Magma	1
Neal's Yard Dairy	3
Pleasures of past times	6
Reign Vintage	4
Stanfords	5

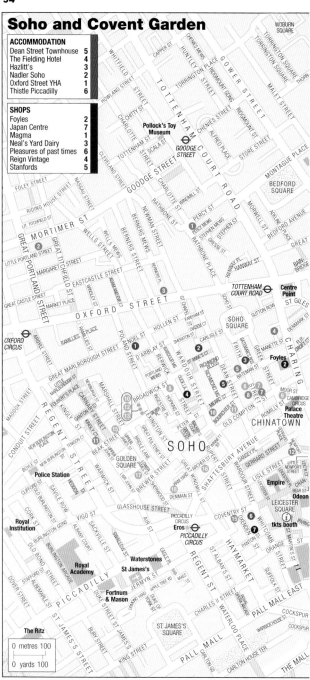

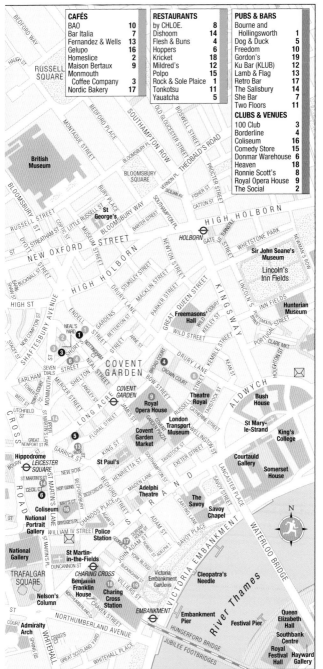

CAFÉS

BAO	10
Bar Italia	7
Fernandez & Wells	13
Gelupo	16
Homeslice	2
Maison Bertaux	9
Monmouth	
Coffee Company	3
Nordic Bakery	17

RESTAURANTS

by CHLOE.	8
Dishoom	14
Flesh & Buns	4
Hoppers	6
Kricket	18
Mildred's	12
Polpo	15
Rock & Sole Plaice	1
Tonkotsu	11
Yauatcha	5

PUBS & BARS

Bourne and	
Hollingsworth	1
Dog & Duck	5
Freedom	10
Gordon's	19
Ku Bar (KLUB)	12
Lamb & Flag	13
Retro Bar	17
The Salisbury	14
She Bar	7
Two Floors	11

CLUBS & VENUES

100 Club	3
Borderline	4
Coliseum	16
Comedy Store	15
Donmar Warehouse	6
Heaven	18
Ronnie Scott's	8
Royal Opera House	9
The Social	2

Covent Garden Market

runs parallel to Shaftesbury Avenue. The old-school pubs, seedy shops, boutiques, cafés and bars here are typical of the area and a good barometer of the latest Soho fads. The liberal atmosphere of Soho has also made it a permanent fixture on the **gay scene** since the last century, with gay bars, clubs and cafés jostling for position on Old Compton Street. Its cross-streets – Greek, Frith and Dean – feature a tempting mix of old-school Italian cafés, jazz clubs, members' bars and new restaurants.

Carnaby Street

MAP P.54, POCKET MAP E15
⊖ Oxford Circus.

Carnaby Street was famous as the fashion focus of London's Swinging Sixties. A victim of its own hype, it quickly declined into an avenue of overpriced tack, and so it remained for several decades. Nowadays, it's pedestrianized and smart again, but dominated by chains – for any sign of contemporary London fashion, you have to go round the corner to **Foubert's Place** and **Newburgh**

Street. Kingsly Court, tucked away just off Carnaby Street, hosts some of the better dining and drinking options.

Pollock's Toy Museum

MAP P.54, POCKET MAP E12
1 Scala St ⊖ Goodge Street ☎ 020 7636 3452, ⓦ www.pollockstoys.com. Mon–Sat 10am–5pm. £7.

This highly atmospheric, doll's house-like toy museum is housed above a wonderful toy shop. Its collections include a fine example of the Victorian paper theatres popularized by Benjamin Pollock, who sold them under the slogan "a penny plain, two pence coloured". The other exhibits range from vintage teddy bears to Sooty and Sweep, and from Red Army soldiers to wax dolls, filling every nook and cranny of the museum's six tiny, rickety rooms and its two winding stairways – be sure to look out for the dalmatian, Dismal Desmond.

Covent Garden Piazza

MAP P.54, POCKET MAP H15
⊖ Covent Garden.

Cleopatra's Needle

London's oldest monument, **Cleopatra's Needle** (Map p.54, Pocket Map J16) languishes little-noticed on the busy Victoria Embankment, guarded by two Victorian sphinxes (facing the wrong way). The 60ft-high, 180-ton stick of granite actually has nothing to do with Cleopatra – it's one of a pair erected in Heliopolis in 1475 BC (the other one is in New York's Central Park) and taken to Alexandria by Emperor Augustus fifteen years after Cleopatra's suicide. This obelisk was presented to Britain in 1819 by the Turkish viceroy of Egypt, but nearly sixty years passed before it finally made its way to London. It was erected in 1878, above a time capsule containing, among other things, the day's newspapers, a box of hairpins, a railway timetable and pictures of the country's twelve prettiest women.

London's oldest planned square, laid out in the 1630s by Inigo Jones, Covent Garden Piazza was initially a great success – its novelty value alone ensured a rich and aristocratic clientele for the surrounding properties. Over the next century, though, the tone of the place fell as the fruit and vegetable **market** expanded, and theatres and coffee houses began to move in. Eventually, a large covered market was constructed in the middle of the square, but when the market closed in 1974, it was very nearly demolished to make way for an office development. Instead, the elegant Victorian market hall and its largely pedestrianized, cobbled piazza were restored to house shops, restaurants and craft stalls. The piazza is now one of London's major tourist attractions.

St Paul's Church

MAP P.54, POCKET MAP H15
Bedford St ⊖ Covent Garden ☎ 020 7836 5221, Ⓦ actorschurch.org. Mon–Fri 8.30am–5pm, Sat depending on events, Sun 9am–1pm. Free.
The proximity of so many theatres has earned this church the nickname of the "**Actors' Church**", and it's filled with memorials to international thespians from Boris Karloff to Gracie Fields. The space in front of the church's Tuscan portico – where Eliza Doolittle

was discovered selling violets by Henry Higgins in George Bernard Shaw's *Pygmalion* – is now a legalized venue for the piazza's buskers and street performers, who must audition for a slot months in advance. Round the back, the **churchyard** provides a tranquil respite from the activity outside.

London Transport Museum

MAP P.54, POCKET MAP H15
Covent Garden Piazza ⊖ Covent Garden ☎ 020 7379 6344, Ⓦ ltmuseum.co.uk. Daily 10am–6pm. £17.50 (kids free).

London Transport Museum

Half-price theatre tickets

The Society of London Theatre (Ⓦwww.tkts.co.uk) runs the **TKTS booth** in Leicester Square (Mon–Sat 10am–7pm, Sun 11am–4.30pm), which sells tickets for all the West End shows for the same day and two days ahead, with discounts of up to fifty percent. On average, you're looking at £20–40 per ticket.

Housed in the piazza's former flower market, the ever-popular London Transport Museum is a surefire hit for families with kids under 10. To follow the story of London's transport chronologically, head for Level 2, where you'll find a reconstructed 1829 Shillibeer's Horse Omnibus, which provided the city's first regular horse-bus service. Level 1 tells the story of the world's first underground system and contains a lovely 1920s Metropolitan line carriage, fitted out in burgundy and green with pretty, drooping lamps. Down on the ground floor, you can peep inside the first tube train, from the 1890s, whose lack of windows earned it the nickname "the padded cell". Most of the interactive stuff is aimed at kids, but visitors of all ages should check out the tube driver simulator. You can buy reproductions of the Tube's stylish maps and posters, many commissioned from well-known artists, at the shop on the way out.

Royal Opera House
MAP P.54, POCKET MAP H15
Bow St ⊖ Covent Garden ⓘ 020 7304 4000, Ⓦ www.roh.org.uk.
The arcading in the northeast corner of the piazza was rebuilt as part of the multi-million pound refurbishment of the Royal Opera House whose Neoclassical facade, dating from 1811, opens onto Bow Street. The market's spectacular wrought-iron **Floral Hall** now serves as the opera house's impressive first-floor foyer and champagne bar; the next level up is a terrace overlooking the piazza, beyond the *Amphitheatre* bar/restaurant. Excellent **backstage tours** of the opera house (book in advance; usually Mon–Sat 10.30am, 12.30 & 2.30pm; £12) give you a sense of the huge scale of the operation, and depending on the day's schedule, can include a look-in at ballet rehearsals.

Freemasons' Hall
MAP P.54, POCKET MAP H14
60 Great Queen St ⊖ Covent Garden ⓘ 020 7395 9257, Ⓦ www.freemasonry.london. museum. Mon–Sat 10am–5pm. Free.
It's difficult to miss the austere, Pharaonic mass of the Freemasons' Hall, built as a memorial to all the masons who died in World War I. The interior is worth a peek for the **Grand Temple** alone, whose pompous, bombastic decor is laden with heavy symbolism. To see it, you must sign up for one of the free guided tours (Mon–Fri 11am, noon, 2, 3 & 4pm, some tours on Sat, check in advance). There's a museum of masonic regalia, and a shop, too.

Benjamin Franklin House
MAP P.54, POCKET MAP H16
36 Craven St ⊖ Charing Cross ⓘ 020 7839 2006, Ⓦ benjaminfranklinhouse. org. Architectural tour Mon noon, 1pm, 2pm, 3.15pm & 4.15pm. £6. Historical Experience tour Wed–Sun noon, 1pm, 2pm, 3.15pm & 4.15pm. £8.
From 1757 to 1775, **Benjamin Franklin** (1706–90) lived in London espousing the cause of the British colonies (of which the US was then one), before

returning to America to help draft the Declaration of Independence and the US Constitution. Wisely, the curators have left Franklin's house pretty much empty, eschewing any attempt to install period furniture. Instead, aided by a costumed guide and a series of impressionistic audiovisuals, visitors are transported back to the time of Franklin, who lived here with his "housekeeper" in cosy domesticity while his wife and daughter languished in Philadelphia. Note that visits are by guided tour only and should be booked in advance. Shorter tours focusing on the history of the building run on Mondays.

Victoria Embankment

MAP P.54, POCKET MAP J16–H19
⊖ Temple or Embankment.

Built between 1868 and 1874, the Victoria Embankment was the inspiration of civil engineer **Joseph Bazalgette**, whose project simultaneously relieved congestion along the Strand, provided an extension to the underground railway and sewage systems, and created a new stretch of parkland, now dotted with statues and memorials, and a riverside walk – no longer much fun due to the volume of traffic that barrels along it, though it does afford some good views over the river.

Somerset House

MAP P.54, POCKET MAP J16
Victoria Embankment ⊖ Temple ⓘ 020 7845 4600, ⓦ www.somersethouse.org. uk. Courtyard & terrace daily 8am–11pm. Exhibition spaces Mon, Tues, Sat & Sun 10am–6pm, Wed–Fri 11am–8pm. Free.

Sole survivor of the grand edifices which once lined this stretch of the riverfront, Somerset House's four wings enclose an elegant and surprisingly large courtyard. From March to October, a wonderful 55-jet fountain spouts straight from the courtyard's cobbles; in winter, an ice rink is set up in its

place. The monumental Palladian building itself was begun in 1776 by William Chambers as a purpose-built governmental office development, but now houses a series of exhibition spaces, and puts on events throughout the year. Various free **guided tours** are available (Tues, Thurs & Sat; get tickets from information desk in South Building from 10.30am).

In the house's north wing is the **Courtauld Gallery** (daily 10am–6pm; £8; ⓦ www. courtauld.ac.uk), chiefly known for their dazzling permanent collection of Impressionist and Post-Impressionist paintings. It is currently closed for refurbishment until at least 2020, but key pieces of the collection will be displayed in temporary exhibitions around London and further afield during this time. Among the most celebrated works are a small-scale version of Manet's nostalgic *Bar at the Folies-Bergère,* Renoir's *La Loge* and Degas' *Two Dancers,* plus a whole heap of Cézanne's canvases, including one of his series of *Card Players.* The Courtauld also boasts a fine selection of works by the likes of Bellini, Brueghel, Rubens, van Dyck, Tiepolo and Cranach the Elder.

Embankment Gardens

Shops

Foyles

MAP P.54, POCKET MAP G14
107 Charing Cross Rd ⊖ Tottenham
Court Road. Mon–Sat 9.30am–9pm, Sun
11.30am–6pm.
Long-established, famous and
huge bookshop with an excellent
selection of titles old and new,
plus a jazz music store, a café and
a gallery.

Japan Centre

MAP P.54, POCKET MAP F16
35b Panton St ⊖ Piccadilly Circus. Mon–
Sat 10am–9.30pm, Sun 11am–8pm.
This basement shop and food
centre is cram-packed with
everything Japanese: *the* place to
get every variety of noodle, sushi
ingredients, fresh miso, sake and
Japanese whiskies. Also has food
counters for ramen and other
treats.

Magma

MAP P.54, POCKET MAP G14
29 Shorts Gardens ⊖ Covent Garden. Mon–
Sat 11am–7pm, Sun 11am–6pm.

Neal's Yard Dairy

It's difficult to leave this sleek store
empty-handed, filled as it is with
beautifully designed, whimsical and
affordable gifts, toys, homeware,
stationery, books and gizmos.

Neal's Yard Dairy

MAP P.54, POCKET MAP G14
17 Shorts Gardens ⊖ Covent Garden. Mon–
Sat 10am–7pm.
London's finest cheese shop, with
a huge selection of quality cheeses
from around the British Isles, as
well as a few exceptionally good
ones from Europe. They're happy
for you to taste before you buy.

Pleasures of past times

MAP P.54, POCKET MAP G16
11 Cecil Court ⊖ Leicester Square. Tues–
Fri 11am–6pm, Sat noon–6pm (ring the
bell if needed).
Treasure trove for secondhand
showbiz books, including vintage
titles and curiosities, rare finds,
posters, prints and old postcards.

Reign Vintage

MAP P.54, POCKET MAP F15
12 Berwick St ⊖ Oxford Circus. Mon–Sat
11am–8pm, Sun 11am–7pm.
In the heart of rapidly gentrifying
Berwick Street, this spruce
secondhand shop is a cut above
its rivals, sourcing its gear from
Europe and helpfully organizing it
by colour and style.

Stanfords

MAP P.54, POCKET MAP G15
7 Mercer Street ⊖ Covent Garden. Mon–Sat
9am–8pm, Sun 11.30am–6pm.
The world's largest specialist travel
bookshop, stocking pretty much any
map of anywhere, plus a huge range
of guides, travel literature and gifts.

Cafés

BAO

MAP P.54, POCKET MAP E15
53 Lexington St ⊖ Piccadilly Circus.
Mon–Sat noon–3pm & 5.30–10pm, Sun
noon–5pm.

Minimalist *BAO* is a firm favourite for authentic Taiwanese food. Reservations aren't taken, and queues snake down the road for the moreish, fluffy steamed buns.

Bar Italia

MAP P.54, POCKET MAP F15

22 Frith St ⊖ Tottenham Court Road. Mon–Sat 7am–5am, Sun 7am–midnight.

This tiny coffee bar is a Soho institution, serving espressos, croissants and sandwiches around the clock – as it has been since the 50s.

Fernandez & Wells

MAP P.54, POCKET MAP E15

43 Lexington Street ⊖ Piccadilly Circus. Mon–Fri 8am–11pm, Sat 11am–11pm.

Excellent gourmet sandwiches, charcuterie and cheeses and small plates for around £5–8, plus great coffee and amazing cakes for around £2, at this small urban-rustic café – licensed with a good list of wines and sherries.

Gelupo

MAP P.54, POCKET MAP F15

7 Archer St ⊖ Piccadilly Circus. Mon–Thurs 11am–11pm, Fri & Sat 11am–midnight, Sun noon–11pm.

The place for artisan gelatos, sorbets and granitas – from roasted plum to burnt caramel and bitter chocolate sorbet (flavours change every day) – and good strong Italian coffee.

Homeslice

MAP P.54, POCKET MAP G14

13 Neal's Yard ⊖ Covent Garden. Daily noon–11pm.

Buzzing place offering wood-fired thin-crust gourmet pizzas with inventive toppings plus fizz on tap; £5 per slice, £20 for a 20-inch pizza.

Maison Bertaux

MAP P.54, POCKET MAP G15

28 Greek St ⊖ Leicester Square or Tottenham Court Road. Mon–Sat 8.30am–10.30pm, Sun 9.30am–7.30pm.

Maison Bertaux

Long-standing, old-fashioned and wonderfully French patisserie with two floors inside and charming street-side tables. Fabulous cakes, tarts and croissants in a lively, pretty setting.

Monmouth Coffee Company

MAP P.54, POCKET MAP G14

27 Monmouth St ⊖ Covent Garden. Mon–Sat 8am–6.30pm.

The marvellous aroma hits you when you walk in to this cosy coffee house. Pick your coffee from a fine selection, buy the beans to take home, and grab a pastry to go.

Nordic Bakery

MAP P.54, POCKET MAP E15

14a Golden Square ⊖ Piccadilly Circus. Mon–Fri 7.30am–8pm, Sat 8.30am–7pm, Sun 9am–7pm.

Stylish Nordic independent café and bakery, where the lofty ceilings and huge windows create a welcoming space to enjoy coffee, rye bread sandwiches and Scandi pastries – try the berry or cinnamon buns.

Flesh & Buns

Restaurants

by CHLOE.

MAP P.54, POCKET MAP J15
34–43 Russell St ⊖ Covent Garden.
Mon–Wed & Sun 10am–10pm, Thurs–Sat 10am–11pm.

Riding the vegan wave, the quirky US fast-food brand has opened in Covent Garden and added some British twists – like tofu fish'n'chips – to its on-trend menu of vegan mac'n'cheese, meatballs and salads.

Dishoom

MAP P.54, POCKET MAP G15
12 Upper St Martin's Lane ⊖ Leicester Square ⊕ 020 7420 9320. Mon–Thurs 8am–11pm, Fri 8am–midnight, Sat 9am–midnight, Sun 9am–11pm.

Re-creating the atmosphere of the Persian cafés of Old Bombay, this is a buzzy place which serves delicious Indian food; the breakfasts are a hit too. Arrive early, or be prepared to queue.

Flesh & Buns

MAP P.54, POCKET MAP G15
41 Earlham St ⊖ Covent Garden ⊕ 020 7632 9500. Mon & Tues noon–3pm & 5–10pm, Wed–Fri noon–3pm & 5–11pm, Sat noon–11pm, Sun noon–9.30pm.

Enjoy delicious rice buns with meat or fish, washed down with sake, at this loud, friendly, rock'n'roll *izakaya*-style basement restaurant; lunch or pre-theatre set menu £22 for two courses.

Hoppers

MAP P.54, POCKET MAP F15
49 Frith St ⊖ Leicester Square. Mon–Thurs noon–2.20pm & 5.30–10.30pm, Fri & Sat noon–10.45pm, Sat noon–10.30pm.

Outstanding, moreish Sri Lankan food – fiery, unusual curries are accompanied by "hoppers", bowl-shaped rice pancakes, or rotis. No reservations; come early.

Kricket

MAP P.54, POCKET MAP E16
12 Denman St ⊖ Piccadilly Circus ⓦ kricket.co.uk. Mon–Sat noon–2.30pm & 5–10.30pm.

It started life as a pop-up in a shipping container food market in South London, but *Kricket* has now transplanted to Soho, where it serves sophisticated, gently spiced cocktails alongside a delicious menu of small sharing plates of intriguing Indian dishes. The menu changes seasonally, but the samphire pakora (£7) and Keralan fried chicken (£8.50) are firm favourites.

Mildred's

MAP P.54, POCKET MAP E15
45 Lexington St ⊖ Oxford Circus ⊕ 020 7494 1634. Mon–Sat noon–11pm.

This cheery veggie restaurant is a Soho stand-by, serving a wholesome, delicious and varied menu of burgers, curries and pies, as well as wicked but wonderful puddings. Mains £12; no bookings.

Polpo

MAP P.54, POCKET MAP E15
41 Beak St ⊖ Piccadilly Circus ⊕ 020 7734 4479. Mon–Sat 11.30am–11pm, Sun 11.30am–10pm.

Fabulous bar-restaurant modelled on a Venetian *bacaro*. Small plates from £6 – try the crab and chilli linguine, *pizzette* or any of the *polpette* (meatballs). Reservations for lunch; limited ones for dinner – you may have to queue.

Rock & Sole Plaice

MAP P.54, POCKET MAP H14
47 Endell St ⊖ Covent Garden ⓘ 020 7836 3785. Mon–Sat 11.30am–10.30pm, Sun noon–10.30pm.
Pricey fish-and-chip shop (from £15), where they do all the staples just right; you eat in or at one of the pavement tables.

Tonkotsu

MAP P.54, POCKET MAP F15
63 Dean St ⊖ Tottenham Court Road ⓘ 020 7437 0071. Mon–Fri noon–3pm & 5–10.30pm, Sat 11.30am–10.30pm, Sun 11.30am–10pm.
Slurpable, silky home-made ramen noodles in rich, savoury stocks, with pork belly, seafood or veggie options – the first in a rapidly expanding franchise. Prices start from £10.

Yauatcha

MAP P.54, POCKET MAP E15
15–17 Broadwick St ⊖ Piccadilly Circus ⓘ 020 7494 8888. Mon–Sat noon–10pm, Sun noon–10.30pm, patisserie counter till 11pm.
Sleek, contemporary Chinese teahouse-restaurant serving up dim sum (£6–12) and classy patisserie throughout the day.

Pubs and bars

Bourne and Hollingsworth

MAP P.54, POCKET MAP F13
28 Rathbone Place ⊖ Goodge Street. Mon & Tues 5pm–12.30am, Wed–Sat 5pm–1.30am.
Prohibition-style vintage cocktail bar in a tucked-away basement, offering a playful, changing cocktail menu.

Dog & Duck

MAP P.54, POCKET MAP F15
18 Bateman St ⊖ Tottenham Court Road. Mon–Thurs 11.30am–11pm, Fri 11.30am–11.30pm, Sat 11am–11.30pm, Sun noon–10.30pm.
Tiny Nicholson's pub that retains much of its old character, with beautiful Victorian tiling and mosaics, plus a decent range of real ales.

Freedom

MAP P.54, POCKET MAP F15
66 Wardour St ⊖ Piccadilly Circus. Mon–Thurs 4pm–3am, Fri & Sat 2pm–3am, Sun 4–10.30pm.
Established gay bar, popular with a straight/gay Soho crowd. It's a good spot for evening drinks, and the basement hosts various cabaret and club nights.

Gordon's

MAP P.54, POCKET MAP H17
47 Villiers St ⊖ Embankment. Mon–Sat 11am–11pm, Sun noon–10pm.
Cavernous, shabby, atmospheric wine bar specializing in ports and sherries. The excellent and varied wine list, decent buffet food and genial atmosphere make this a

Gordon's

favourite with local office workers, who spill outdoors in the summer.

Ku Bar (KLUB)

MAP P.54, POCKET MAP G15
30 Lisle St ⊖ Leicester Square. Mon–Sat 10pm–3am, Sun noon–midnight. Club till 5am last Fri & Sat of month.

The Lisle Street original, with a downstairs club open late, is one of Soho's largest and best-loved gay bars, serving a scene-conscious yet low-on-attitude clientele. It's joined by a stylish sibling bar on Frith Street.

Lamb & Flag

MAP P.54, POCKET MAP G15
33 Rose St ⊖ Leicester Square or Covent Garden. Mon–Sat 11am–11.30pm, Sun noon–10.30pm.

Small, popular historic pub hidden away down an alley between Garrick Street and Floral Street where the Poet Laureate, John Dryden, was beaten up in 1679 by a group of thugs, hired most probably by his rival poet, the Earl of Rochester.

The Salisbury

Retro Bar

MAP P.54, POCKET MAP H16
2 George Court, off Strand ⊖ Charing Cross
Ⓦ www.retrobarlondon.co.uk. Mon–Fri noon–11pm, Sat 2–11pm, Sun 2–10pm.

Indie/retro gay bar tucked down a quiet alleyway, playing 1970s and 80s rock, pop, rockabilly and alternative sounds, and featuring regular pub quizzes and DJ nights.

The Salisbury

MAP P.54, POCKET MAP G16
90 St Martin's Lane ⊖ Leicester Square. Mon–Thurs 11am–11pm, Fri & Sat 11am–midnight, Sun 11am–10.30pm.

Well-preserved Victorian pub with cut, etched and engraved windows, bronze lampstands, Art Nouveau light fittings and a fine lincrusta ceiling.

She Bar

MAP P.54, POCKET MAP F15
23 Old Compton St ⊖ Leicester Square. Mon–Thurs 4–11.30pm, Fri & Sat 4pm–12.30am, Sun 4–10.30pm.

Rather swish lesbian bar in the heart of Soho, with regular DJ nights and drinks offers; women-only at busy times.

Two Floors

MAP P.54, POCKET MAP E15
3 Kingly St ⊖ Oxford Circus. Mon–Thurs noon–11.30pm, Fri & Sat noon–midnight, Sun noon–10.30pm.

Soho pub/bar with craft beers and cool cocktails in the bare-bones ground-floor space, and a tiki bar in the basement. It gets very crowded.

Clubs and venues

100 Club

MAP P.54, POCKET MAP E14
100 Oxford St ⊖ Tottenham Court Road
☏ 020 7636 0933, Ⓦ www.the100club.co.uk.

Fun venue whose history stretches back to 1942 and takes in Louis Armstrong, Glenn Miller and the

Sex Pistols. Now hosts eclectic rock and indie, with some jazz.

Borderline

MAP P.54, POCKET MAP F14
Orange Yard, off Manette St ⊖ Tottenham Court Road ☎ 020 3871 7777, Ⓦ www.theborderlinelondon.com.
Consistently good live music with an indie edge, ranging from nu-folk to punk, plus lively club nights.

Coliseum

MAP P.54, POCKET MAP G16
St Martin's Lane ⊖ Leicester Square ☎ 020 7845 9300, Ⓦ www.eno.org.
Home to the English National Opera, which differs from its Royal Opera House counterpart in that all its operas are sung in English, productions tend to be more experimental, and tickets cost a lot less.

Comedy Store

MAP P.54, POCKET MAP F16
1a Oxendon St ⊖ Piccadilly Circus ☎ 020 7024 2060, Ⓦ www.thecomedystore.co.uk.
Venerable alternative-comedy venue, with improv by in-house comics and a regular stand-up bill. Weekends are busiest, with two shows – book ahead.

Donmar Warehouse

MAP P.54, POCKET MAP G15
41 Earlham St ⊖ Covent Garden ☎ 020 3282 3808, Ⓦ www.donmarwarehouse.com.
Excellent theatre noted for its new plays, top-quality reappraisals of the classics and star-studded casts.

Heaven

MAP P.54, POCKET MAP H17
Villiers St ⊖ Charing Cross Ⓦ www.heavennightclub-london.com.
Wildly popular, iconic gay club pulling a mixed, up-for-it crowd for big-name G-A-Y weekend nights and Popcorn Mondays.

Ronnie Scott's

MAP P.54, POCKET MAP F15
47 Frith St ⊖ Tottenham Court Road ☎ 020

Royal Opera House

7439 0747, Ⓦ www.ronniescotts.co.uk.
The most famous jazz club in London, this small and atmospheric place with smart decor is pricey (tickets around £30), but still hosts the best jazz acts in town.

Royal Opera House

MAP P.54, POCKET MAP H15
Bow St ⊖ Covent Garden ☎ 020 7304 4000, Ⓦ www.roh.org.uk.
The ROH can't quite shake its reputation for elitism, and certainly its lavish operas are expensive – though ballet tickets are a little cheaper. Tickets are best booked well in advance, though every Friday at 1pm 49 tickets for performances for the following week are released online.

The Social

MAP P.54, POCKET MAP D13
5 Little Portland St ⊖ Oxford Circus Ⓦ www.thesocial.com. Mon–Wed 3pm–midnight, Thurs 3pm–1am, Fri 12.30pm–1am, Sat 6pm–1am.
Retro club-bar with eclectic live music and great DJs playing everything from afro to electronica to a truly hedonistic, hard-drinking crowd.

Bloomsbury

Bloomsbury was built in grid-plan style from the 1660s onwards, and the formal, bourgeois Georgian squares laid out then remain the area's main distinguishing feature. In the twentieth century, Bloomsbury acquired a reputation as the city's most learned quarter, dominated by the dual institutions of the British Museum and London's central universities, and home to many of London's chief book publishers, but perhaps best known for its literary inhabitants, among them T.S. Eliot and Virginia Woolf. To its north are the busy main-line train stations of Euston, St Pancras and King's Cross – beyond which, straddling the canal, is one of the city's most dynamic redeveloped quarters.

British Museum

MAP P.68, POCKET MAP G13

Great Russell St ⊖ Tottenham Court Road
☎ 020 7323 8299, ⓦ britishmuseum.org.
Daily 10am–5.30pm, Fri until 8.30pm. Free.
Major special exhibitions around £17.

One of the great museums of the world, the BM contains an incredible collection of antiquities, prints, drawings and books. Begun in 1823, the building itself is the grandest of London's Greek Revival edifices, with its central **Great Court** featuring a remarkable curving glass-and-steel roof designed by Norman Foster. At the Court's centre stands the copper-domed former **Round Reading Room** of the British Library, where Karl Marx penned *Das Kapital* (currently closed to the public). Enquire at the information

Great Court, British Museum

desk in the Great Court about free room tours, highlights tours (Fri–Sun 11.30am & 2pm; £14) and audioguides (£7).

The BM's collection of **Roman and Greek antiquities** is unparalleled, and is most famous for the Parthenon sculptures, better known as the **Elgin Marbles** after the British aristocrat who walked off with the reliefs in 1801. Elsewhere, the **Egyptian collection** is easily the most significant outside Egypt, ranging from monumental sculptures to the ever-popular mummies and their ornate outer caskets. Also on display is the **Rosetta Stone**, which enabled French professor Champollion to finally unlock the secret of Egyptian hieroglyphs. Other highlights include a splendid series of **Assyrian reliefs** from Nineveh, and several extraordinary artefacts from **Mesopotamia** such as the enigmatic *Ram in the Thicket* (a goat statuette in lapis lazuli and shell) and the remarkable hoard of goldwork known as the Oxus Treasure.

The leathery half-corpse of the 2000-year-old **Lindow Man**, discovered in a Cheshire bog, and the Anglo-Saxon treasure from the **Sutton Hoo** ship burial, by far the richest single archeological find made in Britain, are among the highlights of the **Europe** collection, which ranges from the twelfth-century **Lewis chessmen** carved from walrus ivory to avant-garde Russian ceramics celebrating the 1917 revolution.

The **Enlightenment Gallery**, which once housed the King's Library, directly off the Great Court in the east wing, displays some of the museum's earliest acquisitions and curios, brought back from the far reaches of the British Empire. Just north of the Great Court stands magnificent *Hoa Hakananai'a*, a *moai* stone head sculpture from Easter Island (Rapa Nui). Take the stairs down from here for the museum's superb **African galleries** in the basement. And in the north wing

Foundling Museum

of the museum, closest to the back entrance on Montague Place, there are also fabulous **Asian** treasures including an extraordinary collection of ancient Chinese porcelain.

Foundling Museum

MAP P.68, POCKET MAP J4
40 Brunswick Square ⊖ Russell Square
☎ 020 7841 3600, ⊛ foundlingmuseum. org.uk. Tues–Sat 10am–5pm, Sun 11am–5pm. £10.

This museum tells the fascinating story of the **Foundling Hospital**, London's first home for abandoned children founded in 1756 by retired sea captain Thomas Coram. As soon as it was opened, it was besieged, and soon forced to reduce its admissions drastically and introduce a ballot system. Among the most tragic exhibits are the tokens left by the mothers in order to identify the children should they ever be in a position to reclaim them: these range from a heart-rending poem to a simple enamel pot label reading "ale". The museum also boasts an impressive **art collection** including works by Hogarth, Gainsborough and Reynolds, now hung in carefully

BLOOMSBURY

preserved eighteenth-century interiors of the original hospital.

Charles Dickens Museum

MAP P.68, POCKET MAP K4
48 Doughty St ⊖ Russell Square ☏ 020 7405 2127, ⓦ www.dickensmuseum.com.
Tues–Sun 10am–5pm. £9.50.

Dickens moved to this house, now a museum, in 1837 shortly after his marriage to Catherine Hogarth, and they lived here for two years, during which time he wrote *Nicholas Nickleby* and *Oliver Twist*. Catherine gave birth to two of their children in the bedroom here, and her youngest sister, who lived with them, died tragically in Dickens' arms. Much of the house's furniture belonged to Dickens, at one time or another, and there's an early portrait miniature painted by his aunt in 1830. The museum puts on special exhibitions in the adjacent house, no. 49, where you'll also find a café.

Wellcome Collection

MAP P.68, POCKET MAP H4
183 Euston Rd ⊖ Euston or Euston Square ☏ 020 7611 2222, ⓦ wellcomecollection.org. Tues–Sat 10am–6pm, Thurs until 10pm, Sun 11am–6pm. Free.

Excellent temporary exhibitions on topical scientific issues are staged in the ground-floor gallery of the Wellcome Collection, founded by American-born pharmaceutical magnate Henry Wellcome (1853–1936). On the first floor, as part of the permanent collection, **Medicine Man** showcases the weird and wonderful collection of historical and scientific artefacts amassed by Wellcome himself. These range from Florence Nightingale's moccasins to a sign for a Chinese doctor's hung with human teeth, and from erotic figurines to phallic amulets – in other words, this section is an absolute must. Next door, **Medicine Now** focuses on

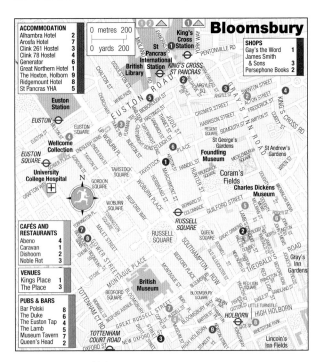

contemporary medical questions, while the top-floor **reading room** is a quirky, well-designed space for private study and perusing more gruesome exhibits.

British Library

MAP P.68, POCKET MAP H3
96 Euston Rd ⊖ King's Cross St Pancras
🌐 0330 333 1144, Ⓦ www.bl.uk. Treasures gallery Mon & Fri 9.30am–6pm, Tues–Thurs 9.30am–8pm, Sat 9.30am–5pm, Sun 11am–5pm. Free.

The red-brick brutalism of the British Library may be horribly out of fashion, but the public exhibition galleries inside are superb. The first place to head for is the dimly lit gallery of **Treasures of the British Library**, where a superlative selection of ancient manuscripts, maps, documents and precious books, including the *Magna Carta*, are displayed. You can also see the Gutenberg Bible, the first to be printed using moveable type; other exhibits, such as Shakespeare first editions, regularly change. The special exhibitions, for which there is sometimes an admission charge, are always excellent.

St Pancras and King's Cross stations

MAP P.68, POCKET MAP J3
Euston Rd.

Completed in 1876, the former Midland Grand Hotel's majestic sweep of Neo-Gothic lancets, dormers and chimney-pots forms the facade of **St Pancras Station**, where Eurostar trains arrive. The adjacent **King's Cross Station**, opened in 1850, is a mere shed in comparison, albeit one with a spectacular semi-circular, glass-roofed concourse on the side. King's Cross is more famous as the station from which **Harry Potter** and his wizarding chums leave for school on the *Hogwarts Express* from platform 9¾. The scenes from the films were shot between platforms 4 and 5, and a station trolley is now embedded in the new concourse

John Betjeman statue, St Pancras Station

wall, providing a perfect photo opportunity for passing Potter fans.

King's Cross canal district

MAP P.68, POCKET MAP J2
⊖ King's Cross Ⓦ kingscross.co.uk. Visitor Centre 11 Stable St Mon–Fri 10am–5pm, Sat 10am–4pm.

To the north of King's Cross, a stretch of Regent's Canal and a cluster of Victorian industrial buildings form focal points for a 67-acre redevelopment project, housing a mixture of high-tech commercial, academic and residential projects. A former granary building, built in 1852 by Lewis Cubitt, architect of King's Cross Station, is home to **Central Saint Martins** school of art, in front of which 1080 fountains jets embedded in the ground dance away in **Granary Square** – irresistible for children on hot days. It's worth exploring the surrounds (you can book a free guided tour). There are galleries, restaurants, weekend markets and pleasant green spaces: some of the area's old **gasholders** have been refurbished, one enclosing a small patch of green, while a footbridge takes you over to **Camley Street Natural Park** (re-opening spring 2019; free).

Shops

Gay's the Word

MAP P.68, POCKET MAP J4

66 Marchmont St ⊖ Russell Square. Mon–Sat 10am–6.30pm, Sun 2–6pm.

An extensive collection of LGBTQ classics, contemporary fiction and non-fiction, plus cards, calendars and weekly lesbian discussion groups and readings.

James Smith & Sons

MAP P.68, POCKET MAP G14

53 New Oxford St ⊖ Tottenham Court Road. Mon, Tues, Thurs & Fri 10am–5.45pm, Wed 10.30am–5.45pm, Sat 10am–5.15pm.

A survivor from an earlier time (it was established in 1830), this beautiful and venerable shop purveys portable seats and canes, but its main trade is in umbrellas.

Persephone Books

MAP P.68, POCKET MAP J12

59 Lamb's Conduit St ⊖ Russell Square. Mon–Fri 10am–6pm, Sat 11am–5pm, Sun noon–4pm.

Lovely bookshop offspring of a publishing house that specializes in neglected early and mid-

James Smith & Sons

twentieth-century writing, mostly by women.

Cafés and restaurants

Abeno

MAP P.68, POCKET MAP H13

47 Museum St ⊖ Tottenham Court Road ☎ 020 7405 3211. Daily noon–10pm.

Japanese place that specializes in *okonomiyaki* (£10–21), a stuffed cabbage, egg and ginger pancake prepared before your eyes. Noodles and set menus, too; reservations recommended.

Caravan

MAP P.68, POCKET MAP J2

1 Granary Square ⊖ King's Cross St Pancras ☎ 020 7101 7661. Mon–Fri 8am–10.30pm, Sat 10am–10.30pm, Sun 10am–4pm. Bar till late.

A trailblazer on the hip King's Cross scene – which has since expanded to five locations – this buzzy spot, occupying a huge old grain store, serves fabulous Modern European food and coffee to a lively, in-the-know crowd. Small plates £7–10; pizzas from £9.

Dishoom

MAP P.68, POCKET MAP J2

5 Stable St ⊖ King's Cross St Pancras ☎ 020 7420 9321. Mon–Wed 8am–11pm, Thurs & Fri 8am–midnight, Sat 9am–midnight, Sun 9am–11pm.

Dishoom, a mini-chain of gorgeous Old Bombay-style restaurants, has nailed sepia-tinted cool and serves great food. The rich black dhal is a winner.

Noble Rot

MAP P.68, POCKET MAP J12

51 Lamb's Conduit St ⊖ Russel Square ☎ 020 7242 8963, ⓦ noblerot.co.uk. Mon–Sat noon–11pm.

A stylish, classic wine bar and restaurant, known for its extensive range of wines by the glass. The restaurant, which serves high-quality dishes with Mediterranean influences and impeccable British ingredients (mains £18–25), can be booked, while bar tables are walk-in only.

Pubs and bars

Bar Polski
MAP P.68, POCKET MAP J13
11 Little Turnstile ⊖ Holborn. Mon 4–11pm, Tues–Thurs 12.30–11pm, Fri 12.30–11.30pm, Sat 6–11pm.
Great Polish bar in an alley near Holborn tube, offering flavoured vodkas and beers, and good, cheap Polish food.

The Duke
MAP P.68, POCKET MAP J12
7 Roger St ⊖ Russell Square or Holborn. Mon–Sat noon–11pm.
Cosy neighbourhood pub with lots of interwar design details. Good, simple food, too.

The Euston Tap
MAP P.68, POCKET MAP H4
190 Euston Road ⊖ Euston. Mon–Sat noon–late, Sun noon–10pm.
A huge selection of ales packed into a tiny space – this pub occupies the two original entrance lodges to the old Euston station, and serves a regularly changing selection of cask and craft ales.

The Lamb
MAP P.68, POCKET MAP J12
94 Lamb's Conduit St ⊖ Russell Square. Mon–Wed 11am–11pm, Thurs–Sat 11am–midnight, Sun noon–10.30pm.
Marvellously well-preserved Victorian pub of mirrors, polished wood and "snob" screens. The excellent Young's ales round things off splendidly.

Museum Tavern
MAP P.68, POCKET MAP G13
49 Great Russell St ⊖ Tottenham Court Road. Mon–Thurs 11am–11.30pm, Fri & Sat 11am–midnight, Sun 10am–10pm.

The Lamb greenery

Large and characterful old pub, opposite the British Museum, and once the drinking hole of Karl Marx. Good range of ales.

Queen's Head
MAP P.68, POCKET MAP J4
66 Acton St ⊖ King's Cross St Pancras. Mon & Sun noon–11pm, Tues–Sat noon–midnight.
Laidback little Victorian pub offering craft ales, ciders and a good whisky list, plus simple food. Regular live jazz and bar-room piano.

Venues

Kings Place
MAP P.68, POCKET MAP J2
90 York Way ⊖ King's Cross St Pancras ☏ 020 7520 1490, ⓦ kingsplace.co.uk.
Eclectic venue with several spaces for acoustic and classical music of all stripes, plus spoken word performances and comedy, galleries and other events.

The Place
MAP P.68, POCKET MAP H4
17 Duke's Rd ⊖ Euston ☏ 020 7121 1100, ⓦ theplace.org.uk.
Excellent small dance theatre presenting the work of new choreographers and student performers, and hosting dance from across the globe, as well as new operas.

The City

The City is where London began, and its boundaries today are only slightly larger than those marked by the Roman walls and their medieval successors. However, you'll find few visible leftovers of London's early days, since four-fifths of it burned down in the Great Fire of 1666. The majority of Londoners lived and worked in or around the City up until the eighteenth century – nowadays, it's primarily one of the world's main financial centres and although three hundred thousand commuters work here, fewer than ten thousand actually live here. The City is only really busy Monday to Friday during the day, so if you're looking for nightlife, you're best off heading for Clerkenwell, which lies on the City's northwest fringe.

Temple

MAP P.74, POCKET MAP K15

⊖ **Temple.**

Temple is the largest and most complex of the **Inns of Court**, where, since medieval times, every aspiring barrister in England and Wales has had to study in order to qualify for the bar. Despite the fact that only a few very old buildings survive here, the overall atmosphere is like that of an Oxbridge college and the maze of courtyards and passageways is fun to explore – especially after dark, when Temple is gas-lit.

Medieval students ate, attended lectures and slept in the **Middle Temple Hall** (Mon–Fri 10–11.30am & 3–4pm; free), still the Inn's main dining room. Constructed in the 1560s, the hall

Temple Church

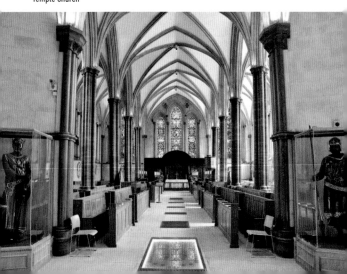

provided the setting for many great Elizabethan masques and plays – probably including Shakespeare's *Twelfth Night*, which is believed to have been premiered here in 1602. The hall is worth a visit for its fine hammerbeam roof, wooden panelling and decorative Elizabethan screen.

The complex's oldest building, **Temple Church** (Mon, Tues, Thurs & Fri 10am–4pm, Wed 2–4pm but times can vary; £5; Ⓦ www.templechurch.com) was built in 1185 by the Knights Templar, the military monks who protected pilgrims heading for the Holy Land. Despite wartime damage, the original round church – modelled on the Holy Sepulchre in Jerusalem – still stands, with its striking Purbeck-marble piers, recumbent marble effigies of knights and tortured grotesques grimacing in the spandrels of the blind arcading. The church features in both the book and the film of *The Da Vinci Code* by Dan Brown.

Fleet Street

MAP P.74, POCKET MAP K6–L6
⊖ Temple.

In the nineteenth century, all the major national and provincial dailies had their offices and **printing presses** in and around Fleet Street. Computer technology rendered the presses here obsolete in the 1980s, however, and within a decade or so all the newspaper headquarters had gone, leaving just a couple of landmarks to testify to five hundred years of printing history. The most remarkable is the city's first glass curtain-wall construction, the former **Daily Express** building at no. 127, with its sleek black Vitrolite facade.

St Bride's

MAP P.74, POCKET MAP L6
Fleet St ⊖ Blackfriars or Temple Ⓦ www.stbrides.com. Mon–Fri 8am–6pm, Sat 10am–3.30pm, Sun 10am–6.30pm. Free.

Lincoln's Inn chapel

To get a sense of Fleet Street in the days when the press dominated the area, head for the "journalists' and printers' cathedral", St Bride's Church, which boasts Wren's tallest and most exquisite spire (said to be the inspiration for the tiered wedding cake). The crypt contains a little museum with a few artefacts dating back to the site's Roman origins.

Lincoln's Inn

MAP P.74, POCKET MAP K14
Lincoln's Inn Fields ⊖ Chancery Lane ⓘ 020 7405 1393, Ⓦ www.lincolnsinn.org.uk. Mon–Fri 7am–7pm. Free.

Lincoln's Inn, on the east side of Lincoln's Inn Fields, was the first of the Inns of Court, and in many ways is the prettiest, having miraculously escaped the ravages of the Blitz. Famous alumni include Thomas More, Oliver Cromwell and Margaret Thatcher. The main entrance is the diamond-patterned, red-brick Tudor gateway on Chancery Lane, adjacent to which is the early seventeenth-century **chapel** (Mon–Fri 9am–5pm), with its unusual fan-vaulted open undercroft and, on the first floor, a

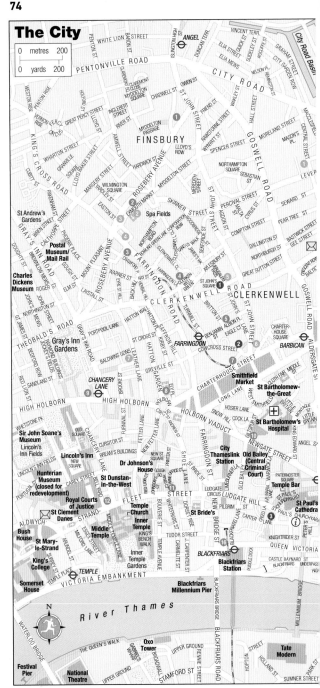

The City

| 0 | metres | 200 |
| 0 | yards | 200 |

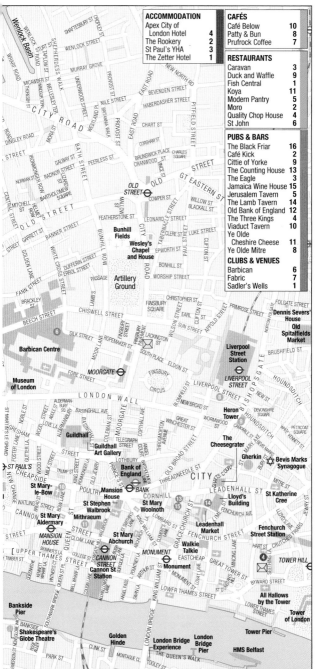

ACCOMMODATION

Apex City of London Hotel	4
The Rookery	2
St Paul's YHA	3
The Zetter Hotel	1

CAFÉS

Café Below	10
Patty & Bun	8
Prufrock Coffee	7

RESTAURANTS

Caravan	3
Duck and Waffle	9
Fish Central	1
Koya	11
Modern Pantry	5
Moro	2
Quality Chop House	4
St John	6

PUBS & BARS

The Black Friar	16
Café Kick	2
Cittie of Yorke	9
The Counting House	13
The Eagle	3
Jamaica Wine House	15
Jerusalem Tavern	5
The Lamb Tavern	14
Old Bank of England	12
The Three Kings	4
Viaduct Tavern	10
Ye Olde Cheshire Cheese	11
Ye Olde Mitre	8

CLUBS & VENUES

Barbican	6
Fabric	7
Sadler's Wells	1

late Gothic nave, hit by a zeppelin in World War I and much restored since. The Inn's oldest building, the fifteenth-century **Old Hall** (closed), where the lawyers used to live and where Dickens set the case Jarndyce and Jarndyce in *Bleak House*, features a fine timber roof, linenfold panelling and an elaborate, early Jacobean screen.

Sir John Soane's Museum

MAP P.74, POCKET MAP J14
12–14 Lincoln's Inn Fields ⊖ Holborn
☎ 020 7405 2107, ⓦ www.soane.org. Wed–
Sun 10am–5pm. Free.

The chief architect of the Bank of England, **John Soane** (1753–1837) designed this house not only as a home and office but also as a place to stash his large collection of art and antiquities. Arranged much as it was in his lifetime, the ingeniously planned house has an informal, treasure-hunt atmosphere and intriguing spatial tricks, created with Soane's trademark domes, mirrors and skylights. The star exhibits are **Hogarth**'s satirical *Election* series and his merciless morality tale *The Rake's Progress,* as well as the alabaster Egyptian sarcophagus of Seti I rejected by the British Museum. Note that the museum is extremely popular,

so you may have to queue – and leave bags in the cloakroom. To see Soane's private apartments, which include a display of his architectural models, you need to join a free tour (Wed–Sun 1.15pm & 2pm; sign up as soon as you arrive), or highlights tour (Thurs & Fri noon, Sat & Sun 11am & noon; £12.50).

Dr Johnson's House

MAP P.74, POCKET MAP L6
17 Gough Square ⊖ Blackfriars or
Temple ☎ 020 7353 3745, ⓦ www.
drjohnsonshouse.org. May–Sept Mon–Sat
11am–5.30pm; Oct–April Mon–Sat
11am–5pm. £7; cash only.

Despite appearances, Dr Johnson's House is the only authentic eighteenth-century building on Gough Square. It was here the great savant, writer and lexicographer lived from 1747 to 1759 whilst compiling the 41,000 entries for the first dictionary of the English language. The panelled rooms of the house are peppered with period furniture and lined with portraits and etchings, including one of Johnson's servant Francis Barber. A first-edition of the great *Dictionary* is on display, and you can flick through a reproduction to discover some wonderfully arcane words, such as lucubration (to study by candlelight).

Dr Johnson's House

Old Bailey

MAP P.74, POCKET MAP L6
Newgate St ⊖ St Paul's ☎ 020 7192 2739, ⓦ cityoflondon.gov.uk. Mon–Fri 10am–12.40pm & 2–3.40pm. Free.

The **Central Criminal Court** is more popularly known as the Old Bailey after the street on which it stands, which used to form the outer walls of the medieval city. It was built on the site of the notoriously harsh Newgate Prison, where folk used to come to watch public hangings. The current, rather pompous Edwardian building is distinguished by its green dome, surmounted by a gilded statue of Justice, unusually depicted without blindfold, holding her sword and scales. The country's most serious criminal court cases take place here, and have included, in the past, the trials of Lord Haw-Haw, the Kray twins, and the Guildford Four and Birmingham Six "IRA bombers". You can watch the proceedings from the visitors' gallery, but large bags, cameras, mobiles and food and drink are not allowed in, and there is no cloakroom.

Smithfield

MAP P.74, POCKET MAP L5
⊖ Farringdon ⓦ smithfieldmarket.com.

For more than three centuries Smithfield was a popular venue for **public executions**: the Scottish hero, William Wallace, was hanged, disembowelled and beheaded here in 1305, and the Bishop of Rochester's cook was boiled alive in 1531, but the local speciality was burnings, which reached a peak in the mid-sixteenth century during the reign of "Bloody" Mary, when hundreds of Protestants were burned at the stake for their beliefs. These days, Smithfield is dominated by its historic **meat market**, housed in a colourful and ornate Victorian market hall on Charterhouse Street; try to get here early – the activity starts around 2am and you should arrive by 7am

Statue of Justice on the Old Bailey

to catch the action; monthly tours are available (6 or 6.45am; £12.50; book online).

Postal Museum and Mail Rail

MAP P.74, POCKET MAP K4
15–20 Phoenix Place ⊖ King's Cross or Farringdon. ☎ 0300 0300 700, ⓦ postalmuseum.org. Daily 10am–5pm. Museum & Mail Rail £17.05, museum only £11. Book timed ticket for Mail Rail in advance at busy times.

Faced with rising city congestion and an increased demand for speedy postal delivery, in the early 1900s Royal Mail came up with an ingenious solution: the **Mail Rail**. Some 6.5 miles of narrow tunnels were constructed to run east–west under the centre of London for mini-trains to transport the city's post. It opened in 1927 and operated until 2003. Now, a mile-long stretch has been developed as a tourist attraction – tiny electric trains whizz you along the tunnels for 20 minutes, as a former rail engineer provides the audio tour – look out for the train "graveyard" below. It's an intriguing experience, and the exhibits on the history of

St Bartholemew-the-Great

the service are excellent. Just up the road (and part of the same operation), the **Postal Museum** niftily combines a history of the postal services with exhibits of vintage vehicles and rare stamps, and hands-on fun – add your own face to a stamp and so on. It's not cheap, but is a good few hours of interest, and very kid-friendly.

St Bartholomew-the-Great

MAP P.74, POCKET MAP L5
Cloth Fair ⊖ Barbican ☏ 020 7600 0440, Ⓦ www.greatstbarts.com. Mon–Fri 8.30am–5pm, Sat 10.30am–4pm, Sun 8.30am–8pm; mid-Nov to mid-Feb Mon–Fri closes 4pm. £5.

Begun in 1123, St Bartholomew-the-Great is London's oldest and most atmospheric parish church. Its half-timbered Tudor gatehouse on Little Britain incorporates a thirteenth-century arch that once formed the entrance to the nave; above, a wooden statue of St Bartholomew stands holding the knife with which he was flayed. One side of the medieval cloisters survives to the south, immediately to the right as you enter the church.

The rest is a confusion of elements, including portions of the transepts and, most impressively, the chancel, where stout Norman pillars separate the main body of the church from the ambulatory. There are various pre-Fire monuments to admire, the most prominent being the tomb of Rahere, court jester to Henry I, which shelters under a fifteenth-century canopy north of the main altar.

St Bartholomew's Hospital Museum

MAP P.74, POCKET MAP L5
West Smithfield ⊖ Barbican ☏ 020 3465 5798. Tues–Fri 10am–4pm. Free.

Among the medical artefacts, this hospital museum boasts some fearsome amputation instruments, a pair of leather "lunatic restrainers", some great jars with labels such as "poison – for external use only", and a cricket bat autographed by W.G. Grace, who was a student at Bart's in the 1870s. To see the magnificent **Great Hall** you must go on one of the fascinating guided tours (Fri 2pm; £7), which take in Smithfield and the surrounding area as well; the meeting point is the Henry VIII gate.

Museum of London

MAP P.74, POCKET MAP M5
150 London Wall ⊖ Barbican ☏ 020 7001 9844, ⓦ museumoflondon.org.uk. Daily 10am–6pm. Free.

Despite London's long pedigree, very few of its ancient structures are still standing. However, numerous Roman, Saxon and Elizabethan remains have been discovered and are now displayed at the Museum of London. The permanent exhibition provides an imaginative and educational trot through London's past from prehistory to the present day. Specific exhibits to look out for include the Bucklersbury Roman mosaic; sculptures from the temple of Mithras, discovered in the City in 1954 (see page 82); a model of Old St Paul's; the Lord Mayor's heavily gilded coach (still used for state occasions); and the cauldron from the 2012 Olympic Games. The real strength of the museum, though, lies in the excellent temporary exhibitions, lectures, walks and films it organizes throughout the year.

Guildhall

MAP P.74, POCKET MAP M6
Gresham St ⊖ Bank or Mansion House ☏ 020 7332 3700, ⓦ www.cityoflondon. gov.uk. Hall: daily 10am–4.30pm (Sun May–Sept only). Galleries: Mon–Sat 10am–5pm, Sun noon–4pm. Free.

Situated at the geographical centre of the City, Guildhall has been the area's administrative seat for over eight hundred years. It remains the headquarters of the **City of London Corporation**, the City's governing body, and

City churches

The City is crowded with churches (ⓦ london-city-churches. org.uk) – well over forty at the last count, the majority of them built or rebuilt by Wren after the Great Fire. Those particularly worth seeking out include **St Dunstan in the West**, its neo-Gothic tower dominating Fleet Street (Mon–Fri 10am–4pm; ⊖ Temple; MAP P.74, POCKET MAP K6) and **St Mary Abchurch** (Mon–Fri 11am–3pm; ⊖ Cannon Street; MAP P.74, POCKET MAP N6) on Abchurch Lane, unique for an unusual and vast dome fresco painted by a local parishioner and lit by oval lunettes; the superlative lime-wood reredos is by Gibbons. On Lombard Street, **St Mary Woolnoth** (Mon–Fri 9.30am–4.30pm; ⊖ Bank; MAP P.74, POCKET MAP N6) is a typically idiosyncratic creation of Nicholas Hawksmoor, one of Wren's pupils, featuring an ingenious lantern lit by semicircular clerestory windows and a striking altar canopy held up by barley-sugar columns. **St Mary Aldermary** on Queen Victoria Street (Mon–Fri 11am–3pm; ⊖ Mansion House; MAP P.74, POCKET MAP M6) is Wren's most successful stab at Gothic, with fan vaulting in the aisles and a panelled ceiling in the nave, where a café sets up every day. Finally on Walbrook is Wren's most spectacular church interior after St Paul's, **St Stephen Walbrook** (Mon–Thurs 10am–4pm, Fri 10am–3pm, Fri 10am–3.30pm; ⊖ Bank; MAP P.74, POCKET MAP M6), where sixteen Corinthian columns are arranged in clusters around a central dome, and the dark-wood furnishings are again by Grinling Gibbons.

St Paul's Cathedral

is used for grand civic occasions. Architecturally, however, it's not quite the beauty it once was, having been badly damaged in both the Great Fire and the Blitz, and somewhat scarred by the addition of a grotesque 1970s concrete cloister and wing.

Nonetheless, the **Great Hall**, basically a postwar reconstruction on the fifteenth-century walls, is worth a look if there isn't an event going on. In 1553 the venue for the high-treason trials of Lady Jane Grey and her husband, Lord Dudley, the hall is home to a handful of vainglorious late eighteenth- and early nineteenth-century monuments, replete with lions, cherubs and ludicrous allegorical figures.

Also worth a visit is the purpose-built **Guildhall Art Gallery**, which contains one or two exceptional works, such as Rossetti's *La Ghirlandata*, plus a massive painting depicting the 1782 Siege of Gibraltar, commissioned by the Corporation. The gallery also hosts regular temporary exhibitions. In the basement, you can view the remains of a **Roman** amphitheatre, dating from around 120 AD, which was discovered during the gallery's construction.

St Paul's Cathedral

MAP P.74, POCKET MAP M6

St Paul's ☎ 020 7246 8348 or ☎ 020 7246 8357, ⓦ www.stpauls.co.uk. Mon–Sat 8.30am–4.30pm. £16 online (£18 on gate). Designed by **Christopher Wren** and completed in 1710, St Paul's remains a dominating presence in the City despite the encroaching tower blocks. It's topped by an enormous lead-covered dome that's second in size only to St Peter's in Rome, and its showpiece west facade is particularly magnificent. However, compared to its great rival, Westminster Abbey, St Paul's is a soulless but perfectly calculated architectural set piece, a burial place for captains rather than kings.

The best place to appreciate the building's glory is from beneath the **dome**, adorned (against Wren's wishes) by trompe l'oeil frescoes. The most richly decorated section of the cathedral is the **chancel**, where the late Victorian mosaics of birds, fish, animals and greenery are particularly spectacular. The intricately carved oak and lime-wood choir stalls, and the imposing organ case, are the work of Wren's master carver, Grinling Gibbons.

Beginning in the south aisle, a series of stairs leads to the dome's three galleries, the first of which is the internal **Whispering Gallery**, so called because of its acoustic properties – words whispered to the wall on one side are distinctly audible over one hundred feet away on the other, though you often can't hear much above the hubbub. Of the two exterior galleries, the best views are from the tiny **Golden Gallery**, below the golden ball and cross which top the cathedral.

Although the nave is crammed full of overblown monuments to military types, burials in St Paul's are confined to the **crypt**, reputedly the largest in Europe. The whitewashed walls and bright lighting make this one of London's least atmospheric mausoleums, but **Artists' Corner** here does boast as many painters and architects as Westminster Abbey has poets, including Christopher Wren himself. The star tombs, though, are those of Nelson and Wellington, both occupying centre stage and both with more fanciful monuments upstairs.

It's well worth attending one of the cathedral's **services**, if only to hear the ethereal choir, who perform during most evensongs (Mon–Sat 5pm), and on Sundays at 10.15am and 3.15pm.

Paternoster Square

MAP P.74, POCKET MAP L6
🚇 St Paul's.

The Blitz destroyed the area immediately to the north of St Paul's, incinerating all the booksellers' shops and around six million books. In their place a modernist pedestrianized piazza was built, only to be torn down in the 1980s and replaced with post-classical office blocks in Portland stone and a Corinthian column topped by a gilded urn. One happy consequence of the square's redevelopment is that **Temple Bar**, the gateway which used to stand at the top of Fleet Street, has found its way back to London after over a hundred years of exile in a park in Hertfordshire. Designed by Wren himself, the triumphal arch, looking weathered but clean, now forms the entrance to Paternoster Square, with the Stuart monarchs, James I and Charles II, and their consorts occupying the niches.

Bank of England

MAP P.74, POCKET MAP M6
Threadneedle St 🚇 Bank ☏ 020 7601 5545, 🌐 bankofengland.co.uk. Mon–Fri 10am–5pm. Free.

Established in 1694 by William III to raise funds for the war against France, the Bank of England stores the official gold reserves of many of the world's central banks. All that remains of the original building, on which John Soane spent the best part of his career (from 1788

City skyscrapers

Throughout the 1990s, most people's favourite modern building in the City was Richard Rogers' glitzy **Lloyd's Building** – a startling array of glass and blue steel pipes. Lloyd's was eclipsed in the mid-2000s by its near neighbour, Norman Foster's 590ft-high, glass diamond-clad **Gherkin**, which has endeared itself to Londoners thanks to its cheeky shape.

The City skyline continues to sprout yet more skyscrapers, with Richard Rogers' 737ft wedge-shaped office block **The Cheesegrater** (the Leadenhall Building) leading the charge. Close by is the **Scalpel**, a 620ft twisted angular shard of glass, completed in 2018. Still to be finished is the vast, 912ft **22 Bishopsgate**; several even taller constructions are planned, including the 1016ft **1 Undershaft** which will equal the **Shard** in height. More controversial has been Rafael Viñoly's 525ft **Walkie Talkie**, on Fenchurch Street, which features a public "sky garden", as well as bars and restaurants on the top floor (20 Fenchurch St; ☏ 020 7337 2344, 🌐 skygarden.london; Mon–Fri 10am–6pm, Sat & Sun 11am–9pm; book free tickets in advance; bars and restaurants open longer).

onwards), is the windowless outer curtain wall, which wraps itself round the 3.5-acre island site. However, you can view a reconstruction of Soane's Bank Stock Office, with its characteristic domed skylight, in the **museum** (free), which has its entrance on Bartholomew Lane. The permanent exhibition here includes the Bank's original charter and specimens of notes and coins issued by the Bank over the centuries – along with some fakes – plus a gold bar you can feel the weight of. It also attempts to explain the Bank's work in maintaining financial stability through some fairly laboured interactive displays comparing the Bank to a ship's captain in turbulent seas.

Mithraeum (Temple of Mithras)

MAP P.74, POCKET MAP M6
12 Walbrook ⊖ Bank or Cannon Street
Ⓦ londonmithraeum.com. Tues–Sat
10am–6pm, Sun noon–5pm; 20min timed
slots for temple. Free.

In 1954, as the rubble of World War II was being cleared for new developments in the City, archeologists made an extraordinary discovery: the remains of a Roman Temple of Mithras, dedicated to the mysterious all-male cult, and including several sculptures, most famously the head of Mithras – on display at the Museum of London (see page 79). The archeological dig attracted crowds of Londoners, and initially, so as not to disrupt the planned building, the temple remains were reconstructed outside 100m away, where they remained until 2011. In 2017, they were returned to near their original spot, two floors under the new Bloomberg headquarters, and are now presented more accurately, and atmospherically, with sounds and lights used to evoke a sense of cultish mystery. Displayed on the ground floor are some of the numerous archeological finds from the site, including a wooden tablet that is one of the City's earliest financial records, and a tiny amber amulet.

Bevis Marks Synagogue

Mansion House

MAP P.74, POCKET MAP M6

Mansion House Place ⊖ Bank ☎ 020 7397 9306, ⓦ cityoflondon.gov.uk. Access only via group tours.

The Lord Mayor's sumptuous Neoclassical lodgings were designed in 1753. The building's grandest room is the columned **Egyptian Hall** with its barrel-vaulted, coffered ceiling. Also impressive is the vast collection of gold and silver tableware, the mayor's 36-pound gold mace and the pearl sword given by Elizabeth I. Scattered about the rooms are an impressive array of Dutch and Flemish paintings.

Leadenhall Market

MAP P.74, POCKET MAP N6

Leadenhall St ⊖ Monument ⓦ leadenhallmarket.co.uk. Mon–Fri 10am–6pm.

Leadenhall Market's picturesque cobbles and graceful Victorian cast-ironwork date from 1881. Inside, the traders cater mostly for the lunchtime City crowd – the shops, restaurants and bars here are a mix of high-end and lunchtime chains.

Bevis Marks Synagogue

MAP P.74, POCKET MAP N6

Bevis Marks ⊖ Aldgate ☎ 020 7621 1188, ⓦ sephardi.org.uk/bevis-marks/. Mon, Wed & Thurs 10.30am–2pm, Tues & Fri 10.30am–1pm, Sun 10.30am–12.30pm. Guided tours Wed & Fri 11.30am, Sun 11am. £5.

Hidden behind a modern red-brick office block, the Bevis Marks Synagogue was built in 1701 by Sephardic Jews who had fled the Inquisition in Spain and Portugal. It's the country's oldest surviving synagogue, and the roomy, rich interior gives an idea of just how wealthy the worshippers were at the time. The Sephardic community has now dispersed across London and the congregation has dwindled, but the magnificent array of

Leadenhall Market

chandeliers ensure that it's a popular venue for candle-lit Jewish weddings.

Monument

MAP P.74, POCKET MAP N6

Monument St ⊖ Monument ☎ 020 7403 3761, ⓦ themonument.org.uk. Daily: April–Sept 9.30am–5.30pm; Oct–March 9.30am–5pm. £5; cash only.

The Monument was designed by Wren to commemorate the **Great Fire of London**, which raged for five days in early September 1666 and destroyed four-fifths of the City. A plain Doric column crowned with spiky gilded flames, it stands 202ft high, making it the tallest isolated stone column in the world; if it were laid out flat it would touch the site of the bakery where the Fire started, east of the Monument. The bas-relief on the base depicts Charles II and the Duke of York in Roman garb conducting the emergency relief operation. The 311 steps to the viewing gallery once guaranteed an incredible view; nowadays it is somewhat dwarfed by the buildings surrounding it.

Cafés

Café Below

MAP P.74, POCKET MAP M6
St Mary-le-Bow, Cheapside ⊖ St Paul's or
Mansion House. Mon–Fri 7.30am–10am &
11.30am–2.30pm
A rare City gem: a café set in a
wonderful Norman church crypt,
serving excellent, good-value bistro-
style food.

Patty & Bun

MAP P.74, POCKET MAP N5
22 Liverpool St ⊖ Liverpool St. Mon & Tues
11.30am–10pm, Wed & Thurs 11.30am–
11pm, Fri 7.30–10am & 11.30am–11pm,
Sat noon–10pm, Sun noon–9pm.
Spawned from a raved-about food
truck, this is dude food incarnate –
succulent burgers on brioche buns
from £9, plus spicy sides – cheese
balls with hot sauce for £4.50 –
and hangover-busting breakfasts
(Fri only).

Prufrock Coffee

MAP P.74, POCKET MAP K5
23–25 Leather Lane ⊖ Chancery Lane or
Farringdon. Mon–Fri 8am–6pm, Sat & Sun
10am–5pm.

Modern Pantry

Super-hip shrine to the coffee bean,
with a barista school on site. Good
food, too.

Restaurants

Caravan

MAP P.74, POCKET MAP K4
11–13 Exmouth Market ⊖ Farringdon
☎ 020 7833 8115. Mon–Fri 8am–10.30pm,
Sat 10am–10.30pm, Sun 10am–4pm. Bar
open late.
Creative brunches, modern fusion
food and home-roasted coffee are
on offer at this relaxed, cool all-day
place. Small and large plates £7–20.

Duck and Waffle

MAP P.74, POCKET MAP N5
Heron Tower, 110 Bishopsgate ⊖ Aldgate
☎ 020 3640 7310. Daily 24hr.
Forty floors up, this smart place
offers amazing City views and
hipster comfort food with creative
flair. The signature dish features
waffles, duck confit, fried duck egg
and mustard maple syrup (£18),
while 2am offerings include spiced
duck doughnuts (£12).

Fish Central

MAP P.74, POCKET MAP M4
149–155 Central St ⊖ Old Street ☎ 020
7253 4970. Mon–Thurs 11.30am–10.30pm,
Fri 11.30am–11pm, Sat 11am–10.30pm.
Sitting on the edge of the Barbican/
City and Clerkenwell's council
estates, this is both a reliable chippy
and a smart fish restaurant.

Koya

MAP P.74, POCKET MAP M6
10–12 Bloomberg Arcade ⊖ Bank or
Cannon Street ⓦ koya.co.uk. Mon–Sat
11.30am–10.30pm, Sun 10am–6pm.
The huge, swish headquarters of
Bloomberg in London has, as well
as the Mithraeum (see page 82),
an arcade of carefully selected new
restaurants, including a branch of
Caravan (see above), and this small,
authentic udon noodle bar, serving
delicately flavoured hot and cold
noodle dishes (from £11).

Modern Pantry

MAP P.74, POCKET MAP L4

47 St John's Square ⊖ Farringdon ⊕ 020 7553 9210. Mon 8–11am & noon–9pm, Tues–Fri 8–11am & noon–10pm, Sat 9am–4pm & 6–10pm, Sun 9am–4pm.

An elegant contemporary restaurant/café offering outstanding fusion cooking with an explosion of nuanced flavours. Mains from £16; small plates from £7. The Pantry, their tiny deli/shop, does delicious takeaway salad boxes (Mon–Fri 8am–3pm).

Moro

MAP P.74, POCKET MAP K4

34–36 Exmouth Market ⊖ Angel or Farringdon ⊕ 020 7833 8336. Mon–Sat noon–2.30pm & 5.15–10.40pm, Sun 12.30–3.30pm & 5–9.45pm.

This attractive restaurant is a place of pilgrimage for disciples of the chef's Moorish cookbooks. Food is excellent and reservations recommended. Tapas (around £4–6) served all day. Mains £18–24.

Quality Chop House

MAP P.74, POCKET MAP K4

88–94 Farringdon Rd ⊖ Farringdon ⊕ 020 7278 1452. Mon–Sat noon–2.30pm & 6–10pm, Sun noon–4pm.

Beautiful old dining room, butchers and wine bar with a daily changing menu focusing on the best cuts of British meat and freshest produce. Mains from £18; steaks from £41; express lunch menu £19.50 for two courses.

St John

MAP P.74, POCKET MAP L5

26 St John St ⊖ Farringdon ⊕ 020 7251 0848. Mon–Fri noon–3pm & 6–11pm, Sat 6–11pm, Sun 12.30–4pm.

Pared-down former smokehouse close to Smithfield meat market that's become famous for serving outstanding British dishes, often involving unfashionable animal parts. Mains £16–30.

The Black Friar

Pubs and bars

The Black Friar

MAP P.74, POCKET MAP L6

174 Queen Victoria St ⊖ Blackfriars. Mon–Fri 10am–11pm, Sat 9am–11pm, Sun noon–10.30pm.

A gorgeous pub, with Art Nouveau marble friezes of boozy monks and a highly decorated alcove – all original, dating from 1905. A lovely fireplace and an unhurried atmosphere make this a relaxing place to drink.

Café Kick

MAP P.74, POCKET MAP K4

43 Exmouth Market ⊖ Farringdon or Angel. Mon–Thurs 11am–11pm, Fri & Sat 11am–midnight, Sun noon–10.30pm.

This ramshackle, memorabilia-packed French-style café/bar is great fun, the friendly atmosphere enlivened by its busy table-football games. A daytime menu of sandwiches and hearty soups gives way in the evening to nachos and sharing boards.

The Three Kings

Jamaica Wine House

MAP P.74, POCKET MAP N6
St Michael's Alley ⊖ Bank. Mon–Fri
11am–11pm.

Located down a narrow alleyway, on the site of London's first coffee house (1652), this old City institution is known locally as the "Jam Pot". Today, it's a Shepherd Neame pub, divided into four large "snugs" by original high wooden-panelled partitions.

Jerusalem Tavern

MAP P.74, POCKET MAP L5
55 Britton St ⊖ Farringdon. Mon–Fri
noon–11pm.

Converted Georgian coffee house – the frontage dates from 1810 – that has retained much of its original character. Better still, the excellent draught beers are from St Peter's Brewery in Suffolk. Something of a gem in these parts.

The Lamb Tavern

MAP P.74, POCKET MAP N6
10–12 Leadenhall Market ⊖ Monument or Bank. Mon–Fri 11am–11pm.

It's almost exclusively standing room only (both inside and out) at this historic Young's pub situated in the middle of beautiful Leadenhall Market. *Old Tom's Bar* downstairs offers good cheese/sausage platters.

Cittie of Yorke

MAP P.74, POCKET MAP K13
22 High Holborn ⊖ Chancery Lane. Mon–Sat noon–11pm.

A venerable London lawyers' pub now run by Sam Smith's. Head for the vaulted cellar bar or the grand quasi-medieval wine hall at the back with its rows of cosy cubicles.

The Counting House

MAP P.74, POCKET MAP N6
50 Cornhill ⊖ Bank. Mon–Fri 10am–11pm.

An inspired Fuller's bank conversion, the magnificent interior featuring high ceilings, marble pillars, mosaic flooring and a large, oval island bar, plus an enormous glass dome.

The Eagle

MAP P.74, POCKET MAP K4
159 Farringdon Rd ⊖ Farringdon. Mon–Sat noon–11pm, Sun noon–5pm.

London's first gastropub continues to produce excellent Mediterranean food from its little open kitchen, but still feels more like a pub than a restaurant, with a refreshingly unpretentious vibe.

Old Bank of England

MAP P.74, POCKET MAP K14
194 Fleet St ⊖ Temple or Chancery Lane. Mon–Fri 11am–11pm, Sat noon–9pm.

Not the actual Bank of England, but the former Law Courts' branch, this imposing High Victorian banking hall is now a magnificently opulent Fuller's ale-and-pie pub.

The Three Kings

MAP P.74, POCKET MAP L4
7 Clerkenwell Close ⊖ Farringdon. Mon–Fri noon–11pm.

Tucked away north of Clerkenwell Green, this atmospheric pub has a delightfully eclectic interior and two small rooms upstairs perfect for long occupation. Good craft ales too.

Viaduct Tavern

MAP P.74, POCKET MAP L5
126 Newgate St ⊖ St Paul's. Mon–Fri
10am–11pm.
Fuller's pub situated across from
the Old Bailey, with a glorious
Victorian interior including
walls adorned with oils of faded
ladies representing Commerce,
Agriculture and the Arts.

Ye Olde Cheshire Cheese

MAP P.74, POCKET MAP L6
Wine Office Court, 145 Fleet St ⊖ Temple.
Mon–Fri 11.30am–11pm, Sat noon–11pm.
A seventeenth-century watering
hole – famous chiefly because
of patrons such as Dickens and
Dr Johnson – with several snug,
dark-panelled rooms and real fires.
Popular with tourists, but by no
means exclusively so, and serving
keenly priced Sam Smith's brews.

Ye Olde Mitre

MAP P.74, POCKET MAP L5
1 Ely Court, off Hatton Garden
⊖ Farringdon. Mon–Fri 11am–11pm.
Hidden down a tiny alleyway off
Ely Place or Hatton Garden, this
wonderfully atmospheric Fuller's
pub dates back to 1546, although
it was actually rebuilt in the
eighteenth century. The real ales are
excellent.

Performance at Sadler's Wells

Clubs and venues

Barbican

MAP P.74, POCKET MAP M5
Silk St ⊖ Barbican ⓣ 020 7638 8891,
ⓦ barbican.org.uk.
With the outstanding resident
London Symphony Orchestra,
and top foreign orchestras and big-
name soloists in regular attendance,
the Barbican is one of the city's
best venues for classical music, opera,
theatre, dance and film.

Fabric

MAP P.74, POCKET MAP L5
77a Charterhouse St ⊖ Farringdon ⓣ 020
7336 8898, ⓦ www.fabriclondon.com.
Despite big queues and a confusing
layout, this 2500-capacity club is
one of the world's finest. Live bands
and lengthy DJ line-ups mean you
can hear a huge variety of acts. ID
essential.

Sadler's Wells

MAP P.74, POCKET MAP L3
Rosebery Ave ⊖ Angel ⓣ 020 7863 8000,
ⓦ sadlerswells.com.
Home to Britain's best
contemporary dance companies,
and host to the finest international
outfits, Sadler's Wells also puts on
theatre pieces and children's shows.

The East End

The East End is firmly established as one of the city's most vibrant artistic enclaves, peppered with art galleries and a whole host of cutting-edge bars and clubs. Spitalfields – and in particular Brick Lane – lies at the heart of the old East End, once the first port of call for thousands of immigrants over the centuries, and best known today for hipster cafés, vintage Sunday markets and cheap curries. The scene has now spread north to Shoreditch and Dalston, and east to Bethnal Green and beyond, to the edges of the Olympic Park.

V&A Museum of Childhood

MAP P.90
Cambridge Heath Road ⊖ Bethnal Green
☎ 020 8983 5200, ⓦ www.vam.ac.uk/moc/.
Daily 10am–5.45pm. Free.

The open-plan wrought-iron hall in Bethnal Green, which houses the Museum of Childhood, was part of the original V&A building (see page 125), and was transported to the East End from South Kensington in the late 1860s in order to bring art to the poor. Now it displays a large collection of toys and all things related to childhood, including clockwork and moving toys, classic robots, a Hornby toy train of the *Hogwarts Express* and a remarkable collection of antique dolls' houses upstairs. There are daily hands-on activities and kid-centric events.

Geffrye Museum

MAP P.90, POCKET MAP O3
136 Kingsland Rd ⊖ Hoxton Overground
☎ 020 7739 9893, ⓦ www.geffrye-museum.org.uk. Almshouses tours some

Geffrye Museum

Columbia Road Flower Market

Tues & Wed noon–2pm & Sat 11am–4pm. Gardens 7.30am–4.45pm, Sat when almshouses open 10am–4.45pm. Tours £5. The Geffrye Museum, housed in a grandiose enclave of eighteenth-century ironmongers' almshouses, is essentially a museum of domestic furniture. In 1911, at a time when the East End furniture trade was concentrated in the area, the almshouses were converted into a museum for the "education of craftsmen". The almshouses are rigged out as period living rooms of the urban middle class, ranging from the oak-panelled decor of the seventeenth century to the present, though it is closed for refurbishment until 2020. The gardens remain open, and one of the **almshouses** has been restored to its original condition and can be visited by tour several times a week, which you should book ahead.

Columbia Road Flower Market

MAP P.90, POCKET MAP O3
⊖ Shoreditch High Street Overground or Hoxton Overground. Sun 8am–3pm.
Columbia Road is the city's most popular market for flowers and

plants; it's also the liveliest, with the loud and upfront stallholders catering to an increasingly moneyed clientele. As well as seeds, bulbs, potted plants and cut flowers from the stalls, you'll also find every kind of gardening accessory from the chi-chi shops that line the street, and you can keep yourself sustained with bagels, cakes and coffee from the local cafés.

Wesley's Chapel & House

MAP P.90, POCKET MAP N4
49 City Rd ⊖ Old Street ☎ 020 7253 2262, ⓦ www.wesleyschapel.org.uk & ⓦ wesleysheritage.org.uk. Mon–Sat 10am–4pm (closed Thurs 12.45–1.30pm). Free.
A place of pilgrimage for Methodists from all over the world, Wesley's Chapel was built in 1777, and heralded the coming of age of the faith founded by **John Wesley** (1703–91). The interior is uncharacteristically ornate, with powder-pink columns of French jasper and a superb, Adam-style gilded plasterwork ceiling. Predictably enough, the **Museum of Methodism** in the basement has only a passing reference to

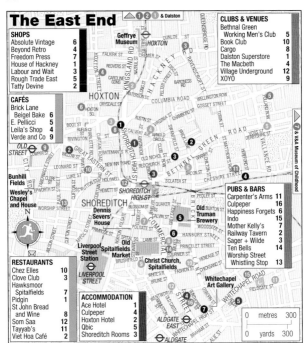

The East End

SHOPS
Absolute Vintage	6
Beyond Retro	4
Freedom Press	7
House of Hackney	1
Labour and Wait	3
Rough Trade East	5
Tatty Devine	2

CAFÉS
Brick Lane	
Beigel Bake	6
E. Pellicci	8
Leila's Shop	4
Verde and Co	9

RESTAURANTS
Chez Elles	10
Clove Club	3
Hawksmoor	
Spitalfields	7
Pidgin	1
St John Bread and Wine	8
Som Saa	12
Tayyab's	11
Viet Hoa Café	2

ACCOMMODATION
Ace Hotel	1
Culpeper	4
Hoxton Hotel	2
Qbic	5
Shoreditch Rooms	3

CLUBS & VENUES
Bethnal Green Working Men's Club	5
Book Club	10
Cargo	8
Dalston Superstore	1
The Macbeth	4
Village Underground	12
XOYO	9

PUBS & BARS
Carpenter's Arms	11
Culpeper	16
Happiness Forgets	6
Indo	15
Mother Kelly's	7
Railway Tavern	1
Sager + Wilde	3
Ten Bells	14
Worship Street Whistling Stop	13

the insanely jealous 40-year-old widow Wesley married, and who eventually left him. Wesley himself spent his last two years in Wesley's House, a delightful Georgian place to the right of the main gates. On display inside are his deathbed and an early shock-therapy machine he was particularly keen on.

Bunhill Fields

MAP P.90, POCKET MAP M4
City Rd ⊖ Old Street. Mon–Fri 8am–7pm or dusk, Sat & Sun 9.30am–7pm or dusk.
The main burial ground for Dissenters or Nonconformists (practising Christians who were not members of the Church of England), Bunhill Fields contains three famous graves in the central paved area: the simple tombstone of poet and artist **William Blake** stands next to a replica of writer **Daniel Defoe**'s, while opposite lies the recumbent statue of John

Bunyan, seventeenth-century author of *The Pilgrim's Progress*.

Whitechapel Art Gallery

MAP P.90, POCKET MAP O5
77–82 Whitechapel High St ⊖ Aldgate East ☎ 020 7522 7888, ⓦ www.whitechapelgallery.org. Tues–Sun 11am–6pm (Thurs until 9pm). Free.
Founded by one of the East End's Victorian philanthropists, Whitechapel Art Gallery is housed in a beautiful crenellated 1899 Arts and Crafts building, embellished with gilded leaves by sculptor Rachel Whiteread, and a neighbouring building, which was once a library. The gallery has an illustrious history of putting on some of London's most innovative exhibitions of contemporary art, events and talks. The ground floor has a well-stocked art bookshop and a stylish **café/wine bar**. The gallery is a good starting point for finding out more about the east

London art scene, particularly on the first Thursday of each month, when it – and some 150 smaller east London galleries – stay open till 9pm and put on events and openings.

Brick Lane

MAP P.90, POCKET MAP 04–05
⊖ Aldgate East or Shoreditch High Street Overground.

Brick Lane lies at the heart of London's Bengali community, whose inexpensive curry houses dominate the southern end of the street. The red-brick chimney halfway up Brick Lane heralds the **Old Truman Brewery**, founded in 1666 and the largest in the world at the end of the nineteenth century. It ceased operations in 1989 and is now at the centre of a whole series of indoor markets – the Backyard Market, Tea Rooms, the Sunday Upmarket and Boiler House food hall (all Sat & Sun) – all of which are buzzing on Sundays, with stalls selling clothes, crafts and food. The streets north of the brewery and the railway arches are the venue for Brick Lane's **Sunday market** (Sun 8am–2pm), which extends along

Sclater Street and Cheshire Street, with stalls selling everything from household tat to antique furniture.

Christ Church, Spitalfields

MAP P.90, POCKET MAP 05
Commercial St ⊖ Liverpool Street ☎ 020 7377 2400, ⓦ ccspitalfields.org. Mon–Fri 10am–4pm, Sun 1–4pm. Free.

Built between 1714 and 1729 by **Nicholas Hawksmoor**, Christ Church features a huge 225ft-high broach spire and giant Tuscan portico. Inside, there's a forest of columned bays, with a lion and a unicorn playing peekaboo on the top of the chancel beam and London's largest Georgian organ.

Old Spitalfields Market

MAP P.90, POCKET MAP 05
Commercial St ⊖ Liverpool Street. ⓦ oldspitalfieldsmarket.com. Mon–Fri 10am–8pm, Sat 10am–6pm, Sun 10am–5pm.

Spitalfields Market was the capital's premier wholesale fruit and vegetable market until 1991. The western 1920s half of the market was replaced by a Norman Foster office development, with glass-box retail units and food traders built

Old Spitalfields Market

The Olympic Park

Dennis Severs' House

MAP P.90, POCKET MAP O5
18 Folgate St ⊖ Liverpool Street ☎ 020
7247 4013, ⓦ www.dennissevershouse.
co.uk. Daytime visits Mon noon–2pm, Sun
noon–4pm. £10. Silent Night Mon, Wed &
Fri 5–9pm. £15.
Visiting the former home of the
American eccentric Dennis Severs
(1948–99) is a bizarre and uncanny
theatrical experience, which Severs
once described as "passing through
a frame into a painting". The house
is entirely candlelit and log-fired,
and decked out as it would have
been over two hundred years ago.
Visitors are free to explore the ten
rooms unhindered, and are left
with the distinct impression that
someone has literally just popped
out – Severs called it a "still-life
drama". The house cat prowls,
there's the smell of gravy bubbling,
and the sound of horses' hooves on
the cobbled street outside. Daytime
visits take place on Sundays and
Mondays; for the candlelit "Silent
Night" visits you must book ahead.

into the old market, although part
of the original facade survives on
the north side of Brushfield Street.
The remaining market now hosts
an eclectic and fairly sophisticated
selection of shops and stalls selling
crafts, clothes and food in the
original red-brick and green-gabled
1893 building, to the east. There's a
vintage market on Thursdays.

The Olympic Park

The focus of the 2012 Olympics was the **Olympic Park**
(ⓦ queenelizabetholympicpark.co.uk), laid out over a series of
islands formed by the River Lee and its various tributaries and
canals. Since the Olympics, the whole area has been replanted
with swathes of grass, trees and flowers, and peppered with
cafés. This, plus an excellent kids' playground, Tumbling Bay,
make it a great park in which to hang out on a sunny day.
The centrepiece of the park is the **Olympic Stadium**, now
used for large concerts, as well as being home to West Ham
United football club. Standing close to the stadium is the **Orbit
Tower** (Mon–Fri 11am–5pm, Sat & Sun 10am–6pm; longer
hours in peak season; £11.50 in advance, £16.50 with slide;
ⓦ arcelormittalorbit.com), a 377ft-high continuous loop of red
recycled steel designed by Anish Kapoor, with a tunnel slide by
Carsten Höller. But the most eye-catching venue is Zaha Hadid's
wave-like **London Aquatics Centre** (daily 6am–10.30pm), four
times over budget, but looking very cool and costing £5.20 for a
swim. Other venues to look out for are the curvy **Velodrome** with
its banked, Siberian pine track and adjacent BMX circuit – part
of the **Lee Valley VeloPark** (ⓦ visitleevalley.org.uk) – and the
Copper Box Arena, now a multi-sports centre. The nearest tube
is Stratford.

Shops

Absolute Vintage

MAP P.90, POCKET MAP O5
14 Hanbury St ⊖ Liverpool Street or
Shoreditch High Street Overground. Daily
11am–7pm.

A Spitalfields treasure-trove of
Twenties to Nineties clobber, with
a good selection of shoes and bags.

Beyond Retro

MAP P.90
110–112 Cheshire St ⊖ Shoreditch
High Street Overground. Mon–Wed, Fri &
Sat 10am–7pm, Thurs 10am–8pm, Sun
11.30am–6pm.

Cavernous warehouse of twentieth-
century classics, with thousands of
goodies including vintage jeans,
1950s frocks and battered cowboy
boots, with an outlet section
offering some serious bargains.

Freedom Press

MAP P.90, POCKET MAP O5
Angel Alley, 84b Whitechapel High St
⊖ Aldgate East. Mon–Sat noon–6pm, Sun
noon–4pm.

Upholding a long East End
tradition of radical politics, this
small anarchist bookshop is packed
with everything from Bakhunin to
Chomsky.

House of Hackney

MAP P.90, POCKET MAP N4
131 Shoreditch High St ⊖ Liverpool Street
or Shoreditch High Street Overground.
Mon–Sat 10am–7pm, Sun 11am–5pm.

Whimsical, high-fashion
homewares, wallpapers, textiles,
clothing and gifts, all designed and
made in England.

Labour and Wait

MAP P.90, POCKET MAP O4
85 Redchurch St ⊖ Shoreditch High Street
Overground. Tues–Fri 11am–6.30pm, Sat &
Sun 11am–6pm.

The hardware, kitchen gear and
cleaning products of your dreams.
From enamel kettles to sharpening
stones, everything is defined
by beautiful design, ingenious
functionality and more than a whiff
of nostalgia.

Rough Trade East

MAP P.90, POCKET MAP O5
Old Truman Brewery, 91 Brick Lane
⊖ Liverpool Street. Mon–Thurs 9am–9pm,
Fri 9am–8pm, Sat 10am–8pm, Sun
11am–7pm.

It started in west London, but the
east London store of this famous
purveyor of vinyl has the edge
in terms of size. It stocks a huge
array of indie, electronica and
more, with listening posts, in store
recommendations, an interesting
selection of books and a small café.
It also hosts in-store appearances
and special gigs by some
impressively high-profile names.

Tatty Devine

MAP P.90, POCKET MAP O4
236 Brick Lane ⊖ Liverpool Street or
Shoreditch High Street Overground. Mon–
Fri 10am–6.30pm, Sat 11am–6pm, Sun
10am–5pm.

This youthful, playful jewellers is
every East End girl's go-to brand
for bold, eye-popping statement
pieces. The laser-cut acrylic
personalized name necklaces are
fabulous.

Beyond Retro

Cafés

Brick Lane Beigel Bake

MAP P.90, POCKET MAP O4
159 Brick Lane ⊖ Shoreditch High Street
Overground. Daily 24hr.

Classic no-frills bagel shop in
the heart of the East End –
unbelievably cheap, even for fillings
such as smoked salmon with cream
cheese (£2) or salt beef (£4.30).

E. Pellicci

MAP P.90
332 Bethnal Green Rd ⊖ Bethnal Green.
Mon–Sat 7am–4pm.

Open since 1900, family-owned
caff *Pellicci's* is one of a dying breed
in London: original 1940s decor,
good-natured banter, giant fry-ups
and inexpensive home-made Italian
comfort food. A beloved East End
institution.

Leila's Shop

MAP P.90, POCKET MAP O4
17 Calvert Ave ⊖ Shoreditch High Street
Overground. Wed–Sat 10am–6pm, Sun
10am–5pm.

Linked to a lovely little deli/
grocer's/farm shop, this simple

E. Pellicci

neighbourhood café serves fresh-
made seasonal, Mediterranean food
and biodynamic wines.

Verde and Co

MAP P.90, POCKET MAP O5
40 Brushfield St ⊖ Liverpool Street.
Mon, Wed & Thurs 10am–7pm, Tues & Fri
8am–8pm, Sat & Sun 10am–5pm.

Gorgeous old Spitalfields store
owned by author Jeanette
Winterson. The picturesque
eighteenth-century shopfront
conceals a deli where coffee, cakes
and simple hot dishes are served to
the lucky few who can bag a seat.

Restaurants

Chez Elles

MAP P.90, POCKET MAP O5
45 Brick Lane ⊖ Aldgate East ☏ 020 7247
9699. Tues–Sat 5.30–10.30pm, Thurs–Sat
also noon–3pm, Sun 11am–4.30pm.

Incongruously set on curry-house-
lined Brick Lane, this pretty, very
French bistro offers rustic Gallic
classics – onion soup, duck confit,
moules – served with charm. Mains
£13.50–20.

Clove Club

MAP P.90, POCKET MAP N4
Shoreditch Town Hall, 380 Old St ⊖ Old
Street ☏ 020 7729 6496. Mon 6–11.30pm,
Tues–Sat noon–2.30pm & 6–11.30pm.

At the vanguard of Shoreditch's
foodie scene, offering tasting menu
(£110) and shorter five-course
menus (Mon–Thurs £75) and
sharing plates at the bar. Delicious,
inventive cooking, if you can
stomach the prepaid ticket booking
system.

Hawksmoor Spitalfields

MAP P.90, POCKET MAP O5
157a Commercial St ⊖ Liverpool Street or
Shoreditch High Street ☏ 020 7426 4850.
Mon–Fri noon–2.30pm & 5–10.30pm, Sat
noon–3pm & 5–10.30pm, Sun noon–9pm.

One for serious meat lovers,
the *Hawksmoor* restaurants
(there are five in London; this

was the first) serve some of the best steaks in town (from £20; sauces and sides extra), as well as seafood and excellent cocktails, all in a sophisticated, leather and mahogany interior.

Pidgin

MAP P.90

52 Wilton Way ⊖ Hackney Central Overground ☏ 020 7254 8311. Tues–Fri 6–11pm, Sat & Sun 1–2.30pm & 6–11pm. Outstanding food – contemporary, punchy and influenced by Asian flavours – on a weekly changing four-course menu (£49). Dishes run the gamut from pigeon pie to aubergine with Szechuan pepper – the surprise element simply adds to the pleasure.

St John Bread and Wine

MAP P.90, POCKET MAP O5

94–96 Commercial St ⊖ Liverpool Street ☏ 020 7251 0848, ⊚ stjohngroup.uk.com/spitalfields. Mon–Fri 9–11.30am, noon–4pm & 6–11pm, Sat & Sun 9am–noon, 1–4pm & 6–11pm (Mon & Sun till 10pm).
A more casual, canteen-style version of Clerkenwell's *St John* restaurant (see page 85), this branch also serves traditional and unusual cuts of meat, so expect offal and game on the menu – devilled kidneys, pigeon and rabbit – from £14 for a main.

Som Saa

MAP P.90, POCKET MAP O5

43a Commercial St ⊖ Aldgate East ☏ 020 7324 7790. Tues–Sat noon–2.30pm & 6–10.30pm.
Forget tired green chicken curry – this Thai food is a cut above the rest, with fresh, surprising dishes (£10–16) such as stir-fried clams with turmeric or Burmese-style pork belly and shoulder curry.

Tayyab's

MAP P.90

83–89 Fieldgate St ⊖ Whitechapel ☏ 020 7247 6400. Daily noon–11.30pm.
This busy place has been serving good, freshly cooked,

Pidgin

straightforward Punjabi food for over forty years. Prices remain low, booking is essential and service is speedy and slick. Unlicensed but you can bring your own alcohol. Mains around £7–10.

Viet Hoa Café

MAP P.90, POCKET MAP O3

70–72 Kingsland Rd ⊖ Hoxton Overground ☏ 020 7729 8293. Mon–Fri noon–3.30pm & 5.30–11.30pm, Sat & Sun 12.30–11.30pm. Simple Vietnamese restaurant on a street heaving with similar places. Big portions and lots of spicy noodle soups to choose from.

Pubs and bars

Carpenter's Arms

MAP P.90

73 Cheshire St ⊖ Bethnal Green Overground. Mon–Wed 4–11.30pm, Thurs & Sun noon–11.30pm, Fri & Sat noon–12.30am.
Bought by the notorious Reggie Kray for his beloved mum, this welcoming pub has cleaned up its act, offering craft lagers, good food and a relaxed neighbourhood vibe.

Mother Kelly's

Culpeper
MAP P.90, POCKET MAP O5
40 Commercial St ⊖ Liverpool Street.
Mon–Thurs 11am–midnight, Fri & Sat
11am–2am, Sun 11am–11pm. Rooftop
Tues–Sun only.
This light-filled, casually stylish
gastropub has a secret: a gorgeous
plant-filled roof terrace where they
serve a simple menu of small plates
(£5–14) that incorporate the plants
they grow. A more substantial
menu is served in the first floor
restaurant and friendly, ground-
floor pub. All dishes are deftly
prepared and the menu changes
regularly (mains £13–17).

Happiness Forgets
MAP P.90, POCKET MAP N4
8–9 Hoxton Square ⊖ Old Street. Daily
5–11pm. Fri & Sat till 3am.
This intimate, candlelit basement
bar is a great place to hunker
down and sip on inventive, strong
cocktails, from the "Tokyo Collins"
to the "Perfect Storm".

Indo
MAP P.90
133 Whitechapel Rd ⊖ Aldgate East. Mon–
Thurs & Sun noon–1am, Fri & Sat till 3am.
Small and dark bar, with an
unpretentious crowd, good pizzas
and a decent range of beers.
Despite its size, you can often find
a comfortable spot.

Mother Kelly's
MAP P.90
251 Paradise Row ⊖ Bethnal Green. Mon
4–11pm, Tues–Thurs & Sun noon–11pm, Fri
& Sat noon–midnight.
One of a number of interesting
ventures occupying a strip of
railway arches in Bethnal Green,
this stripped-back space is a great,
welcoming place for sampling some
of London – and the world's – craft
beers, with 23 on tap at any time
(served in third-, half- of full pints),
plus huge fridges of beers to tempt
you. Food is simple sharing boards
of meats and cheeses.

Railway Tavern
MAP P.90
2 Jude St ⊖ Dalston Kingsland
Overground. Mon–Thurs 4–11pm, Fri &
noon–midnight, Sun noon–10.30pm.
Tucked away on a quiet corner
behind Dalston's main drag, this
is a good-looking, feel-good local,
decked out in vintage railway decor,
with well-kept cask ales, tasty Thai
food and live music.

Sager + Wilde
MAP P.90, POCKET MAP O3
193 Hackney Rd ⊖ Hoxton. Mon–Wed
5pm–midnight, Thurs & Fri 5pm–1am, Sat
noon–1am & Sun noon–midnight.
Gorgeous wine bar in a gussied-up
old East End corner site, with a
fabulous wine selection and cheese
sharing plates and toasties. Prices
can mount (glasses £6–18), but the
quality is impeccable.

Ten Bells
MAP P.90, POCKET MAP O5
84 Commercial St ⊖ Shoreditch High
Street. Mon–Wed & Sun noon–midnight,
Thurs–Sat noon–1am.
Lively historic Spitalfields pub
with beautiful Victorian tiling and
a cocktail bar upstairs. Live music
and DJs at the weekend.

Worship Street Whistling Stop
MAP P.90, POCKET MAP N4
63 Worship St ⊖ Old Street. Mon & Tues

5pm–midnight, Wed & Thurs 5pm–1am, Fri & Sat 5pm–2am.

Shabbily opulent cocktail bar with a speakeasy gin palace vibe and a menu of wildly creative cocktails.

Clubs and venues

Bethnal Green Working Men's Club

MAP P.90

42–44 Pollard Row ⊖ Bethnal Green ☏ 020 7739 7170, ⓦ www.workersplaytime.net.

At once hip and friendly, this old-school venue offers cool post-war decor and an impeccable booking policy: burlesque, disco, swing, ska, cabaret, indie, the lot.

Book Club

MAP P.90, POCKET MAP N4

100–106 Leonard St ⊖ Old Street ⓦ wearetbc.com. Mon–Wed 9am–midnight, Thurs–Fri 9am–2am, Sat 10am–2am, Sun 10am–midnight.

Enjoy "thinking and drinking" at this eclectic cross-platform basement club. Hip-hop quizzes, drawing classes, stand-up diary reading, rip-roaring DJ nights – there's always something exciting going on.

Cargo

MAP P.90, POCKET MAP N4

83 Rivington St ⊖ Old Street ⓦ www.cargo-london.com.

Small, popular venue in what was once a railway arch. Hosts a variety of live acts, including jazz, hip-hop, indie and folk, and an excellent line-up of club nights.

Dalston Superstore

MAP P.90

117 Kingsland High St ⊖ Dalston Kingsland ☏ 020 7254 2273, ⓦ dalstonsuperstore.com.

Outrageous, camp and great fun, this Dalston stalwart is nominally a LGBTQ bar/club but welcomes all, bringing synth-pop, disco, techno, house, soul and funk to a wild-dancing crowd.

The Macbeth

MAP P.90, POCKET MAP N3

70 Hoxton St ⊖ Old Street ☏ 020 7749 0600, ⓦ themacbeth.co.uk.

A brilliantly eclectic selection of fun club nights celebrating everything from Bieber to Beyoncé, plus live bands and pop-culture themed events. Check out the roof terrace.

Village Underground

MAP P.90, POCKET MAP N4

54 Holywell Lane ⊖ Shoreditch High Street Overground ☏ 020 7422 7505, ⓦ villageunderground.co.uk.

Nonprofit, genre-bending arts venue and creative hub (studios include tube carriages and shipping containers and changing street art) with an always intriguing roster of gigs, club nights and theatre. Cool, experimental and progressive.

XOYO

MAP P.90, POCKET MAP N4

32–37 Cowper St ⊖ Old Street ⓦ xoyo.co.uk.

Huge Shoreditch club whose legendary weekend club nights and regular live gigs pull in the biggest names in everything from dance music to indie rock.

Dalston Superstore

The Tower and Docklands

One of the city's main tourist attractions, the Tower of London was the site of some of the goriest events in the nation's history, and is somewhere all visitors should try and get to see. Immediately to the east are the remains of what was the largest enclosed cargo-dock system in the world, built in the nineteenth century to cope with the huge volume of goods shipped in along the Thames from all over the Empire. No one thought the area could be rejuvenated when the docks closed in the 1960s, but since the 1980s, warehouses have been converted into luxury flats, waterside penthouse apartments have been built and the huge high-rise office development of Canary Wharf is now London's second financial centre.

Tower of London

MAP P.100, POCKET MAP O7
⊖ Tower Hill ☎ 020 3166 6000, �🌐 www.
hrp.org.uk. March–Oct Mon & Sun
10am–5.30pm, Tues–Sat 9am–5.30pm;
Nov–Feb Mon & Sun 10am–4.30pm, Tues–
Sat 9am–4.30pm. From £22.50 online.

One of the most perfectly preserved medieval fortresses in the country, the Tower of London sits beside

Beefeater, Tower of London

the Thames surrounded by a wide, dry moat. Begun by William the Conqueror, the Tower is chiefly famous as a place of imprisonment and death, though it has been used variously as a royal residence, armoury, mint, menagerie, observatory and – a function it still serves – a safe-deposit box for the Crown Jewels. Before you set off, join one of the free guided tours, given by the Tower's **Beefeaters** (officially known as Yeoman Warders). As well as giving a good introduction to the history, these ex-servicemen relish hamming up the gory stories.

Visitors today enter the Tower along Water Lane, but in times gone by most prisoners were delivered through **Traitors' Gate**, on the waterfront. The nearby **Bloody Tower** saw the murders of 12-year-old Edward V and his 9-year-old brother, and was used to imprison Walter Raleigh on three separate occasions.

The central **White Tower** is the original "Tower", begun in 1076. Now home to part of the Royal Armouries, and its hands-on "Armouries in Action" displays, it's worth visiting for the beautiful

Tower Bridge

Norman Chapel of St John, on the second floor. To the west of the White Tower is the execution spot on **Tower Green** where seven highly placed but unlucky individuals were beheaded, among them Henry VIII's second and fifth wives.

The **Crown Jewels** are the major reason so many people flock to the Tower, but the moving walkways which take you past the loot are disappointingly swift, allowing you just seconds' viewing during peak periods. The oldest piece of regalia is the twelfth-century Anointing Spoon, but the vast majority of exhibits, including the Imperial State Crown, postdate the Commonwealth (1649–60). Among the jewels are three of the largest cut diamonds in the world, including the legendary Koh-i-Noor, set into the Queen Mother's Crown in 1937.

Tower Bridge

MAP P.100, POCKET MAP O7

🚇 Tower Hill ☎ 020 7403 3761, ⓦ www. towerbridge.org.uk. Daily: April–Sept 10am–5.30pm; Oct–March 9.30am–5pm. £8.70 online.

Tower Bridge ranks with Big Ben as the most famous of all London landmarks. Completed in 1894, its Neo-Gothic towers are clad in Cornish granite and Portland stone, but conceal a steel frame which, at the time, represented a considerable engineering achievement. The **raising of the bascules** (from the French for "see-saw") remains an impressive sight – check the website to find out when the bridge is opening. It's free to walk across the bridge, but you must pay to gain

Docklands Light Railway

The best way to visit Docklands is to take the Docklands Light Railway or **DLR** (ⓦ www.tfl.gov.uk/dlr), whose driverless trains run on overhead tracks, and give out great views over the cityscape. DLR trains set off from Bank tube and from Tower Gateway, close to Tower Hill tube and the Tower of London.

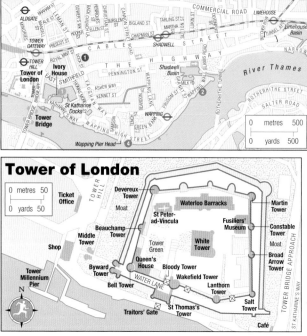

access to the **elevated walkways** linking the summits of the towers – closed from 1909 to 1982 due to their popularity with prostitutes and the suicidal. The views are good both out over the river and directly down through the glass floors, and you get to see the giant, defunct, coal-fired boilers in the **Victorian Engine Rooms** on the south side of the bridge.

St Katharine Docks

MAP P.100, POCKET MAP O7

⊖ Tower Hill.

Built in the late 1820s to relieve the congestion on the River Thames, St Katharine Docks were originally surrounded by high walls to protect the warehouses used to store luxury goods – ivory, spices, carpets and cigars – shipped in from all over the Empire. Nowadays, the docks are used as an upmarket marina, and the old warehouses house shops, pubs and restaurants. More

interesting, however, are the old **swing bridges** over the basins (including one from 1828), the boats themselves – you'll often see beautiful old sailing ships and Dutch barges – and the attractive **Ivory House** warehouse, with its clock tower, at the centre of the three basins. At its peak this warehouse received over 200 tons of ivory annually.

Wapping High Street

MAP P.100

⊖ Wapping Overground.

Once famous for its boatyards and its three dozen riverside pubs, Wapping's Victorian atmosphere has been preserved, and as it lies just a short walk east of the Tower, this is easily the most satisfying part of Docklands to explore. Halfway along Wapping High Street is **Wapping Pier Head**, the former entrance to the London Docks, flanked by grand, curvaceous

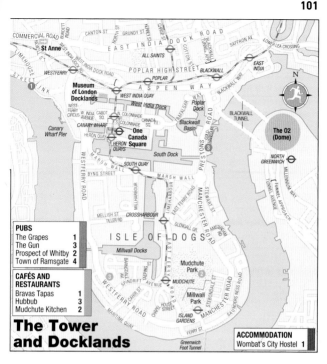

PUBS

The Grapes	1
The Gun	3
Prospect of Whitby	2
Town of Ramsgate	4

CAFÉS AND RESTAURANTS

Bravas Tapas	1
Hubbub	3
Mudchute Kitchen	2

The Tower and Docklands

ACCOMMODATION

Wombat's City Hostel	1

Regency terraces. Here, you'll find one of the few surviving stairs down to the river beside the **Town of Ramsgate** pub; beneath the pub are the dungeons where convicts were chained before being deported to Australia. It was also at the *Town of Ramsgate* that "Hanging" Judge Jeffreys was captured trying to escape disguised as a collier following the victory of William of Orange in 1688.

St Anne's Church

MAP P.100

5 Newell St ⊖ Westferry DLR.

Designed in 1714 by **Nicholas Hawksmoor**, and dominated by a gargantuan west tower, St Anne's boasts the highest church clock in London. Inside is a superb organ built for the Great Exhibition in 1851. In the graveyard Hawksmoor erected a pyramidal structure carved with masonic symbols, now hopelessly eroded; opposite is a

war memorial with relief panels depicting the horrors of trench warfare.

Canary Wharf

MAP P.100

⊖ Canary Wharf & DLR.

The geographical and ideological heart of the new **Docklands** is Canary Wharf, once a destination for bananas (from the Canary Islands – hence the name). An established business district, this is the one Docklands area that you can happily stroll around, taking in the architecture and having a drink overlooking one of the old wharves – or chill out at Crossrail Roof Garden (daily until sunset), a partially enclosed garden. Canary Wharf's name is, of course, synonymous with Cesar Pelli's landmark tower, officially known as **One Canada Square**. It was Britain's tallest building between 1990 and 2012 (before the Shard).

Museum of London Docklands

MAP P.100

West India Quay ⊖ West India Quay ☎ 020 7001 9844, ⓦ www.museumoflondon.org. uk/docklands. Daily 10am–6pm. Free.

The last surviving Georgian warehouses of the West India Docks lie on the far side of a floodlit floating bridge at **West India Quay**. Amidst the dockside bars and restaurants, you'll find Warehouse No. 1, built in 1803 for storing rum, sugar, molasses, coffee and cotton, and now home to the Museum of London Docklands. Spread over several floors, the museum's exhibits chart the history of London's docks on both sides of the river from Roman times to the present day. Highlights include a model of old London Bridge; an eight-foot long watercolour showing the "legal quays" in the 1790s, just before the enclosed docks eased congestion; and a reconstructed warren of late nineteenth-century shops and cobbled dockland streets. Those with kids should head for Mudlarks, on the ground floor, where children can learn a bit about pulleys and ballast, drive a DLR train or simply romp around the soft play area.

The O2 (Dome)

MAP P.100

⊖ North Greenwich ⓦ www.theo2.co.uk.

Clearly visible from the east bank of the Isle of Dogs, the Dome, or **O2**, is a 23,000-seat events arena, designed by Richard Rogers for the millennium celebrations. Over half a mile in circumference, 160ft in height and held up by a dozen, 300ft-tall yellow steel masts, it's the largest of its kind in the world. You can climb the outside of the Dome (Jan to mid-Feb Fri–Sun; mid-Feb to Dec daily, times vary; £28–35), though the views are better from the nearby Emirates Airline cable car (daily at least 9am–10pm; £3.50 with Oyster card).

The O2

Cafés and restaurants

Bravas Tapas

MAP P.100, POCKET MAP O7
St Katharine Docks ⊖ Tower Hill ☎ 020
7481 1464. Mon–Sat noon–10.30pm, Sun
noon–10pm.

Attractive Spanish restaurant
with a sunny dockside terrace,
serving tasty tapas (Moorish
spiced lamb chops, crispy foie
gras-stuffed quail; £5–15) and
Spanish wines.

Hubbub

MAP P.100
269 Westferry Rd ⊖ Mudchute DLR.
Mon–Wed 11am–11pm, Thurs & Fri
11am–midnight, Sat 10am–midnight, Sun
10am–10.30pm.

An oasis in the Docklands desert,
this café-bar is in a former
church, now arts centre, and does
great breakfasts, wraps and hot
specials.

Mudchute Kitchen

MAP P.100
Mudchute City Farm, Pier St
⊖ Mudchute DLR ☎ 020 3069 9290.
Tues–Fri 9.30am–3pm, Sat & Sun
9.30am–5pm.

Good home-made food (£3.50–8)
– cooked breakfasts, panini, jacket
potatoes – children's meals and
farmside seating in this kiddie-
focused city farm (farm daily
9am–5pm; free).

Pubs

The Grapes

MAP P.100
76 Narrow St ⊖ Westferry DLR. Mon–Sat
noon–11pm, Sun noon–10.30pm.

A lovely, narrow little pub on a
quiet street, with lots of seafaring
paraphernalia and a great riverside
balcony out back. The ales are good
and there's an expensive restaurant
upstairs.

Prospect of Whitby

The Gun

MAP P.100
27 Coldharbour ⊖ Canary Wharf or South
Quay or Blackwall DLR. Mon–Sat 11am–
midnight, Sun 11.30am–11.30pm.

Legendary dockers' pub, once the
haunt of Lord Nelson, and now
a classy gastropub. Its cosy back
bar has a couple of snugs, and
the outside deck offers unrivalled
views.

Prospect of Whitby

MAP P.100
57 Wapping Wall ⊖ Wapping Overground.
Mon–Thurs noon–11pm, Fri & Sat noon–
midnight, Sun noon–10.30pm.

Steeped in history, this is London's
most famous riverside pub, with
a pewter bar, flagstone floor,
ancient timber beams and stacks
of maritime memorabilia. Decent
beers and terrific views too.

Town of Ramsgate

MAP P.100
62 Wapping High St ⊖ Wapping
Overground. Mon–Wed & Sun noon–11pm,
Thurs–Sat noon–midnight.

Dark, narrow, medieval pub
located by Wapping Old Stairs,
which once led down to Execution
Dock. Admiral Bligh and Fletcher
Christian were regular drinking
partners here in pre-Mutiny days.

South Bank and around

The South Bank has a lot going for it. As well as the massive waterside arts centre, it's home to a host of tourist attractions including the enormously popular London Eye. With most of London's key sights sitting on the north bank of the Thames, the views from here are the best on the river, and thanks to the wide, traffic-free riverside boulevard, the whole area can be happily explored on foot. And a short walk from the South Bank lie one or two lesser-known but nonetheless absorbing sights such as the Imperial War Museum, which contains the country's only permanent exhibition devoted to the Holocaust.

Southbank Centre

MAP P.105, POCKET MAP J17

⊖ Waterloo Ⓦ www.southbankcentre.co.uk.

The Southbank Centre is home to a whole variety of artistic institutions, the most attractive of which is the **Royal Festival Hall**, built in 1951 for the Festival of Britain and one of London's chief concert venues (see page 109). Their riverside location, the avenue of trees, fluttering banners, buskers and skateboarders, and the weekend food stalls draw in visitors, particularly in summer when weekend festivals, pop-up venues and outside bars are added to the mix. The **Queen Elizabeth Hall** is the complex's second music venue, while the **Hayward Gallery** (Mon & Wed–Sun 11am–7pm, Thurs till 9pm; exhibitions around £15) puts on large modern and contemporary art shows in its spacious, concrete galleries. You'll find secondhand bookstalls outside the nearby **BFI Southbank**, the city's chief arts cinema.

South Bank from Hungerford Bridge

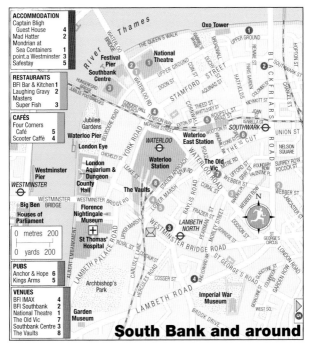

ACCOMMODATION
Captain Bligh
Guest House 4
Mad Hatter 2
Mondrian at
Sea Containers 1
point.a Westminster 3
Safestay 5

RESTAURANTS
BFI Bar & Kitchen 1
Laughing Gravy 2
Masters
Super Fish 3

CAFÉS
Four Corners
Café 5
Scooter Caffè 4

PUBS
Anchor & Hope 6
Kings Arms 5

VENUES
BFI IMAX 4
BFI Southbank 2
National Theatre 1
The Old Vic 7
Southbank Centre 3
The Vaults 8

South Bank and around

National Theatre

MAP P.105, POCKET MAP K17

Waterloo ⓦ nationaltheatre.org.uk.

Looking like a brutalist masterpiece
or a multistorey car park,
depending on whom you ask, the
National Theatre is an institution
first mooted in 1848 but only
realized in 1976. The three
auditoriums within are superb
and can be visited on excellent
backstage tours (1hr; £11), for
which you should book online
in advance. You can also peek
behind the scenes via the Sherling
Backstage Walkway (Mon–Sat
9.30am–7.30pm).

Oxo Tower

MAP P.105, POCKET MAP L7

Southwark

The Oxo Tower started life as a
Victorian power station before
being converted in the 1930s into
a meat-packing factory for the
company that makes Oxo stock

cubes – the lettering is spelt out
in the windows of the main tower.
The building now contains an
exhibition space on the ground
floor (daily 11am–6pm), plus flats
for local residents, sandwiched
between a series of retail workshops
for designers on the first and second
floors, and a swanky restaurant,
bar and brasserie on the top floor.
To enjoy the view without food
or drink, visit the **public viewing
gallery** (daily 10am–1pm).

London Eye

MAP P.105, POCKET MAP J18

Waterloo or Westminster ⓣ 0871 781
3000, ⓦ www.londoneye.com. Daily from
10am; closing time varies (6–8.30pm, 9pm
July & Aug weekends). Closed 2 weeks in
Jan. From £24.30 online.

The London Eye is now one of
the city's most famous landmarks.
Standing an impressive 443ft
high, it's the largest **Ferris wheel**
in Europe, weighing over 2000

tonnes, yet as simple and delicate as a bicycle wheel. It's constantly in slow motion, which means a full-circle "flight" in one of its 32 pods should take around thirty minutes – that may seem a long time, but in fact it passes incredibly quickly. Book in advance (and online to save money) as on arrival you'll still have to queue to be loaded on.

London Aquarium

MAP P.105, POCKET MAP J18
County Hall, Riverside Walk ⊖ Waterloo or Westminster ⓦ www.sealife.co.uk. Oct–mid July Mon–Fri 10am–6pm, Sat & Sun 9.30am–7pm; mid-July–Sept daily 9.30am–7pm. From £21 online.

The most popular attraction in County Hall, the vast former council building by the London Eye, is the London Aquarium, laid out on two subterranean levels. With some super-large tanks, and everything from dog-face puffers and piranhas to the bowmouth guitarfish, this is an attraction that's pretty much guaranteed to please kids. The sea turtles and sharks are always popular. Impressive in scale, the aquarium also has a walk-through underwater tunnel. Ask at the main desk for the times of presentations and feeding times.

London Dungeon

MAP P.105, POCKET MAP J18
County Hall, Westminster Bridge Rd ⊖ Waterloo or Westminster ⓦ www. thedungeons.com. Mid-Aug–mid July Mon–Wed, Fri & Sun 10am–5pm, Thurs 11am–5pm, Sat 10am–6pm; mid-July–mid-Aug daily 10am–6pm. From £21 online.

Inside the County Hall is the ever-popular horror-fest, the London Dungeon. Young teenagers and the credulous probably get the most out of the life-sized tableaux of folk being hanged, drawn and quartered and tortured, the general hysteria being boosted by actors in period garb. Visitors are led through a series of live-action period scenarios, dwelling on the most gruesome London legends from Sweeney Todd to the inevitable Jack the Ripper section, ending with the "Drop Ride to Doom".

Florence Nightingale Museum

MAP P.105, POCKET MAP J19
Lambeth Palace Rd ⊖ Waterloo or Westminster ⓣ 020 7188 4400, ⓦ www. florence-nightingale.co.uk. Daily 10am–5pm. £7.50.

Hidden among the outbuildings of **St Thomas' Hospital**, the Florence

London Aquarium

Nightingale Museum celebrates the devout woman who revolutionized the nursing profession by establishing the first school of nursing at St Thomas' in 1860 and publishing her *Notes on Nursing*, which emphasized the importance of hygiene, decorum and discipline. Exhibits include the white lantern that earned her the nickname "The Lady with the Lamp"; Athena, her stuffed pet owl; and a panel on the remarkable **Mary Seacole**, the Jamaican nurse who cared for soldiers in the Crimea itself; a statue of her stands in the hospital grounds.

Garden Museum

MAP P.105, POCKET MAP J9
Lambeth Palace Rd ⊖ Westminster or Lambeth North ☎ 020 7401 8865, ⓦ www.gardenmuseum.org.uk. Mon–Fri & Sun 10.30am–5pm, Sat 10.30am–4pm. £10; tower only £3.

Housed in the former church of **St Mary-at-Lambeth**, this museum pays homage to John Tradescant, gardener to James I and Charles I, whose sarcophagus is located in the **graveyard** garden (another belongs to Captain Bligh, the commander of the *Bounty*). Tradescant amassed an "Ark" – a cabinet of curiosities – a few items of which are displayed in the museum, along with all sorts of gardening memorabilia, horticultural artworks and interactive displays. It's a charming hotch-potch of stuff, and you can also climb the 131 steps of the church tower for unsurpassed views across to the Houses of Parliament. There's a good café-restaurant on-site.

Imperial War Museum

MAP P.105, POCKET MAP L9
Lambeth Rd ⊖ Lambeth North ☎ 020 7416 5000, ⓦ www.iwm.org.uk. Daily 10am–6pm. Free.

Housed in a domed building that was, until 1930, the central portion of the infamous "Bedlam" lunatic asylum, the Imperial

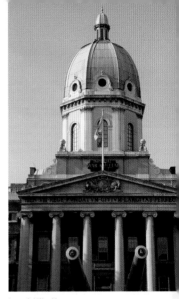

Imperial War Museum

War Museum holds by far the best collection of militaria in the capital. The treatment of the subject matter is impressively wide-ranging and fairly sober, with the main hall's display of guns, rockets, tanks and fighter planes shown alongside such objects as a car destroyed by a suicide bomb in Baghdad in 2007, installed by artist Jeremy Deller. There's a large, extremely thorough series of galleries on **World War I** which includes a walk-through **trench**, and a section telling the story of family life during the Blitz. The museum's **art galleries** on the third floor are well worth a visit for their superb exhibitions of war artists, official and unofficial. Entered from the fourth floor, the harrowing **Holocaust Exhibition** (not recommended for children under 14) pulls few punches, and has made a valiant attempt to avoid depicting the victims of the Holocaust as nameless masses by focusing on individual cases, interspersing the archive footage with eyewitness accounts from contemporary survivors.

Cafés

Four Corners Café

MAP P.105, POCKET MAP K19
12 Lower Marsh ⊖ Waterloo. Mon–Fri
7.30am–6.30pm, Sat 9am–5pm.
Sweet little travel-themed indie
place serving excellent coffee along
with great pastries, sandwiches,
beers and cocktails. The guidebook
exchange is a nice touch.

Scooter Caffe

MAP P.105, POCKET MAP K19
132 Lower Marsh ⊖ Waterloo. Mon–Thurs
8.30am–11pm, Fri 8.30am–midnight, Sat
10am–midnight, Sun 10am–11pm.
This quirky café-bar is charmingly
boho, all vintage memorabilia and
mismatched furniture. Coffee, wine
and snacks served with a smile.

Restaurants

BFI Bar & Kitchen

MAP P.105, POCKET MAP K17
BFI Southbank ⊖ Waterloo ☎ 020
7401 9000. Mon–Sat 10am–11pm, Sun
10am–10.30pm.
This smart, buzzy restaurant/bar (to
the side of the BFI, rather than the

Anchor & Hope

busier riverfront one), convenient
for a pre- or post-movie supper, is
the best of the South Bank chains
– it's run by Benugo. Portions are
small for the price, but the Modern
British food has some creative
flashes; two course pre-film menu
for £22.

Laughing Gravy

MAP P.105, POCKET MAP L8
154 Blackfriars Rd ⊖ Southwark ☎ 020
7998 1707. Mon–Thurs noon–3pm &
5–10pm, Fri noon–3pm & 5–10.30pm,
Sat noon–4pm & 5–10.30pm, Sun
noon–4.30pm.
Warm, welcoming brasserie serving
a menu of robust Modern British
food in a brick-lined dining room
with a cosy, neighbourhood vibe.
Mains £14–26.

Masters Super Fish

MAP P.105, POCKET MAP L8
191 Waterloo Rd ⊖ Waterloo ☎ 020
7928 6924. Mon 5.30–10.30pm, Tues–Sat
noon–3pm & 5.30–10.30pm.
An old-fashioned, unpretentious
fish-and-chip restaurant, which
serves up huge portions with all
the trimmings: gherkins, pickled
onions and a few complimentary
prawns. Mains £9–13.

Pubs

Anchor & Hope

MAP P.105, POCKET MAP L8
36 The Cut ⊖ Southwark. Mon 5–11pm,
Tues–Sat 11am–11pm, Sun 12.30–3.15pm.
Gastropub that dishes up truly
excellent, yet simple grub: Modern
European and creative, with
mouthwatering puds. You can't
book a table, except for Sunday
lunch.

Kings Arms

MAP P.105, POCKET MAP K7
25 Roupell St ⊖ Waterloo. Mon–Fri
11am–11pm, Sat noon–11pm, Sun
noon–10.30pm.
Terrific local on a quiet Victorian
terraced street: the front part is a

traditional drinking area, while the tastefully cluttered rear is a glass and wood conservatory-style space where they serve good-value and tasty Thai food.

Venues

BFI IMAX

MAP P.105, POCKET MAP K17
1 Charlie Chaplin Walk ⊖ Waterloo ☎ 0330 333 7878, ⓦ www.bfi.org.uk.
Remarkable glazed drum housing Britain's largest screen, showing 2D and 3D films – mostly superhero franchises, action movies and family entertainment – in a vertiginous auditorium.

BFI Southbank

MAP P.105, POCKET MAP K17
South Bank ⊖ Waterloo ☎ 020 7928 3232, ⓦ www.bfi.org.uk.
Known for its attentive audiences and an exhaustive, eclectic programme that includes directors' seasons, talks and themed series. Around eight films daily are shown in the vast NFT1 and three smaller screens.

National Theatre

MAP P.105, POCKET MAP K17
South Bank ⊖ Waterloo ☎ 020 7452 3000, ⓦ www.nationaltheatre.org.uk.
The NT consists of three separate theatres – the 1150-seater Olivier, the proscenium-arched Lyttelton and the experimental Dorfman – and puts on a programme ranging from Greek tragedies to Broadway musicals. Some productions sell out months in advance, and prices aren't low, though the Travelex ticket scheme releases hundreds of seats at £15 for each show.

The Old Vic

MAP P.105, POCKET MAP K8
The Cut, South Bank ⊖ Waterloo ☎ 0844 871 7628, ⓦ oldvictheatre.com.
This elegant old theatre was founded in 1818 and shows a mixture of high-profile new plays

National Theatre

and imaginative stagings of classic works, drawing big-name actors.

Southbank Centre

MAP P.105, POCKET MAP J17
South Bank ⊖ Waterloo ☎ 020 7960 4200, ⓦ www.southbankcentre.co.uk.
The SBC has three concert venues. The 2500-seat Royal Festival Hall (RFH) is tailor-made for large-scale choral and orchestral works, and is home to the Philharmonia and the London Philharmonic. The lugubrious Queen Elizabeth Hall (QEH) is used for chamber concerts, solo recitals and contemporary work, while the Purcell Room is the most intimate venue.

The Vaults

MAP P.105, POCKET MAP K18
Leake Street ⊖ Waterloo ☎ 020 7401 9603, ⓦ thevaults.london.
Just off Lower Marsh, you'll find Leake Street, a graffiti-covered tunnel which has attracted the city's street artists for a decade. It's an area to watch, with bars and restaurants opening up in the arcades along here, but long-time residents are The Vaults, a warren of theatre spaces and bars, known for immersive theatre and other inventive shows.

Bankside and Borough

In Tudor and Stuart London, the chief reason for crossing the Thames to Southwark was to visit the then disreputable Bankside entertainment district around the south end of London Bridge. Four hundred years on, Londoners have rediscovered the area, thanks to wholesale regeneration that has engendered a wealth of new attractions along the riverside – with the charge led by the mighty Tate Modern. And with a traffic-free, riverside path connecting most of the sights, plus the magnificent, gourmet Borough Market to tempt you (see page 116), this is easily one of the most enjoyable areas of London in which to hang out.

Millennium Bridge

MAP P.112, POCKET MAP L6–L7
⊖ **Southwark.**

The first new bridge to be built across the Thames since Tower Bridge opened in 1894, the sleek, stainless-steel Millennium Bridge is London's sole pedestrian-only river crossing. A suspension bridge of innovative design, it famously bounced up and down when it first opened and had to be closed immediately for two years for repairs. It still wobbles a bit, but most people are too busy enjoying the spectacular views across to St Paul's Cathedral and Tate Modern to notice.

Millennium Bridge

Tate Modern

MAP P.112, POCKET MAP L7
Bankside ⊖ Southwark ⓣ 020 7887 8888,
ⓦ www.tate.org.uk. Daily 10am–6pm,
Fri & Sat until 10pm. Charge for special
exhibitions. Free.

Bankside is dominated by the
austere power station transformed
by the Swiss duo Herzog &
de Meuron into Tate Modern,
where the Tate shows off its
vast collection of international
modern art. Opened in 2000 as
the world's largest modern art
gallery, astonishingly it has since
doubled in size, with a brick-clad,
twisting eleven-storey extension
by the same architects. This is
the **Blavatnik Building**; the
original power station is the **Boiler
House**. Linking the two is the
stupendously large **Turbine Hall**,
normally used to display one huge
installation. You can enter from the
riverside – which brings you to the
bridge spanning the Turbine Hall –
the west side, with a ramp sloping
down to level 0 of the Turbine Hall;
or via the piazza on the south side.
Level 0 of the Blavatnik Building,
directly off the Turbine Hall, is
the power station's original **Tanks**
– roughly finished, large circular
spaces for performance art, film
and large installations. Levels 2, 3
and 4 of both wings are the main
gallery spaces (level 3 of the Boiler
House is dedicated to temporary
exhibitions). The curators have
eschewed the usual chronological
approach and gone instead for
hanging works according to themes
and ideas, so you'll find works
by the likes of Picasso, Brancusi,
Lichtenstein, Riley and Hepworth
alongside newer names as befits
the particular exhibit. Increasingly
Tate also displays works by artists
from across the globe. They also

Extension at Tate Modern

regularly rehang the galleries, so
expect things to change between
visits. Given the size – there are
around eight hundred works on
show – you need to devote the best
part of a day to do it justice, or be
very selective. It's worth picking up
a plan (£1) or multimedia guide
(£4.50). If you're not sure where to
begin, take the escalator to level 2
of the Boiler House for the small
Start Display, which features a
few of Tate's most famous works,
including Matisse's *The Snail*
(1953), as an introduction to the
collection. Also on level 2, you'll
find rooms dedicated to Joseph
Beuys – at the centre of the Artists
and Society exhibition that links
politics, social movements and
art – and Mark Rothko, whose
abstract Seagram Murals have their
own shrine-like room. Finally, take
the time to enjoy the magnificent
views – out over the river from the
restaurant on level 6 of the main

Tate to Tate

The **Tate Boat** shuttles between Tate Britain and Tate Modern
every forty minutes; journey time is twenty minutes (£8.30).

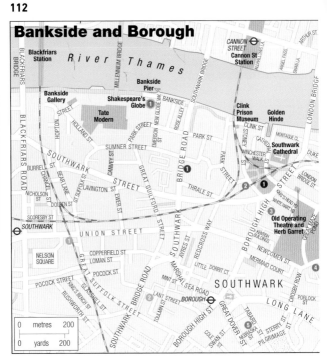

Bankside and Borough

building, or from the spectacular viewing level at the top of the Blavatnik Building.

Shakespeare's Globe Theatre

MAP P.112, POCKET MAP M7
21 New Globe Walk ⊖ Southwark or London Bridge ⊕ 020 7902 1400, Ⓦ www.shakespearesglobe.com. Daily 9am–5pm. Exhibition £15 online; £12 in person.
Dwarfed by the Tate Modern, but equally remarkable in its own way, Shakespeare's Globe Theatre is an open-air reconstruction of the polygonal playhouse where most of the Bard's later works were first performed. Sporting the first new thatched roof in central London since the 1666 Great Fire, the theatre puts on plays by Shakespeare and his contemporaries, both outside and in the indoor candlelit theatre (see page 117). To find out more about Shakespeare and Bankside, visit the Globe's stylish **exhibition**, whose imaginative hands-on displays really hit the spot. Visitors also get taken on an informative half-hour **guided tour** round the theatre itself, except in the afternoons during the summer season, when you can only visit the exhibition. Tours of Shakespeare's Southwark and the Sam Wanamaker Playhouse are on offer too.

Golden Hinde

MAP P.112, POCKET MAP M7
St Mary Overie Dock, Cathedral St ⊖ London Bridge ⊕ 020 7403 0123, Ⓦ goldenhinde.com. Daily: April–Oct 10am–6pm; Nov–March 10am–5pm. Check in advance; often closed for events. Entry £5; events vary.
An exact replica of the galleon in which **Francis Drake** sailed around the world from 1577 to 1580, this modern version of the *Golden Hinde* circumnavigated the globe for some twenty

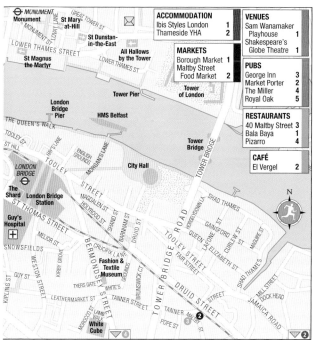

years before eventually settling permanently in Southwark. The ship is surprisingly small, and its original crew of eighty-plus must have been cramped to say the least. They put on lots of activities for kids – such as all-important pirate training – and host evening gigs for grown-ups.

Clink Prison Museum

MAP P.112, POCKET MAP N7

1 Clink St ⊖ London Bridge ☏ 020 7403 0900, ⓦ clink.co.uk. July–Sept daily 10am–9pm; Oct–June Mon–Fri 10am–6pm, Sat & Sun 10am–7.30pm. £7.50.

Housed in the suitably dismal confines of an old cellar, this museum explores the history of the former **Clink Prison**, which once stood close by. The prison began as a medieval dungeon for disobedient clerics under the Bishop of Winchester's Palace – the **rose window** of the Great Hall has survived just east of the

museum – and later became a dumping ground for Bankside lowlife, before being burnt to the ground by rioters in 1780. The exhibition features a handful of prison-life tableaux and plenty of graphic descriptions of the torture and horror experienced by the prisoners.

Southwark Cathedral

MAP P.112, POCKET MAP M7

Cathedral St ⊖ London Bridge ☏ 020 7367 6700, ⓦ www.southwarkcathedral. org.uk. Visitor hours: Mon–Fri 9am–5pm, Sat 9.30am–3.45pm & 5–6pm & Sun 12.30–3pm & 4–6pm. Free.

Of the original thirteenth-century Augustinian priory church of St Mary Overie, only the choir and retrochoir now remain, separated by a tall and beautiful stone Tudor screen; they're thought to be the oldest Gothic structures left in London. The nave was rebuilt in the nineteenth century, but

HMS Belfast

the cathedral contains numerous interesting monuments, from a thirteenth-century oak effigy of a knight to an early twentieth-century memorial to Shakespeare (his brother is buried here). Above the memorial is a stained-glass window featuring a whole cast of characters from the plays.

Old Operating Theatre and Herb Garret

MAP P.112, POCKET MAP N7
9a St Thomas St ⊖ London Bridge ⊕ 020 7188 2679, ⊚ oldoperatingtheatre.com. Mon 2–5pm, Tues–Sun 10.30am–5pm. £6.50.

By far the most educational – and strangest – of Southwark's museums is the Old Operating Theatre. Visitors must climb up to the attic of a former church tower, which houses an old hospital **apothecary**, with displays explaining the painful truth about pre-anaesthetic operations. These took place in the adjacent women's **operating theatre**, designed in 1821 "in the round", literally like a theatre, so that students (and members of high society) could view the proceedings.

The Shard

MAP P.112, POCKET MAP N7
32 London Bridge ⊖ London Bridge ⊕ 0844 499 7111, ⊚ theviewfromtheshard.com. April–Oct daily 10am–10pm; Nov–March Mon–Wed & Sun 10am–7pm, Thurs–Sat 10am–10pm; can change because of events. From £21.50 online in advance.

London's – and the country's – tallest building, Renzo Piano's 1016ft-high, tapered, glass-clad skyscraper **The Shard**, once seen as hubristic, has become part of the cityscape since it topped out in 2012. It houses a mixture of flats, restaurants, a hotel and expensive top-floor viewing platforms (the uppermost open to the sky). The views are sublime, making everything else in London look small, from the unicycle of the London Eye to the tiny box that is St Paul's Cathedral, while the model railway of London Bridge is played out below you.

HMS Belfast

MAP P.112, POCKET MAP N7
The Queen's Walk ⊖ London Bridge ⊕ 020 7940 6300, ⊚ hmsbelfast.iwm.org.uk. Daily 10am–6pm. From £13.90 online.

An 11,550-ton **Royal Navy cruiser**, HMS *Belfast* saw action both in World War II and in the Korean War, and has been permanently moored on the Thames since 1971. The most enjoyable aspect of a visit is exploring the maze of cabins and scrambling up and down the vertiginous ladders. Be sure to check out the top Flag Deck for the views and the claustrophobic lowest levels, the Boiler and Engine rooms.

City Hall

MAP P.112, POCKET MAP N7
The Queen's Walk ⊖ London Bridge or Tower Hill ☎ 020 7983 4000, Ⓦ london.gov.uk. Mon–Thurs 8.30am–6pm, Fri 8.30am–5.30pm. Free.

Bearing a striking resemblance to a giant car headlight, Norman Foster's startling glass-encased City Hall is the headquarters for the **Greater London Authority** and the Mayor of London. Visitors are welcome to stroll up the helical walkway, visit the café and watch proceedings from the second floor. The outside amphitheatre, "the Scoop", is a venue for free events in summer.

Bermondsey Street

MAP P.112, POCKET MAP N8
⊖ London Bridge.

Bermondsey, the area east of London Bridge, was once famous for its wharves, tanneries and factories. The wharves along the river underwent extensive redevelopment in the 1980s, particularly east of Tower Bridge around Butler's Wharf, while the area's old high street has been transformed over the last decade or so into an appealing stretch of cafés, pubs, art galleries and restaurants; you'll also find small breweries and street food stalls at weekends at nearby Maltby Street, and gourmet delights at Borough Market (see page 116). For contemporary art, the biggest

player around is the White Cube gallery at nos. 144–152 (Tues–Sat 10am–6pm, Sun noon–6pm; free; Ⓦ whitecube.com). On Bermondsey Square, the venerable Bermondsey antique market takes place early on Friday mornings (6am–2pm).

Fashion & Textile Museum

MAP P.112, POCKET MAP N8
83 Bermondsey St ⊖ London Bridge or Borough ☎ 020 7407 8664, Ⓦ www.ftmlondon.org. Tues–Sat 11am–6pm, Thurs until 8pm, Sun 11am–5pm (closes between exhibitions). £9.90.

Lifelong dream of Zandra Rhodes, fashion's *grande dame extraordinaire*, the FTM is an arresting sight – daubed in yellow, pink and orange. The museum's exhibitions are wide-ranging – from vintage frocks to specialist textile shows. Items on display draw from her own vast collection and beyond, and are exhibited with care and flair.

City Hall

Markets

Borough Market

MAP P.112, POCKET MAP M7

8 Southwark St ⊖ London Bridge. Wed & Thurs 10am–5pm, Fri 10am–6pm, Sat 8am–5pm.

Fine-food heaven, Borough has long been *the* London institution for gourmets, and attracts suppliers from all over the UK who converge to sell organic and artisan goodies from around the world. There's also a global array of street food vendors most days of the week, and cooking displays in the glass foyer (Thurs 1–2.30pm). The Victorian market hall, with its slender wrought-iron columns, is lovely. Prices are high and Saturdays can be a crush; arrive early.

Maltby Street Food Market

MAP P.112, POCKET MAP O8

Maltby St ⊖ Tower Bridge. Sat 10am–5pm, Sun 11am–4pm.

Near Borough Market, this street food hot spot huddles under the railway arches near Tower Bridge. Most action is

Maltby Street Food Market

on the lively Ropewalk, with its pop-up bars, cafés and snack stalls – plus tap rooms for several of the microbreweries that cluster here.

Restaurants

40 Maltby Street

MAP P.112, POCKET MAP O8

40 Maltby St ⊖ Bermondsey ⊕ 020 7237 9247. Food served Wed & Thurs 6–9.30pm, Fri 12.30–2.30pm & 6–9.30pm, Sat noon–3.30pm & 6–9.30pm, Sun noon–3.30pm.

Hunker down in this market wine bar for exceptional, gutsy food and natural wines. Dishes £5–15. No reservations.

Bala Baya

MAP P.112, POCKET MAP L8

Arch 25, Old Union Yard Arches, 229 Union St ⊖ Borough or Southwark ⊕ 020 8001 7015. Mon–Fri noon–3pm & 5–11pm, Sat 10.30am–4pm & 6–11pm, Sun 10.30am–5pm.

Nestled under the railway arches, among a clutch of new restaurants, this minimal place draws on the style and flavours of Tel Aviv. Grab a pitta for lunch – with braised beef and tahini, or salmon and pomegranate molasses (£7–9) – or linger over small plates and cocktails come evening.

Pizarro

MAP P.112, POCKET MAP N8

194 Bermondsey St ⊖ London Bridge ⊕ 020 7378 9455. Mon–Sat noon–10.45pm, Sun noon–9.45pm.

Smart restaurant run by José Pizarro, one of London's finest Spanish chefs – his sherry/tapas bar, *José*, nearby at no. 104, is also terrific. With its short menu of unfussy, beautifully executed food, Spanish wines and sherries, it's at the heart of Bermondsey's foodie scene. Tapas, coffee and pastries served all day. Mains £15–35.

Pubs

George Inn

MAP P.112, POCKET MAP M7
77 Borough High St ⊖ London Bridge.
Daily 11am–11pm.

London's only surviving galleried
coaching inn, dating from the
seventeenth century, and now
owned by the National Trust.
Expect lots of wonky flooring,
half-timbering, a good range of
real ales and a fair smattering of
tourists.

Market Porter

MAP P.112, POCKET MAP M7
9 Stoney St ⊖ London Bridge. Mon–Fri
6–8.30am & 11am–11pm, Sat noon–11pm,
Sun noon–10.30pm.

Handsome corner pub by Borough
Market, with an interesting
range of real ales and decent
food. Outrageously popular, as
evidenced by the masses that
spill out onto the surrounding
pavements.

The Miller

MAP P.112, POCKET MAP N8
96 Snowsfields ⊖ London Bridge. Mon–
Wed noon–11pm, Thurs noon–midnight, Fri
noon–1am, Sat 4pm–1am.

A big, fun – sometimes raucous
– and slightly studenty pub,
the *Miller* has lots of outdoor
space, an impressive craft beer
and cider selection, ping-pong
table (till 8pm), pool and table
football.

Royal Oak

MAP P.112, POCKET MAP M8
44 Tabard St ⊖ Borough. Mon–Fri
11am–11pm, Sat noon–11pm, Sun
noon–9pm.

Lovingly unchanging Victorian
pub that has the air of a village
local, and opts simply for serving
a superb stock of real ales (mild,
pale and old) from Harveys
Brewery in Sussex. Good old-
fashioned pub grub and excellent
Sunday roasts.

Globe Theatre

Venues

Sam Wanamaker Playhouse

MAP P.112, POCKET MAP M7
21 New Globe Walk ⊖ Southwark or
London Bridge ☏ 020 7401 9919, ⓦ www.
shakespearesglobe.com.

Attached to Shakespeare's Globe
theatre, this Jacobean-style indoor
venue presents an intriguing
programme of Shakespeare, early
theatre and music events – all in an
intimate and atmospheric, candlelit
space.

Shakespeare's Globe Theatre

MAP P.112, POCKET MAP M7
21 New Globe Walk ⊖ Southwark or
London Bridge ☏ 020 7401 9919, ⓦ www.
shakespearesglobe.com. April–Oct.

This thatch-roofed replica of the
famous Elizabethan theatre (see
page 112) uses natural light and
the minimum of scenery, and
puts on fun, historically authentic
and critically acclaimed plays by
Shakespeare and his contemporaries
– though they do experiment with
new stagings – with Yard tickets
(standing-room only) for £5.

Kensington and Chelsea

London's wealthiest district, the Royal Borough of Kensington and Chelsea is particularly well-to-do in the area south of Hyde Park. The moneyed feel here is evident in the flash shops and swanky bars as well as the plush houses and apartments. The most popular area for tourists, meanwhile, is South Kensington, where three of London's top museums stand side by side. Further south, Chelsea has a slightly more bohemian pedigree, although these days, it's really just another wealthy west London suburb. To the north, Notting Hill is rammed solid with trendy – but wealthy – media folk, yet retains a strong Moroccan and Portuguese presence, as well as vestiges of the African-Caribbean community who initiated – and still run – Carnival, the city's largest street party.

Wellington Arch

MAP P.120, POCKET MAP B18
Hyde Park Corner ⊖ Hyde Park Corner
☏ 020 7930 2726, Ⓦ www.english-heritage.org.uk. Daily: April–Sept 10am–6pm; Oct 10am–5pm; Nov–March 10am–4pm. £6.
Standing in the midst of one of London's busiest traffic interchanges, Wellington Arch was

Wellington Arch

erected in 1828 to commemorate Wellington's victories in the Napoleonic Wars. In 1846, it was topped by an equestrian statue of the Duke himself, which was later replaced by Peace driving a four-horse chariot. Inside, you can view an informative exhibition on the arch and temporary exhibitions and take a lift to the top of the monument, where the exterior balconies offer a bird's-eye view of the surrounding area.

Apsley House

MAP P.120, POCKET MAP B18
Hyde Park Corner ⊖ Hyde Park Corner
☏ 020 7499 5676, Ⓦ www.english-heritage.org.uk. April–Oct Wed–Sun 11am–5pm; Nov–March Sat & Sun 11am–5pm. £11.
The former London residence of the "Iron Duke", Apsley House contains a plethora of Wellington memorabilia and gifts he received, though the highlight here is the **art collection**, much of which used to belong to the King of Spain. Among the best pieces, displayed in the Waterloo Gallery on the first floor, are works by de Hooch, van Dyck, Velázquez, Goya, Rubens and Murillo. The famous, more

The Serpentine in Hyde Park

than twice life-size, nude statue of Napoleon by Antonio Canova stands at the foot of the main staircase. It was disliked by the sitter, not least for the figure of Victory in the emperor's hand, which appears to be trying to fly away.

Hyde Park

MAP P.120, POCKET MAP E7

ⓦ royalparks.org.uk. Daily 5am–midnight. Seized from the Church by Henry VIII to satisfy his desire for yet more hunting grounds, Hyde Park was first opened to the public by James I, when refreshments available included "milk from a red cow". Hangings, muggings and duels, the **1851 Great Exhibition** and numerous public events have all taken place here – and it's still a popular gathering point or destination for political demonstrations. For the most part, however, Hyde Park is simply a leisure ground – a wonderful open space that allows you to lose all sight of the city beyond a few persistent tower blocks.

At the treeless northeastern corner is **Marble Arch**, erected in 1828 as a triumphal entry to Buckingham Palace but now stranded on a ferociously busy traffic island at the west end of Oxford Street. This is the most historically charged spot in Hyde Park, as it marks the site of Tyburn gallows, the city's main location for public executions until 1783, when the action moved to Newgate. It's also the location of **Speakers' Corner**, a peculiarly English Sunday tradition, featuring an assembly of soap-box orators, religious extremists and hecklers.

At the centre of the park is the curvaceous lake of the **Serpentine**. Rowing boats and pedalos can be rented (April–Oct daily 10am until dusk; £12/hr) from the boathouse on the north bank, while the lake's popular **Lido** (May Sat & Sun 10am–6pm; June–Aug daily 10am–6pm; £4.80) is situated on the south bank. Nearby is the **Diana Memorial Fountain** (daily: March & Oct 10am–6pm; April–Aug 10am–8pm; Sept 10am–7pm; Nov–Feb 10am–4pm; free), less of a fountain, and more of a giant oval-shaped mini-moat, in which kids can dip their feet.

Kensington and Chelsea

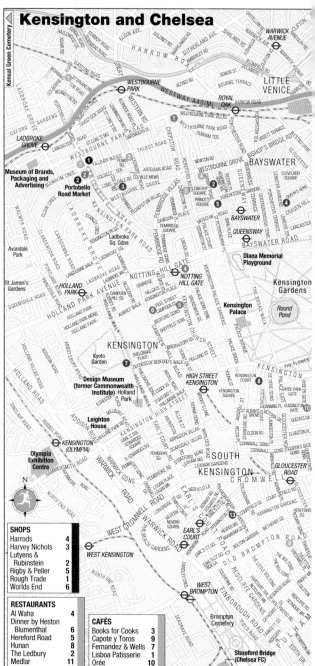

SHOPS

Harrods	4
Harvey Nichols	3
Lutyens & Rubinstein	2
Rigby & Peller	5
Rough Trade	1
Worlds End	6

RESTAURANTS

Al Waha	4
Dinner by Heston Blumenthal	6
Hereford Road	5
Hunan	8
The Ledbury	2
Medlar	11

CAFÉS

Books for Cooks	3
Capote y Toros	9
Fernandez & Wells	7
Lisboa Patisserie	1
Orée	10

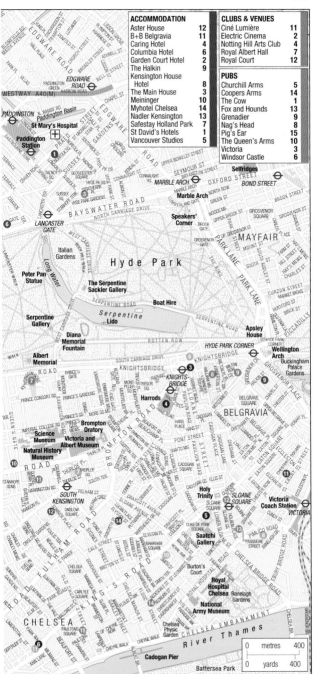

ACCOMMODATION

Aster House	12
B+B Belgravia	11
Caring Hotel	4
Columbia Hotel	6
Garden Court Hotel	2
The Halkin	9
Kensington House Hotel	8
The Main House	3
Meininger	10
Myhotel Chelsea	14
Nadler Kensington	13
Safestay Holland Park	7
St David's Hotels	1
Vancouver Studios	5

CLUBS & VENUES

Ciné Lumière	11
Electric Cinema	2
Notting Hill Arts Club	4
Royal Albert Hall	7
Royal Court	12

PUBS

Churchill Arms	5
Coopers Arms	14
The Cow	1
Fox and Hounds	13
Grenadier	9
Nag's Head	8
Pig's Ear	15
The Queen's Arms	10
Victoria	3
Windsor Castle	6

Kensington Gardens

MAP P.120, POCKET MAP C7

⊖ Queensway, Lancaster Gate or High Street Kensington Ⓦ royalparks.org.uk. Daily 6am–dusk.

The more tranquil, leafier half of Hyde Park, Kensington Gardens is home to **Long Water**, the pretty upper section of the Serpentine and the **Italian Gardens**, a group of five fountains laid out symmetrically in front of an Italianate loggia.

One of the park's best-loved monuments is **Peter Pan**, the fictional character who enters London along the Serpentine in the eponymous tale. The book's author, J.M. Barrie, used to walk his dog in Kensington Gardens, and it was here that he met the five pretty, upper-class Llewelyn Davies boys, who wore "blue blouses and bright red tam o'shanters". They were the inspiration for the book's "Lost Boys", and he eventually became their guardian. Barrie himself paid for the statue, which was erected in secret during the night in 1912. More fun for kids (and also inspired by Peter Pan), is the nearby excellent **Diana Memorial Playground**.

To the south of Peter Pan is the **Serpentine Gallery** (daily 10am–6pm; free; Ⓦ www. serpentinegalleries.org), which has a reputation for lively and often controversial contemporary art exhibitions. Their second building, the **Serpentine Sackler Gallery**, is in a converted gunpowder store with Zaha-Hadid-designed restaurant extension, on the other side of Long Water. The gallery also commissions a leading architect each year to design a summer **pavilion**.

The park's most impressive monument by far, however, is the **Albert Memorial**, erected in 1876. It's as much a hymn to the glorious achievements of the British Empire as to its subject, Queen Victoria's husband, whose gilded image sits under its central canopy, clutching a catalogue for the 1851 Great Exhibition. If you want to learn more about the 169 life-sized depictions of long-gone artists (all men) around the pediment, join one of the monthly guided tours (March–Dec first Sun of month 2pm & 3pm; 45min; £9).

Diana Memorial Playground

Kensington Palace

MAP P.120, POCKET MAP B8
Kensington Gardens ⊖ Queensway or High Street Kensington ☎ 020 3166 6000, ⓦ www.hrp.org.uk. Daily March–Oct 10am–6pm; Nov–Feb 10am–4pm. £19.50.

Bought by William and Mary in 1689, the modestly proportioned Jacobean brick mansion of Kensington Palace was the chief royal residence for the next fifty years. KP, as it's fondly known in royal circles, is best known today as the place where **Princess Diana** lived from her marriage until her death in 1997. Today, it's the official residence of a number of royals including Prince William, Kate Middleton, Prince Harry and Meghan Markle.

The palace is home to the **Royal Ceremonial Dress Collection**, which means you usually get to see a few of the frocks worn by Diana, as well as several of the Queen's dresses. The highlights of the **King's State Apartments** are the trompe-l'oeil ceiling paintings by William Kent, particularly those in the Cupola Room, and the paintings in the King's Gallery by, among others, Tintoretto. Also of interest in the King's Gallery is the wind dial above the fireplace, connected to the palace weather vane, which was built for William III and is still fully functioning. The **Queen's State Apartments** are more modest.

Exhibits also cover the life – and jewels – of **Queen Victoria**, who spent an unhappy childhood under the steely gaze of her strict German mother. According to her diary, her best friends were the palace's numerous "black beetles".

Brompton Oratory

MAP P.120, POCKET MAP D9
Brompton Rd ⊖ South Kensington ☎ 020 7808 0900, ⓦ bromptonoratory.co.uk. Mon–Fri 6.30am–8pm, Sat 6.30am–7.45pm, Sun 7.30am–8pm. Free.

London's most flamboyant Roman Catholic church, Brompton

Brompton Oratory

Oratory was completed in 1886 and modelled on the Gesù church in Rome. The ornate Italianate interior is filled with gilded mosaics and stuffed with sculpture, much of it genuine Italian Baroque, while the pulpit is a superb piece of Neo-Baroque from the 1930s; note the high cherub count on the tester. And true to its architecture, the church practises "smells and bells" Catholicism, with daily Mass in Latin.

Natural History Museum

MAP P.120, POCKET MAP D9
Cromwell Rd ⊖ South Kensington ☎ 020 7942 5000, ⓦ nhm.ac.uk. Daily 10am–5.50pm. Free.

With its 675ft terracotta facade, Alfred Waterhouse's purpose-built mock-Romanesque 1881 colossus ensures the Natural History Museum's status as London's most handsome museum. The collections are as much an important resource for serious zoologists as they are a popular attraction.

The main entrance leads to the vast central **Hintze Hall**, dominated by a huge blue whale skeleton suspended from the ceiling

Natural History Museum

in a dramatic diving pose. To one side, you'll find the **Dinosaur** gallery, where the highlight for many kids is the grisly life-sized animatronic dinosaur tableau. Other child-friendly sections include the **Creepy-Crawlies** room, which features a live colony of leaf-cutter ants and the old-fashioned **Mammals** gallery.

For a visually exciting romp through evolution, head for the **Red Zone** (once the Geology Museum); popular sections include the slightly tasteless Kobe earthquake simulator, and the spectacular display of gems and crystals in the Earth's Treasury.

Little visited compared to the rest of the museum, the **Orange Zone** is dominated by the Cocoon, a giant concrete egg encased within the Darwin Centre's atrium, and home to over 20-million specimens. On the top floors visitors can learn more about the scientific research and specimen collections, and, in the nearby Zoology spirit building, view a small selection of bits and bobs pickled in glass jars (behind the scenes tours available; £10). From

here you can exit via the wildlife garden (April till early Nov).

Science Museum

MAP P.120, POCKET MAP D9
Exhibition Rd ⊖ South Kensington ℹ 0870 870 4868, ⓦ sciencemuseum.org.uk. Daily 10am–6pm, till 7pm in school holidays. Free.

The Science Museum is undeniably impressive, filling its large, multi-level spaces with items from every conceivable area of science, including space travel, telecommunications, time, mathematics, chemistry and medicine. It's been undergoing a huge renovation project, so expect some floor closures until 2019 – and plenty of exciting new exhibits. First off, ask at the information desk for details of the day's events and demonstrations. By the entrance is the Energy Hall – dominated by large pumping engines from the days of steam – the ground floor continues on to Exploring Space, with some impressive rockets and space craft, then Making the Modern World, a display of iconic inventions. Beyond here is the Wellcome

Wing, with its interactive galleries and IMAX cinema (tickets £11). Kids will love the third floor for its hands-on experimentation and whizz-bang science shows at the Wonderlab Interactive gallery (£8), while an endearingly vintage museum feel is retained up in the hangar-like Flight Gallery on the third floor, with some wonderful old flying machines.

Victoria and Albert Museum

MAP P.120, POCKET MAP D9
Entrances on Cromwell & Exhibition roads
⊖ South Kensington ☏ 020 7942 2000,
ⓦ vam.ac.uk. Daily 10am–5.45pm (Fri until 10pm). Free.

In terms of sheer variety and scale, the **V&A** is the greatest museum of applied arts in the world. Beautifully but haphazardly displayed across a seven-mile, four-storey maze of halls and corridors, the V&A's treasures are impossible to survey in a single visit.

The most celebrated of the V&A's exhibits are the **Raphael Cartoons**, seven vast biblical paintings that served as designs for a set of tapestries destined for the Sistine Chapel. Close by, you can view highlights from the UK's largest dress collection and the world's biggest collection of Indian art outside India. In addition, there are extensive Chinese, Islamic and Japanese galleries; a gallery of twentieth-century **objets d'art** to rival the Design Museum; and more Constable **paintings** than Tate Britain. And the V&A's temporary shows – for which you have to pay – are among the best in Britain, some housed in the new subterranean exhibition spaces near the elegant Exhibition Road entrance, where the original Portland stone screen has been opened up to give access onto the gleaming white Sackler Courtyard.

Wading through the huge collection of European sculpture, you come to the surreal **plaster**

casts gallery, filled with copies of European art's greatest hits, from Michelangelo's *David* to Trajan's Column from the forum in Rome (sawn in half to make it fit). The chronologically displayed British and European galleries are superb, with a number of complete period interiors displayed. Before you leave, make sure you check out the museum's beautifully decorated trio of original refreshment rooms, the **Morris, Gamble & Poynter Rooms**, at the back of the main galleries.

Holy Trinity Church

MAP P.120, POCKET MAP F9
Sloane Square ⊖ Sloane Square
☏ 020 7730 7270, ⓦ www.holytrinitysloanesquare.co.uk. Mon–Sat 8.30am–5.30pm, Sun 8.30am–1.30pm. Free.

An architectural masterpiece created in 1890, Holy Trinity is probably the finest **Arts and Crafts** church in London. The east window is the most glorious of the furnishings, a vast, 48-panel extravaganza designed by Edward Burne-Jones, and the largest ever made by Morris & Co. Holy

Victoria and Albert Museum

Trinity is very High Church, filled with the smell of incense, statues of the Virgin Mary and confessionals.

Saatchi Gallery

MAP P.120, POCKET MAP E10

King's Rd ⊖ Sloane Square ☎ 020 7811 3070, ⓦ saatchigallery.com. Daily 10am–6pm. Free for most exhibitions.

On the south side of King's Road, a short stroll from Sloane Square, are the former **Duke of York's Barracks**, now housing upmarket shops and cafés. The main building, erected in 1801 and fronted by a solid-looking Tuscan portico, is home to the privately run Saatchi Gallery. Its fifteen whitewashed rooms – "a study in blandness" according to one art critic – host changing exhibitions of contemporary art.

Royal Hospital Chelsea

MAP P.120, POCKET MAP F10

Royal Hospital Rd ⊖ Sloane Square ☎ 020 7881 5200, ⓦ www.chelsea-pensioners. co.uk. Mon–Fri 10am–4pm; dining hall closed noon–2pm. Free.

Founded as a retirement home for army veterans by Charles II in 1682 and still going strong, the Wren-designed Royal Hospital is worth a visit for the vast, barrel-vaulted **chapel**, with its colourful apse fresco, and the equally grand, wood-panelled **dining hall**, opposite, with its allegorical mural of Charles II and his hospital. In the Secretary's Office, on the east side of the hospital, there's a small **museum**, displaying Pensioners' uniforms, medals and two German bombs.

National Army museum

MAP P.120, POCKET MAP E11

Royal Hospital Rd ⊖ Sloane Square ☎ 020 7881 6606, ⓦ www.nam.ac.uk. Free.

Appropriately housed in a sort of concrete bunker, the National Army Museum has recently been completely remodelled. Beyond the array of historical artefacts, uniforms, medals and artworks – including the skeleton of Napoleon's horse – it re-examines military life and the role of the British Army as an instrument of empire through five themed exhibition areas, including lots of hands-on stuff for kids, and an "assault course" play centre (£5.75).

Portobello Road

Chelsea Physic Garden

MAP P.120, POCKET MAP E11

Royal Hospital Rd ⊖ Sloane Square ⓘ 020 7352 5646, ⓦ www.chelseaphysicgarden. co.uk. April–Oct Mon–Fri & Sun 11am–6pm, July & Aug café & garden Tues & Wed till 10pm; limited winter opening. £10.50.

Hidden from the road by a high wall, Chelsea Physic Garden is a charming little inner-city escape. Founded in 1673, it's the second oldest botanic garden in the country. Unfortunately, it's also rather small, and a little too close to Chelsea Embankment to be a peaceful oasis, but keen botanists will enjoy it nevertheless. There's also a café, which serves home-made cakes.

Portobello Road Market

MAP P.120, POCKET MAP A6

⊖ Notting Hill Gate or Ladbroke Grove. Main market Mon–Sat 9am–6pm; antiques Sat 8am–6pm.

Situated in one of the wealthiest parts of town, Portobello Road Market is always a great spot for a browse and a bargain. Things kick off, at the intersection with Chepstow Villas, with junky antique stalls and classier, pricier antique shops. After a brief switch to fruit and veg around the 1910 **Electric Cinema**, the market gets a lot more fun at Portobello Green, where the emphasis switches to retro clothes and jewellery, records and books. Further up again, the secondhand material becomes pure boot-sale, laid out on rugs on the road. Beyond, **Golborne Road market** (same times as Portobello) is cheaper and less crowded, with attractive antique and retro furniture.

Museum of Brands, Packaging and Advertising

MAP P.120, POCKET MAP A5

111–117 Lancaster Rd ⊖ Ladbroke Grove ⓘ 020 7908 0880, ⓦ www. museumofbrands.com. Mon–Sat 10am–6pm, Sun 11am–5pm. £9.

Museum of Brands

Despite its rather unwieldy title, it's definitely worth popping into this museum, which is based on the private collection of Robert Opie, a Scot whose compulsive collecting has left him with ten thousand yoghurt pots alone. From Victorian ceramic pots of anchovy paste to the alcopops of the 1990s, the displays provide a fascinating social commentary on the times.

Design Museum

MAP P.120, POCKET MAP A8

224–238 Kensington High St ⊖ High St Kensington ⓘ 020 7940 8790, ⓦ designmuseum.org. Daily 10am–6pm, first Fri of month till 8pm. Permanent collection free; charge for special exhibitions.

One of the most striking 1960s buildings in London, a concrete-framed structure with a hyperbolic paraboloid roof and the former home of the Commonwealth Institute, has been taken over by the Design Museum. The permanent exhibition, **Designer Maker User**, features highlights from the museum's collection of design classics and everyday objects, while temporary exhibitions cover fashion, industrial design, graphics, materials and more.

Leighton House

MAP P.120, POCKET MAP A9
12 Holland Park Rd ⊖ High Street Kensington ⓣ 020 7602 3316, ⓦ www.rbkc.gov.uk/museums. Daily except Tues 10am–5.30pm. £9.

Leighton House was built by the architect George Aitchison for Frederic Leighton, President of the Royal Academy and the only artist ever to be made a peer (albeit on his deathbed). "It will be opulence, it will be sincerity", the artist opined before construction commenced in the 1860s. The big attraction is its domed **Arab Hall**. Based on the banqueting hall of a Moorish palace in Palermo, it has a central black marble fountain, and is decorated with Saracen tiles, gilded mosaics and latticework drawn from all over the Islamic world. The other rooms are less spectacular but in compensation are hung with excellent paintings by Lord Leighton and his Pre-Raphaelite friends Edward Burne-Jones, Lawrence Alma-Tadema and John Everett Millais.

Holland Park Kyoto Garden

Holland Park

MAP P.120, POCKET MAP A8
⊖ Holland Park or High Street Kensington. Daily 7.30am–dusk.

Holland Park is laid out in the former grounds of the Jacobean mansion of Holland House – sadly only the east wing survived the war, but it's enough to give an idea of what the place looked like. Several formal gardens are laid out before the house, drifting down in terraces to a café, a restaurant (the former Garden Ballroom) and an art gallery. The most unusual of the gardens is the **Kyoto Garden**, a Japanese-style sanctuary to the northwest of the house, peppered with modern sculpture and complete with koi carp and peacocks.

Kensal Green Cemetery

MAP P.120
Harrow Rd ⊖ Kensal Green ⓣ 020 8969 0152, ⓦ wkensalgreencemetery.com & ⓦ kensalgreen.co.uk. April–Sept Mon–Sat 9am–6pm, Sun 10am–6pm; Oct–March Mon–Sat 9am–5pm, Sun 10am–5pm. Free.

Opened in 1833, Kensal Green Cemetery was the first of the city's commercial graveyards, and contains some of London's most extravagant Gothic tombs. The cemetery is vast, so it makes sense to join one of the **guided tours** (March–Oct every Sun; Nov–Feb 1st & 3rd Sun of month; 2pm at the Anglican Chapel; £7). Graves of the more famous incumbents – Thackeray, Trollope, Siemens and the Brunels – are less interesting architecturally than those on either side of the **Centre Avenue**, which leads from the eastern entrance on Harrow Road. Worth looking out for are Major-General Casement's bier, held up by four grim-looking turbaned Indians; circus manager Andrew Ducrow's conglomeration of beehive, sphinx and angels; and artist William Mulready's neo-Renaissance extravaganza.

Shops

Harrods

MAP P.120, POCKET MAP E8
87–135 Brompton Rd ⊖ Knightsbridge.
Mon–Sat 10am–9pm, Sun 11.30am–6pm.
London's most famous department
store is an enduring landmark of
quirks and pretensions – not least
its dress code (no clothing revealing
intimate parts of the body). It's
notable for its Art Nouveau tiled
food hall, the huge toy department
and its range of designer labels.

Harvey Nichols

MAP P.120, POCKET MAP A19
109–125 Knightsbridge ⊖ Knightsbridge.
Mon–Sat 10am–9pm, Sun 11.30am–6pm.
Absolutely fabulous, darling, with
eight floors of the latest designer
collections and more casual clothing.
The gorgeous cosmetics department
is frequented by A- and Z-listers
alike, while the fifth-floor food hall
offers frivolous goodies at high prices.

Lutyens & Rubinstein

MAP P.120
21 Kensington Park Rd ⊖ Ladbroke
Grove. Mon & Sat 10am–6pm, Tues–Fri
10am–6.30pm, Sun 11am–5pm.
Classy bookshop with a hand-
selected array of classics, titles in
translation, poetry, art books and
literary gifts. A bibliophiles' dream.

Rigby & Peller

MAP P.120, POCKET MAP E10
13 King's Rd ⊖ Sloane Square. Mon–Sat
10am–7pm, Sun noon–6pm.
Once corsetières to HM the
Queen, if that can be counted as a
recommendation, this store stocks a
wide range of beautiful lingerie and
swimwear, with designer names as
well as its own range, for all shapes
and sizes. The personal fitting service
is deemed to be London's best.

Rough Trade

MAP P.120, POCKET MAP A6
130 Talbot Rd ⊖ Ladbroke Grove. Mon–Sat
10am–6.30pm, Sun 11am–5pm.

Harvey Nichols

Legendary indie music specialist
shop, first opened in 1976 at the
height of punk/new wave, with
knowledgeable, friendly staff and a
dizzying array of genres from indie-
pop and electronica to country and
beyond. There is a sister store across
town on Brick Lane (see page 93).

Worlds End

MAP P.120, POCKET MAP D11
430 King's Rd ⊖ Sloane Square. Mon–Sat
10am–6pm.
Iconic Vivienne Westwood outlet,
on the far end of the King's Road,
selling classics, new pieces and
samples, some of them recycled. In
a previous incarnation, when it was
co-owned by Malcolm McLaren, it
sold proto-punk fetishist gear, and
became a magnet for the young
punks who went on to form the
Sex Pistols.

Cafés

Books for Cooks

MAP P.120
4 Blenheim Crescent ⊖ Ladbroke Grove.
Tues–Sat 10am–6pm.

Pasteis de nata at Lisboa Patisserie

Tiny "test kitchen" within London's top cookery bookshop. It's cramped but friendly; this is an experience not to be missed, with tasty dishes at low prices. Make sure you get there in time to grab a table for the set-menu lunch (Tues–Fri noon–1.30pm; check their Twitter account for the day's menu).

Capote y Toros

MAP P.120, POCKET MAP C10
157 Old Brompton Rd ⊖ Gloucester Road or South Kensington. Tues–Sat 6–11.30pm.
Sunny bar with emphasis on sherries (more than 125 available, dozens by the glass), and interesting tapas (mostly £6–12).

Fernandez & Wells

MAP P.120, POCKET MAP D9
8 Exhibition Rd ⊖ South Kensington. Mon–Sat 8am–11pm, Sun 9am–8pm.
This smart little café-bar serves excellent coffee, sandwiches, cheese and charcuterie – and is good for people watching from its outdoor tables, as the throngs pass by on their way to South Ken's museums. Drinks only in the evening.

Lisboa Patisserie

MAP P.120
57 Golborne Rd ⊖ Ladbroke Grove. Mon–Sat 7.30am–7.30pm, Sun 7.30am–7pm.
Authentic Portuguese *pastelaria*, with the best *pasteis de nata* (custard tarts) this side of Lisbon – also coffee, cakes and a friendly atmosphere.

Orée

MAP P.120, POCKET MAP E10
65 King's Road ⊖ Sloane Square. Daily 8am–7pm.
Bakery-patisserie specializing in delicious classic French pastries – immaculate eclairs and Paris-Brest – and a few contemporary flavours (yuzu lemon tart). It also serves open sandwiches, brunch and gluten-free options. Not cheap – but this is the King's Road – and they have branches in Fulham and High Street Ken.

Restaurants

Al Waha

MAP P.120, POCKET MAP B6
75 Westbourne Grove ⊖ Bayswater or Queensway ℡ 020 7229 0806. Daily noon–11.30pm.
Arguably London's most authentic Lebanese restaurant; courteous service and delicious meze, but also mouthwatering main course dishes involving various permutations of grilled chicken and lamb. Mains £12–16.

Dinner by Heston Blumenthal

MAP P.120, POCKET MAP A19
Mandarin Oriental Hotel, 66 Knightsbridge ⊖ Knightsbridge ℡ 020 7201 3833. Mon–Fri noon–2.30pm & 6–10.15pm, Sat & Sun noon–2.30pm & 6.30–10.30pm.
Heston doesn't actually cook here, but one of his former *Fat Duck* chefs serves wildly imaginative food, using old

English recipes that give you a once-in-a-lifetime experience. Mains £33–50; three-course set lunch £45 (Mon–Fri).

Hereford Road

MAP P.120, POCKET MAP B6

3 Hereford Rd ⊖ Bayswater or Notting Hill Gate ☏ 020 7727 1144. Mon–Sat noon–2.30pm & 6–10pm, Sun noon–4pm & 6–10pm.

Highly accomplished English cooking focusing on simple, old-fashioned excellence and seasonal produce. Mains from £14, and set meals, from £13.50 for two courses, on weekday lunchtimes.

Hunan

MAP P.120, POCKET MAP F10

51 Pimlico Rd ⊖ Sloane Square ☏ 020 7730 5712. Mon–Sat 12.30–2pm & 6.30–11pm.

Despite the name, this serves Taiwanese/Chinese fusion food. There's no menu: tell them how spicy you like things, and they will bring you a vast array of small dishes. Lunch from £45.80, dinner from £67.80.

The Ledbury

MAP P.120, POCKET MAP A6

127 Ledbury Rd ⊖ Westbourne Park ☏ 020 7792 9090. Mon & Tues 6.30–9.45pm, Wed–Sun noon–2pm & 6.30–9.45pm.

Aussie chef Brett Graham's modern food – elegant, confident and delicate – well deserves its two Michelin stars. Four-course set menus £80 (lunch) or £125 (dinner).

Medlar

MAP P.120, POCKET MAP D11

438 King's Rd ⊖ Fulham Broadway ☏ 020 7349 1900. Tues–Fri noon–3pm & 6.30–10.30pm, Sat noon–3pm & 6–10.30pm, Sun noon–3pm & 6–9.30pm.

A lovely, upscale place offering French-influenced Modern British food in a welcoming dining room. It's all prix fixe, and excellent value. Three-course lunch £35 Tues–Sun; three-course dinner £53 (£35 on Sun).

Pubs

Churchill Arms

MAP P.120, POCKET MAP B7

119 Kensington Church St ⊖ Notting Hill Gate. Mon–Wed 11am–11pm, Thurs–Sat 11am–midnight, Sun noon–10.30pm.

Very cosy, quirky, flower-festooned pub serving Fuller's beers, Guinness and good Thai food.

Coopers Arms

MAP P.120, POCKET MAP E11

87 Flood St ⊖ Sloane Square. Daily noon–11pm.

Popular, easy-going neighbourhood pub, offering first-rate Young's beer and British pub grub. The gussied-up interior features lots of vintage styling.

The Cow

MAP P.120, POCKET MAP B5

89 Westbourne Park Rd ⊖ Westbourne Park or Royal Oak. Mon–Thurs noon–11pm, Fri & Sat noon–midnight, Sun noon–10.30pm.

Owned by Tom Conran, son of gastro-magnate Terence, this boho pub pulls a lively crowd, due in part to its food, served in the bar

Dinner by Heston Blumenthal

and dining room (dining room Mon–Sat 7–11pm, Sun 12.30–3.30pm), which includes a daily supply of fresh oysters.

Fox and Hounds

MAP P.120, POCKET MAP F10

29 Passmore St ⊖ Sloane Square. Mon–Sat noon–11pm, Sun noon–10.30pm.

On a quiet street near Sloane Square, this tiny Young's pub provides a perfect winter retreat. With its piano, faux books, oil paintings and relaxed, neighbourhood feel, it's a world away from the glitzier options in these parts.

Grenadier

MAP P.120, POCKET MAP B19

18 Wilton Row ⊖ Hyde Park Corner or Knightsbridge. Mon–Sat 11am–11.30pm, Sun noon–11.30pm.

Located in a cobbled mews, this quaint little pub was Wellington's local (his horse mounting block survives outside) and his officers' mess; the original pewter bar survives and the wood-panelled interior is cosy. Serves real ales and pricey food.

Grenadier

Nag's Head

MAP P.120, POCKET MAP A19

53 Kinnerton St ⊖ Hyde Park Corner or Knightsbridge. Daily 11am–11pm.

A convivial, quirky and raffish little pub in a posh mews, with dark wood-panelling, a mobile phone ban and a wealth of tatty nostalgic bric-a-brac attesting to its bohemian credentials. The sunken backroom has a flagstone floor.

Pig's Ear

MAP P.120, POCKET MAP D11

35 Old Church St ⊖ Sloane Square. Mon–Sat noon–11pm, Sun noon–10.30pm.

Deep in Chelsea village, the *Pig's Ear* is a lively, stylish gastropub, where you can enjoy excellent craft ales and seriously good Modern British food.

The Queen's Arms

MAP P.120, POCKET MAP C9

30 Queens Gate Mews ⊖ Gloucester Road or South Kensington. Mon–Sat noon–11pm, Sun noon–10.30pm.

Tucked away in a charming mews just a short walk from both the Royal Albert Hall and South Ken's museums, the Queen's Arm's is a very welcome, relaxed neighbourhood pub in this area.

Victoria

MAP P.120, POCKET MAP D6

10a Strathearn Place ⊖ Lancaster Gate or Paddington. Mon–Sat 11am–11pm, Sun noon–10.30pm.

Fabulously ornate corner pub, with two open fires, much Victorian brass and tilework, and gold-trimmed mirrors. The Fuller's beer here is excellent, too.

Windsor Castle

MAP P.120, POCKET MAP A7

114 Campden Hill Rd ⊖ Notting Hill Gate. Mon–Sat noon–11pm, Sun noon–10.30pm.

Popular, pretty, early Victorian wood-panelled pub with a large courtyard. Good ales, craft beers and classy pub grub – it's a welcoming spot to come across, tucked away in the backstreets of

Royal Albert Hall

one of London's poshest residential neighbourhoods.

Clubs and venues

Ciné Lumière

MAP P.120, POCKET MAP D9
17 Queensberry Place ⊖ South Kensington ⓣ 020 7871 3515, ⓦ www.institut-francais.org.uk.
Predominantly, but by no means exclusively, French films, both old and new (sometimes with subtitles), put on by the Institut Français.

Electric Cinema

MAP P.120
191 Portobello Rd ⊖ Ladbroke Grove ⓣ 020 7908 9696, ⓦ www.electriccinema.co.uk.
One of the oldest cinemas in the country (opened 1911), the Electric is a stunner, with luxury leather armchairs, footstools, two-seater sofas and an excellent bar.

Notting Hill Arts Club

MAP P.120, POCKET MAP B7
21 Notting Hill Gate ⊖ Notting Hill Gate ⓣ 020 7460 4459, ⓦ www.nottinghillartsclub.com.

Arty basement club that's popular for everything from Latin-inspired funk, jazz and disco through to soul, house and indie.

Royal Albert Hall

MAP P.120, POCKET MAP C8
Kensington Gore ⊖ South Kensington or High Street Kensington ⓣ 020 7589 8212, ⓦ www.royalalberthall.com.
Splendid red-brick, terracotta and marble concert hall built in 1871 that serves as the main venue for the annual BBC Proms summer festival of classical music (ⓦ www.bbc.co.uk/proms), and also the place for a whole range of popular shows from opera to pop concerts. Guided tours of the opulent building itself include architectural and behind the scenes options (£13).

Royal Court

MAP P.120, POCKET MAP F10
Sloane Square ⊖ Sloane Square ⓣ 020 7565 5000, ⓦ www.royalcourttheatre.com.
One of the best places in London to catch radical new writing, either in the proscenium arch downstairs theatre or the smaller-scale studio space; the café-bar buzzes pre- and post-performance.

Regent's Park and Camden

Framed by dazzling Nash-designed, magnolia-stuccoed terraces, and home to London Zoo, Regent's Park is a very civilized and well-maintained spot. Nearby Camden, by contrast, has a scruffy feel to it, despite its many well-to-do residential streets. This is partly due to the chaos and fall-out from the area's perennially popular weekend market, centred around Camden Lock on the Regent's Canal. A warren of stalls with an alternative past still manifest in its quirky wares, street fashion, books, records and street food stalls, the market remains one of the city's best-known off-beat attractions.

Regent's Park

MAP P.135, POCKET MAP E4–F4
⊖ Regent's Park, Great Portland Street or Baker Street ⓦ www.royalparks.org.uk. Daily 5am–dusk.

It was under the Prince Regent (later George IV) that Regent's Park began to take its current form – hence its official title – and the public weren't allowed in until 1845 (and even then for just two days of the week). According to John Nash's 1811 masterplan, the park was to be girded by a continuous belt of terraces, and sprinkled with a total of 56 villas, including a magnificent pleasure palace for the prince himself. The plan was never fully realized, but enough was built to create something of the idealized garden city that Nash and the Prince Regent envisaged. Pristine, mostly Neoclassical terraces form a near-unbroken horseshoe around the Outer Circle, which marks the park's perimeter along with a handful of handsome villas.

By far the prettiest section of the park is **Queen Mary's Gardens**, within the central Inner Circle. As well as a pond replete with exotic ducks, and a handsomely landscaped giant rockery, a large slice of the gardens is taken up with a glorious **rose garden**, featuring

Regent's Park

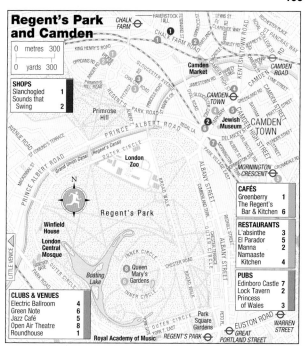

Regent's Park and Camden

| 0 metres | 300 |
| 0 yards | 300 |

SHOPS

| Slanchogled | 1 |
| Sounds that Swing | 2 |

CAFÉS

| Greenberry | 1 |
| The Regent's Bar & Kitchen | 6 |

RESTAURANTS

L'absinthe	3
El Parador	5
Manna	2
Namaaste Kitchen	4

PUBS

Edinboro Castle	7
Lock Tavern	2
Princess of Wales	3

CLUBS & VENUES

Electric Ballroom	4
Green Note	6
Jazz Café	5
Open Air Theatre	8
Roundhouse	1

some four hundred varieties surrounded by a ring of ramblers. Along the eastern edge of the park, the tree-lined **Broad Walk** forms a stately approach (much appreciated by rollerbladers) to the park's most popular attraction, London Zoo.

London Central Mosque

MAP P.135, POCKET MAP E4

146 Park Rd, Regent's Park ⊖ St John's Wood or Marylebone ☏ 020 7725 2212, ⓦ www.iccuk.org.

Prominent on the Regent's Park skyline is the shiny copper dome and minaret of the London Central Mosque, an entirely appropriate addition to the park given the Prince Regent's taste for the Orient. Non-Muslim visitors are welcome to look in at the Islam Gallery.

Regent's Canal

MAP P.135, POCKET MAP J2–A4

⊖ Warwick Avenue or Camden Town.

The Regent's Canal, completed in 1820, was constructed as part of a direct link from Birmingham to the newly built London Docks. After an initial period of heavy usage it was overtaken by the railway, and never really paid its way as its investors had hoped. By some miracle, however, it survived, and its nine miles, 42 bridges, twelve locks and two tunnels stand as a reminder of another age. The lock-less stretch of the canal between **Little Venice** and Camden Town is the busiest, most attractive section, tunnelling through to Lisson Grove, skirting Regent's Park, offering views of London Zoo, and passing straight through the heart of Camden Market. It's also the one section that's served by scheduled narrowboats. Alternatively, you can cycle, walk or jog along the towpath.

Regent's Canal by boat

Three companies run daily boat services on the Regent's Canal between Camden and Little Venice, passing through the Maida Hill tunnel. The narrowboat **Jenny Wren** (March Sat & Sun 12.30pm & 2.30pm; April–Oct daily 12.30pm, 2.30pm, 4.30pm; £15; ☎ 020 7485 4433, ⓦ walkersquay.com) starts off at Camden, goes through a canal lock and heads for Little Venice and then back again; while **Jason's** narrowboats (April–Oct daily from Little Venice 10.30am, 12.30pm, 2.30pm, June–Aug also Sat & Sun 4.30pm; 45min later for Camden; £10 single, £15 return; ⓦ jasons. co.uk) start off at Little Venice (though you can get on at Camden). The **London Waterbus Company** (April–Sept daily 10am, 11am, 12.15pm, 1.45pm & 3pm, one-way at 4.15pm; Oct Thurs & Fri 11am, 1pm & 3pm from Little Venice, noon, 2.15pm & 4pm from Camden, Sat & Sun hourly 11am–4pm; Nov–March Sat & Sun 11am, 1pm & 3pm from little Venice, noon, 2.15pm & 4pm from Camden; £9 single, £14 return; ⓦ londonwaterbus.com) calls in at London Zoo en route; journey time is 45 minutes one-way.

London Zoo

MAP P.135, POCKET MAP F3
Outer Circle, Regent's Park ⊖ Camden Town ☎ 0344 225 1826, ⓦ www.zsl. org/zsl-london-zoo. Daily: April–Aug 10am–6pm; Sept–mid-Oct 10am–5.30pm; mid-Oct–March 10am–4pm. £24.30 online.
The northeastern corner of Regent's Park is occupied by London Zoo. Founded in 1826 with the

London Zoo

remnants of the royal menagerie, the enclosures here are as humane as any inner-city zoo could make them, and kids usually enjoy themselves. In particular they love **Animal Adventure**, the children's zoo (and playground) where they can actually handle the animals, and the regular "Animals in Action" live shows. Highlights include the invertebrate house, the **Gorilla Kingdom**, the walk-through **Rainforest Life** where you might get close-up to a sloth, and **Land of the Lions**, designed to look like India's Sasan Gir National Park. The zoo boasts some striking architectural features, too, such as the 1930s modernist, spiral-ramped concrete former **penguin pool** (where Penguin Books' original colophon was sketched but now unused), designed by the Tecton partnership led by Berthold Lubetkin, who also made the zoo's Round House. The **Giraffe House**, by contrast, was designed in Neoclassical style by Decimus Burton. Other landmark features are the mountainous **Mappin Terraces**, from just before World War I, and the colossal tetrahedral aluminium-framed tent of

The Kerb in Camden market

Lord Snowdon's modern **aviary** (currently undergoing renovation).

Camden Market

MAP P.135, POCKET MAP F1–G2

Camden Town camdenlock.net. Daily 9.30am–6pm, more stalls at weekends.

For all the tourist hordes, Camden Market (in actual fact, a conglomeration of markets) remains a genuinely offbeat place. The tiny crafts market, which began in the 1970s in the cobbled courtyard by **Camden Lock**, has since mushroomed out of all proportion, with everyone trying to grab a piece of the action in the warren-like stretch along Camden High Street and Chalk Farm Road. Encroaching developments and several damaging fires haven't dampened its popularity, and it can be quite a crush at weekends.

Many stalls stay open all week long, alongside a crop of shops, cafés and bars. **Stables Market** (the old horse hospital), on Chalk Farm Road, is good for vintage and antiques, and the vast 90s throwback clubwear emporium Cyberdog. And there are plenty of takeaway food outlets ready to fuel hungry shoppers. Though the quality is mixed, some better stalls have opened up in the Stables, and there's a tempting variety at **Kerb Camden** in West Yard (daily 11am–6 or 7pm, plus some later events; kerbfood.com), which hosts some of London's favourite street food outlets.

Jewish Museum

MAP P.135, POCKET MAP G2

129 Albert St Camden Town 020 7284 7384, www.jewishmuseum.org.uk. Daily 10am–5pm, Fri closes 2pm. £7.50.

Camden is home to London's purpose-built Jewish Museum. On the first floor, there's an engaging exhibition explaining Jewish practices, illustrated by cabinets of Judaica. On the second floor, there's a special Holocaust gallery, which tells the story of Leon Greenman (1920–2008), one of only two British Jews who suffered and survived Auschwitz. The museum also puts on a lively programme of special exhibitions, discussions and concerts, and has a café on the ground floor.

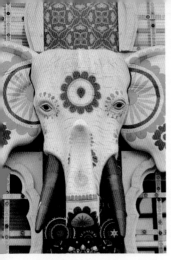

Namaaste Kitchen

Shops

Slanchogled

MAP P.135, POCKET MAP F1
66 Chalk Farm Rd ⊖ Chalk Farm. Mon–Sat
10am–6pm, Sun 11am–6pm.
Unusual, sunny shop selling
arts and crafts materials – paper
and inks, ribbons and transfers,
anything you can imagine – with
lots of creative ideas to inspire.

Sounds that Swing

MAP P.135, POCKET MAP G2
88 Parkway ⊖ Camden Town. Mon–Sat
11am–6pm, Sun noon–6pm.
The bricks-and-mortar store of No
Hit Records offers an impeccable
selection of retro rockabilly, blues,
gospel, ska and the like on vinyl.

Cafés

Greenberry

MAP P.135, POCKET MAP E1
101 Regents Park Rd ⊖ Chalk Farm. Mon &
Sun 9am–3pm, Tues–Sat 9am–10pm.
This buzzy neighbourhood bistro
serves fresh, creative food with
global influences (mains from £13),
weekend brunches, plus home-
made ice cream.

The Regent's Bar & Kitchen

MAP P.135, POCKET MAP F4
Inner Circle, Regent's Park ⊖ Baker Street.
Daily 8am–8pm.
Busy park café with lots of outdoor
seating. It's run by the Benugo
group and serves wood-fired pizza
and Modern European café food.

Restaurants

L'absinthe

MAP P.135, POCKET MAP F2
40 Chalcot Rd ⊖ Chalk Farm. ☎ 020 7483
4848. Mon 8am–3pm, Tues–Fri 8am–3pm
& 6–10pm, Sat 9am–3pm & 6–10pm, Sun
noon–3pm & 6–9pm.
Very French, slightly dated café,
deli and bistro restaurant offering
scrumptious baguettes, tarts,
patisserie and *croques monsieurs*, along
with classic French mains like duck
confit (£17) and steak frites (£23);
two-course weekday lunch £15.

El Parador

MAP P.135, POCKET MAP G3
245 Eversholt St ⊖ Mornington Crescent
☎ 020 7387 2789. Mon–Thurs noon–3pm &
6–11pm, Fri noon–3pm & 6–11.30pm, Sat
6–11.30pm, Sun 6.30–9.30pm.
Head to this cosy local joint for
fabulous tapas (£5–10) – and don't
miss the creative vegetarian dishes.

Manna

MAP P.135, POCKET MAP E1
4 Erskine Rd ⊖ Chalk Farm ☎ 020
7722 8028. Tues–Fri noon–3pm &
6.30–10pm, Sat noon–3pm & 6–10pm, Sun
noon–7.30pm.
Long-established restaurant serving
large portions of very good vegan
food from around the world – with
jackfruit burgers, raw lasagne and
other vegan inventiveness. Mains
£15–16.

Namaaste Kitchen

MAP P.135, POCKET MAP G2
64 Parkway ⊖ Camden Town ☎ 020
7485 5977. Mon–Sat noon–11.30pm, Sun
noon–11pm.

Superb modern Indian restaurant presenting unusual dishes such as venison kebab, or splash out on lobster in Kerala spices (£23), along with familiar favourites like chicken tikka masala (£11). Mains mostly £10–16.

Pubs

Edinboro Castle

MAP P.135, POCKET MAP G2
57 Mornington Terrace ⊖ Camden Town. Mon–Sat noon–11pm, Sun noon–10.30pm.
A huge pub with a standard menu, good beer selection and a large, leafy beer garden. Very popular on hot summer days.

Lock Tavern

MAP P.135, POCKET MAP F1
35 Chalk Farm Rd ⊖ Chalk Farm. Mon–Thurs noon–midnight, Fri & Sat noon–1am, Sun noon–11pm.
Rambling pub with comfy sofas, a leafy terrace and beer garden. There's hipster pub grub and DJs/ live bands playing anything from punk, funk and electro to avant-country.

Princess of Wales

MAP P.135, POCKET MAP F2
22 Chalcot Rd ⊖ Chalk Farm. Mon–Fri 11am–midnight, Sat 10am–midnight, Sun 10am–11.30pm.
Smart, popular gastropub with excellent food. You can eat in the pub, the dining room, or the stylish beer garden with its own Banksy-style mural.

Clubs and venues

Electric Ballroom

MAP P.135, POCKET MAP G2
184 Camden High St ⊖ Camden Town
☎ 020 7485 9007, ⊕ electricballroom. co.uk.
Long-running, grungy venue that hosts rock, metal and indie gigs, plus disco and pop club nights.

Green Note

MAP P.135, POCKET MAP G2
106 Parkway ⊖ Camden Town ☎ 020 7485 9899, ⊕ greennote.co.uk.
Intimate music venue that punches way above its weight with its excellent roots, folk and world music. Good veggie snacks, too.

Jazz Café

MAP P.135, POCKET MAP G2
5 Parkway ⊖ Camden Town ☎ 020 7485 6834, ⊕ thejazzcafelondon.com.
Buzzing venue whose classy music policy explores world music, funk and r'n'b, as well as jazz. If you fancy a sit-down book a seat at one of the restaurant tables.

Open Air Theatre

MAP P.135, POCKET MAP F4
Regent's Park, Inner Circle ⊖ Baker Street ☎ 0844 826 4242, ⊕ openairtheatre.com.
This beautiful space in Regent's Park hosts a tourist-friendly summer programme of Shakespeare, musicals, contemporary theatre and concerts; perfect when the weather's good.

Roundhouse

MAP P.135, POCKET MAP F1
Chalk Farm Rd ⊖ Chalk Farm ☎ 0300 678 9222, ⊕ roundhouse.org.uk.
Camden's barn-like former engine shed puts on a variety of theatrical spectacles, circus performances and excellent live gigs.

Open Air Theatre, Regents Park

Hampstead and Highgate

The high points of north London, both geographically and aesthetically, the elegant, largely eighteenth-century developments of Hampstead and Highgate have managed to cling on to their village origins. Of the two, Highgate is slightly sleepier and more aloof, Hampstead busier and buzzier, with high-profile intelligentsia and discerning pop stars among its residents. Both benefit from direct access to one of London's wildest patches of greenery, Hampstead Heath, where you can enjoy stupendous views over London, as well as outdoor concerts and high art in and around the country mansion of Kenwood House.

Hampstead Heath

MAP P.142
Gospel Oak or Hampstead Heath Overground, or ⊖ Hampstead or Golders Green.

Hampstead Heath is the city's most enjoyable public park, with a wonderful variety of bucolic scenery across its 800 acres. At the park's southern end are the rolling green pastures of **Parliament Hill**, north London's premier spot for kite-flying. On either side are numerous **ponds**, three of which – one for men, one for women and one mixed – you can swim in (daily from 7am; closing time varies; £2; ☎ 020 7485 5757). The thickest woodland is to be found in the West Heath, also the site of the most formal section, **Hill Garden**, a secretive and romantic little gem with eccentric balustraded terraces and a ruined pergola. Beyond lies **Golders Hill Park**, where you can gaze at pygmy goats and fallow

Hampstead Heath

deer, and inspect the impeccably maintained aviaries, home to flamingos, cranes and other exotic birds.

Kenwood House

MAP P.142

⊖ Highgate or Golders Green. ⓦ english-heritage.org.uk. Daily 10am–5pm; Dec–March closes 4pm. Free.

The Heath's most celebrated sight is the whitewashed Neoclassical mansion of **Kenwood House**, set in its own magnificently landscaped grounds at the high point of the Heath. The house is home to a superlative collection of seventeenth- and eighteenth-century art, including masterpieces by Vermeer, Rembrandt, Boucher, Gainsborough and Reynolds. Of the period interiors, the most spectacular is Robert Adam's sky-blue and gold library.

Kenwood House

Keats House

MAP P.142

Keats Grove ⊖ Hampstead or Hampstead Heath Overground ☏ 020 7332 3868, ⓦ cityoflondon.gov.uk. Wed–Sun 11am–5pm. £6.50.

An elegant, whitewashed Regency double villa, Keats House is a shrine to Hampstead's most lustrous figure. Inspired by the tranquillity of the area and by his passion for girl-next-door Fanny Brawne (whose house is also part of the museum), Keats wrote some of his most famous works here before leaving for Rome, where he died of consumption in 1821 aged just 25. The neat, rather staid interior contains books and letters, and the four-poster bed in which the poet first coughed up blood.

2 Willow Road

MAP P.142

⊖ Hampstead or Hampstead Heath Overground ☏ 020 7435 6166, ⓦ nationaltrust.org.uk. March–Oct Wed–Sun 11am–5pm. £7.

An unassuming red-brick terraced house built in the 1930s by the Hungarian-born architect **Ernö Goldfinger** (1902–87), 2 Willow Road gives a fascinating insight into the modernist mindset. This was a state-of-the-art pad when Goldfinger moved in, and as he changed little during the following fifty years, what you see today is a 1930s avant-garde dwelling preserved in aspic, a house at once both modern and old-fashioned. An added bonus is that the rooms are packed with **works of art** by the likes of Henry Moore and Man Ray. Before 3pm, visits are by hour-long guided tour only (11am, noon, 1 & 2pm, 11am tour sometimes booked up by groups); after 3pm the public has unguided, unrestricted access.

Fenton House

MAP P.142

Windmill Hill ⊖ Hampstead ☏ 020 7435 3471, ⓦ nationaltrust.org.uk. March–Oct Wed–Sun 11am–5pm. £8.

Decorated in the eighteenth-century taste, grand Fenton House is home to a collection of European and Oriental ceramics, as well as a superb collection of **early**

Hampstead and Highgate

CAFÉS & RESTAURANTS	
Delicatessen	3
Jin Kichi	1
Louis Patisserie	2

PUBS	
The Flask	1
The Holly Bush	3
Southampton Arms	4
The Spaniards Inn	2

SHOP	
Daunt Books	1

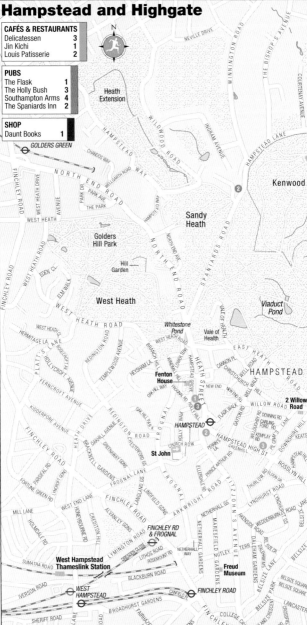

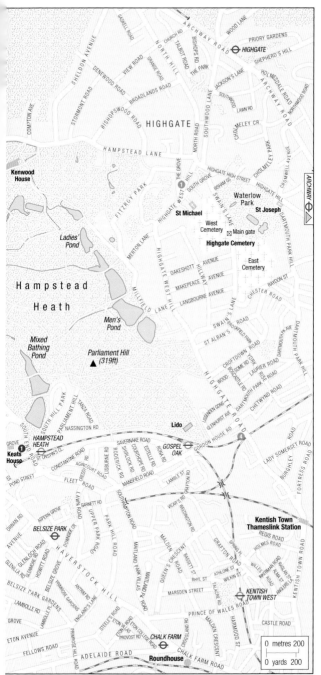

Highgate Cemetery

musical instruments. Experienced keyboard players are let loose on some of the instruments most weeks (Wed 2.30pm) and you can book tickets for one of the occasional **concerts**. Tickets for the house also allow you to take a stroll in the beautiful orchard, kitchen garden and formal **garden**, which features some top-class topiary and herbaceous borders.

Freud Museum

MAP P.142
20 Maresfield Gardens ⊖ **Finchley Road.** ☏ **020 7435 2002,** Ⓦ **freud.org.uk. Wed– Sun noon–5pm. £9.**
Hidden away in the leafy streets of south Hampstead, the Freud Museum is one of the most poignant of London's museums. Having lived in Vienna for his entire adult life, **Sigmund Freud** was forced to flee the Nazis, and arrived in London during the summer of 1938 as a semi-invalid (he died within a year). The ground-floor study and library look exactly as they did when Freud lived here – the collection of erotic antiquities and the famous couch, sumptuously draped in Persian carpets, were all brought here from Vienna. Upstairs, home movies of family life in Vienna are shown continually, and a small room is dedicated to his daughter, Anna, herself an influential child analyst, who lived in the house until her death in 1982.

Highgate Cemetery

MAP P.142
Swain's Lane ⊖ **Archway** ☏ **020 8340 1834,** Ⓦ **highgatecemetery.org.**
Receiving far more visitors than Highgate itself, Highgate Cemetery is London's most famous graveyard. The most illustrious incumbent of the **East Cemetery** (March–Oct daily 10am–5pm; Nov–Feb daily 10am–4pm; £4) is **Karl Marx**. Erected by the Communist movement in 1954, his vulgar bronze bust surmounting a granite plinth is a far cry from the unfussy memorial he had requested; close by lies the much simpler grave of the author George Eliot. The East Cemetery's lack of atmosphere is in part compensated for by the fact that you can wander at will through its maze of circuitous paths.

On the other side of Swain's Lane, the overgrown **West Cemetery**, with its spooky Egyptian Avenue and terraced catacombs, is the ultimate Hammer Horror graveyard, and one of the city's most impressive sights. Visitors can only enter by way of a **guided tour** (Mon–Fri 11am & 1.45pm, book in advance online, Sat & Sun every 30min 11am–4pm, Nov–Feb till 3pm, no advance booking at weekends; £12 includes East Cemetery; no under 8s). Among the prominent graves usually visited are those of artist Dante Gabriel Rossetti, and of lesbian novelist Radclyffe Hall.

Shop

Daunt Books

MAP P.142
51 South End Rd ⊖ Hampstead Heath.
Mon–Sat 9am–6pm, Sun 11am–6pm.
Hampstead branch of this excellent bookshop, which is strong on guidebooks, travel writing and fiction, and has a good kids' section.

Cafés and restaurants

Delicatessen

MAP P.142
46 Rosslyn Hill ⊖ Hampstead ☎ 020 7700 5511. Mon–Thurs & Sun noon–11pm, Sat 6–11pm.
The name is misleading – this is no deli, but a small, buzzing and distinctly high-end kosher restaurant. Its delicious and inventive menu takes inspiration from across the southern Mediterranean and Middle East, so expect flavours of tahini, sumac and preserved lemons, and dishes like Turkish pizza and ras el hanut lamb chops. It's all designed for sharing – starter meze £6.50–9, mains £20–25.

Jin Kichi

MAP P.142
73 Heath St ⊖ Hampstead ☎ 020 7794 6158. Tues–Sat 12.30–2.30pm & 6–10.30pm, Sun closes 10pm.
Cramped, homely and very busy (so book ahead), Jin Kichi offers almost every Japanese dish, though it specializes in grilled skewers of meat (£16–19 for set of seven).

Louis Patisserie

MAP P.142
32 Heath St ⊖ Hampstead. Daily 7.30am–7pm.
This tiny, understated, old-fashioned Hungarian tearoom/ patisserie has long been serving sticky cakes, tea and coffee to a mixed crowd. Also serves cooked breakfasts.

Pubs

The Flask

MAP P.142
77 Highgate West Hill. Bus #210, #270 from ⊖ Archway. Mon–Sat 11.30am–11pm, Sun noon–10.30pm.
Ideally situated at the heart of Highgate village green, this Fuller's pub has a rambling, low-ceilinged interior and a roomy summer terrace – as a result, it's very, very popular at weekends. The pub's original stable block dates back to 1663, and is still fitted with two 17th-century horseboxes.

The Holly Bush

MAP P.142
22 Holly Mount ⊖ Hampstead. Mon–Sat noon–11pm, Sun noon–10.30pm.
A lovely old Fuller's pub (Grade II listed), with a cosy real fire in winter and a charming wooden interior, tucked away in the steep backstreets of Hampstead village. Some guest ales on offer, as well as decent food – expect seasonal, hearty fare.

Southampton Arms

MAP P.142
139 Highgate Rd ⊖ Gospel Oak. Mon–Sat noon–midnight, Sun noon–10.30pm.
You'll find an excellent choice of ales and ciders from small British producers at this friendly pint-sized boozer, with proper sausages, scotch eggs and cheese plates to fill up on. Decoration is simple. No bookings. Cash only.

The Spaniards Inn

MAP P.142
Spaniards Rd ⊖ Hampstead. Mon–Sat noon–11pm, Sun noon–10.30pm.
Curl up in this iconic, creaky sixteenth-century inn, featured in The Pickwick Papers. The building dates back to the 1500s, and the building itself is – unsurprisingly – listed. Perfect for a lazy Sunday afternoon after a walk on the Heath. The large pub garden is packed on sunny days.

Greenwich

Greenwich is one of London's most beguiling spots. Its nautical associations are trumpeted by the likes of the magnificent *Cutty Sark* tea clipper and the National Maritime Museum; its architecture, especially the Old Royal Naval College and the Queen's House, is some of the finest on the river; and its Observatory is renowned throughout the world. With the added attractions of riverside pubs and walks, a large and well-maintained park with superb views across the river and to the Docklands, plus a popular arts and crafts market, you can see why Greenwich is the one place in southeast London that draws large numbers of visitors.

Old Royal Naval College

MAP P.148
Romney Rd ⊖ Cutty Sark DLR ☎ 020 8269 4747, ⓦ www.ornc.org. Grounds daily 8am–11pm. Buildings daily 10am–5pm. Free.

It's entirely appropriate that the Old Royal Naval College is the one London building that makes the most of its riverbank location. Initially intended as a royal palace, Wren's beautifully symmetrical Baroque ensemble was eventually converted into a hospital for disabled seamen in the eighteenth century. From 1873 until 1998 it was home to the Royal Naval College, but now houses the University of Greenwich and the Trinity Laban's college of music.

The two grandest rooms, situated underneath Wren's twin domes,

Old Royal Naval College chapel

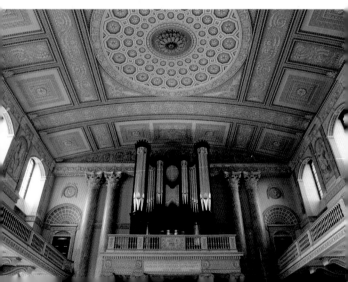

are magnificently opulent and well worth visiting. The **Chapel's** exquisite pastel-shaded plasterwork and spectacular decorative ceiling detail were designed by James "Athenian" Stuart, after a fire in 1799 destroyed the original interior. The magnificent **Painted Hall** features trompe-l'oeil fluted pilasters, and James Thornhill's gargantuan allegorical ceiling painting depicting William and Mary handing down Peace and Liberty to Europe, with a vanquished Louis XIV clutching a broken sword below them. While the Hall is being restored (until 2019), you can book a close-up tour of the works (£10).

National Maritime Museum and Queen's House

National Maritime Museum

MAP P.148

Romney Rd ⊖ Cutty Sark DLR ℹ 020 8858 4422, ⓦ rmg.co.uk. Daily 10am–5pm. Free. The excellent **National Maritime Museum** houses a vast collection of boats and nauticalia, imaginatively displayed in modern, interactive galleries designed to appeal to visitors of all ages; you'll find several hands-on sections for kids throughout the museum. The glass-roofed central courtyard is home to the museum's largest artefacts, among them the splendid 63ft-long gilded **Royal Barge**, designed in Rococo style for Prince Frederick, the much unloved eldest son of George II.

Nearby is a room dedicated to Turner's *Battle of Trafalgar*. On the second floor, a large exhibition on Nelson includes the coat he wore at Trafalgar.

A bright white Palladian villa flanked by colonnades, the **Queen's House** is the focal point of Greenwich's riverside architectural ensemble and an integral part of the Maritime Museum. Inside, one or two features survive from Stuart times, most notably the cuboid Great Hall, the beautiful cantilevered Tulip Staircase and Queen's Presence Chamber, which retains its rich ceiling decoration from the 1630s. The rooms provide

Visiting Greenwich

The most scenic and leisurely way to reach Greenwich is to take a **boat** from one of the piers in central London (every 15–30min peak times). Greenwich can also be reached by **train** from London Bridge (every 10–20min), or by **Docklands Light Railway** (DLR) from Bank or Tower Gateway direct to Cutty Sark. For the best view of the Wren buildings, get out at Island Gardens station to admire the view across the river, and then take the Greenwich Foot Tunnel under the Thames.

You can buy combined tickets for the Observatory and *Cutty Sark* for £19 online; £24.25 in person.

GREENWICH

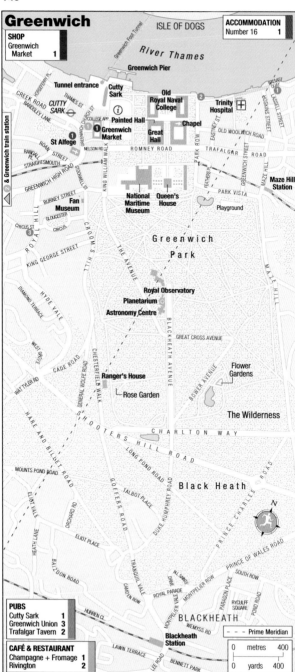

Greenwich

ISLE OF DOGS

ACCOMMODATION
Number 16   1

SHOP
Greenwich
Market   1

River Thames

Greenwich Pier

Greenwich Foot Tunnel

Tunnel entrance

Cutty Sark

Old Royal Naval College

Trinity Hospital

BELFAST WAY

LASSELL STREET

ROSKINS STREET

EASTNEY ST

2

THAMES ST

KOSSEGYN PL

CREEK ROAD

BARDSLEY LANE

CUTTY SARK

COLLEGE APP

GREENWICH CHURCH ST

Painted Hall

Great Hall

Chapel

OLD WOOLWICH ROAD

PARK ROW

TRAFALGAR ROAD

GREENWICH STREET

MAZE HILL

St Alfege

Greenwich Market

1

i

NELSON RD

ROMNEY ROAD

KING WILLIAM WALK

FEATHERS

PARK VISTA

Maze Hill Station

ROAN STREET

RANDALL PL

STRAIGHTSMOUTH

GREENWICH HIGH ROAD

& Greenwich train station

Burney Street

Fan Museum

GLOUCESTER

CIRCUS ST

CIRCUS

National Maritime Museum

Queen's House

Playground

CROOM'S HILL

ROYAL HILL

KING GEORGE STREET

THE AVENUE

Greenwich Park

HYDE VALE

DIAMOND TERRACE

WEST GROVE

CROOM'S HILL

Royal Observatory

Planetarium

Astronomy Centre

BLACKHEATH AVENUE

MAZE HILL

GREAT CROSS AVENUE

CADE ROAD

CHESTERFIELD WALK

CROESTERS THAMES WALK

Ranger's House

Rose Garden

SHOOTERS HILL ROAD

Flower Gardens

The Wilderness

WATT TYLER RD

BOWER AVENUE

C H A R L T O N W A Y

HARE AND BILLET ROAD

MOUNTS POND ROAD

ELIOT VALE

HEATH LANE

ORCHARD RD

ELIOT PLACE

LONG POND ROAD

GOFFERS ROAD

TALBOT PLACE

DUKE HUMPHREY ROAD

B l a c k H e a t h

PRINCE CHARLES ROAD

N

BAIZDON ROAD

TRANQUIL VALE

CAMDEN ROW

ROYAL PARADE

N.L. SANDS

MONTPELIER VALE

MONTPELIER ROW

PRINCE OF WALES ROAD

SOUTH ROW

PARAGON PLACE

RYCLIFF SQUARE

POND ROAD

PUBS
Cutty Sark   1
Greenwich Union   3
Trafalgar Tavern   2

HUBBEN CL

MONTPELIER VALE

WEMYSS RD

B L A C K H E A T H

- - - Prime Meridian

CAFÉ & RESTAURANT
Champagne + Fromage   1
Rivington   2

LAWN TERRACE

LEE ROAD

Blackheath Station

BENNETT PARK

| 0 | metres | 400 |
| 0 | yards | 400 |

a permanent home for the museum's vast maritime **art collection**, while the lavishly restored King's Presence Chamber displays Gentileschi's *Joseph and Potiphar's Wife*, one of the house's original artworks.

Cutty Sark

MAP P.148

King William Walk ⊖ Cutty Sark DLR ⓘ 020 8858 4422, Ⓦ rmg.co.uk. Daily 10am–5pm. £12.15 online; £13.50 in person.

Wedged in a dry dock by the Greenwich Foot Tunnel is the majestic *Cutty Sark*, the world's last surviving **tea clipper**. Launched from the Clydeside shipyards in 1869, the *Cutty Sark* was more famous in its day as a wool clipper, returning from Australia in just 72 days. The vessel's name comes from Robert Burns' *Tam O'Shanter*, in which Tam, a drunken farmer, is chased by Nannie, an angry witch in a short Paisley linen dress, or "cutty sark"; the clipper's figurehead shows her clutching the hair from the tail of Tam's horse. After a devastating fire in 2007, the ship has been beautifully restored from the bunkhouses on deck, to the ship's brass-lined keel. A collection of more than eighty ships' figureheads are lined up beneath the ship's prow.

Greenwich Park

MAP P.148

⊖ Cutty Sark DLR Ⓦ royalparks.org.uk. Daily 6am–dusk.

A welcome escape from the traffic and crowds, Greenwich Park is a great place to have a picnic or collapse under the shade of one of the giant plane trees. The chief delight, though, is the superb view from the steep hill crowned by the Royal Observatory (see below), from which Canary Wharf looms large over Docklands and the Dome. The park is also celebrated for its rare and ancient trees, its royal deer enclosure in "The Wilderness" and its semicircular rose garden.

Fan Museum

MAP P.148

12 Crooms Hill ⊖ Greenwich DLR ⓘ 020 8305 1441, Ⓦ thefanmuseum.org.uk. Tues–Sat 11am–5pm, Sun noon–5pm. £5.

The Fan Museum is a fascinating little place (and an extremely beautiful house) to the west of Greenwich Park, revealing the importance of the fan as a social and political document. The permanent exhibition on the ground floor traces the history of the fan and the materials employed, from peacock feathers to straw, while the temporary exhibitions on the first floor draw from the museum's extensive collection. Outside, there's a tearoom, housed in the kitsch, hand-painted orangery, with afternoon tea served (Tues & Fri–Sun 12.30–4.30pm, no bookings).

Royal Observatory

MAP P.148

Greenwich Park ⊖ Cutty Sark DLR ⓘ 020 8858 4422, Ⓦ rmg.co.uk. Daily 10am–6pm. £13.50.

Established in 1675 by Charles II to house the first Astronomer Royal, John Flamsteed, the Royal Observatory perches on the crest of

Cutty Sark

Greenwich Park's highest hill. The oldest part of the complex is the rather dinky Wren-built red-brick building, whose northeastern turret sports a bright-red time-ball that climbs the mast at 12.58pm and drops at 1pm GMT precise ly; it was added in 1833 to allow ships on the Thames to set their clocks. On the house's balcony overlooking the Thames, you can take a look at a **Camera Obscura**, of the kind which Flamsteed used to make safe observations of the sun.

Flamsteed's chief task was to study the night sky in order to discover an astronomical method of finding the **longitude** of a ship at sea, the lack of which was causing enormous problems for the emerging British Empire. Greenwich's greatest claim to fame, nowadays, is as the home of **Greenwich Mean Time** (GMT) and the Prime Meridian. Since 1884, Greenwich has occupied zero longitude – hence the world sets its clocks by GMT.

The old observatory is now a very popular **museum**. First off, you can see Flamsteed's restored apartments and the Octagon Room, where the king used to show off to his guests. The Time galleries beyond display four of the fabulous marine clocks designed by **John Harrison**, including "H4", which helped him win the Longitude Prize in 1763. In the Meridian Building, you get to see several meridians, including the present-day Greenwich Meridian fixed by the cross hairs in Airy's "Transit Circle", the astronomical instrument that dominates the last room. Reached via the shop (and free to enter), is the Great Equatorial Telescope from 1893.

Astronomers continued to work here until the postwar smog forced them to decamp; in 2018 they returned, as new technology allowed them to circumvent light pollution. The **Annie Maunder Astrographic Telescope** was subsequently installed in the Altazimuth Pavilion; it's not accessible to the public, but its images will be posted online and shown at the Planetarium (see below).

In the **Astronomy Centre** (free entry), housed in the fanciful, domed terracotta South Building, the high-tech galleries give a brief rundown of the Big Bang theory of the universe. You can also watch one of the thirty-minute presentations in the **Planetarium** (£8), introduced by a Royal Observatory astronomer.

The Royal Observatory

Shop

Greenwich Market

MAP P.148

Greenwich Church St 🚇 Cutty Sark or Greenwich DLR & Greenwich train station. Daily 10am–5.30pm. Stalls vary, busiest at weekends.

An attractive historic covered market in the centre of Greenwich, the stalls here change every day, with arts, crafts and plenty of food stalls always on offer; antiques and vintage on Tues, Thurs & Sun. Independent shops nearby offer further treasures, while on weekends flea markets spread further afield.

Café and restaurant

Champagne + Fromage

MAP P.148

34 Church St 🚇 Cutty Sark DLR ☎ 020 8853 3106. Tues–Fri noon–11pm, Sat 11am–11pm, Sun 11am–9pm.

This cool little place gets the balance just right with champagne from small producers, plus artisanal French cheeses, pâtés and charcuterie to nibble on. Baked cheeses, raclette and champagne afternoon teas, too (£48 for two). One of three branches in London.

Rivington

MAP P.148

178 Greenwich High Rd 🚇 Greenwich DLR & train station ☎ 020 8293 9270. Mon–Thurs noon–10pm, Fri noon–11pm, Sat 10am–11pm, Sun 10am–10pm.

There's a lively vibe at this sleek bar/restaurant where the superb gin menu pulls as many people as the creative, flavour-packed Modern British food. Mains from £12 (steaks £26–28).

Greenwich Market

Pubs

Cutty Sark

MAP P.148

Ballast Quay, off Lassell St 🚇 Cutty Sark DLR. Mon–Sat 11.30am–11pm, Sun noon–10.30pm.

This Georgian pub is the best one along Greenwich's riverside, a few paces away from the main tourist drag, with a good range of Young's and guest ales.

Greenwich Union

MAP P.148

56 Royal Hill 🚇 Greenwich DLR & train station. Mon–Fri noon–11pm, Sat 11.30am–11pm, Sun 11.30am–10.30pm.

Owned by the Meantime brewery, this relaxed pub with outdoor terrace offers delicious Meantime craft brews, guest ales and a gastropub menu that includes gourmet burgers.

Trafalgar Tavern

MAP P.148

5 Park Row 🚇 Cutty Sark DLR. Mon–Thurs noon–11pm, Fri noon–1am, Sat 10am–1am, Sun 10am–11pm.

Frequented by the likes of Dickens (and mentioned in *Our Mutual Friend*), William Thackeray and Wilkie Collins, this Regency-style inn is a firm tourist favourite. It has a great riverside position and serves good meals and snacks.

Kew and Richmond

The wealthy suburbs of Kew and Richmond like to think of themselves as apart from the rest of London, and in many ways they are. Both have a distinctly rural feel: Kew, thanks to its outstanding botanic gardens; Richmond, owing to its picturesque riverside setting and its gigantic park. Taking the leafy towpath from Richmond Bridge to one of the nearby stately homes, or soaking in the view from Richmond Park, you'd be forgiven for thinking you were in the countryside. Both Kew and Richmond are an easy tube ride from the centre, but the most pleasant way to reach them is to take one of the boats that plough up the Thames from Westminster.

Syon Park

MAP P.154
Twickenham Rd. Syon Lane train station from Waterloo ☎ 020 8560 0882, ⓦ syonpark.co.uk. House mid-March–Oct Wed, Thurs & Sun 11am–5pm. Gardens mid-March–Oct daily 10.30am–5pm. House & gardens £13; gardens only £8.

From its rather plain, castellated exterior, you'd never guess that **Syon House** boasts London's

Treetop Walkway, Kew Gardens

most opulent eighteenth-century interior. The splendour of Robert Adam's refurbishment is immediately revealed in the pristine Great Hall, an apsed double cube with a screen of Doric columns at one end and classical statuary dotted around the edges. There are several more Adam-designed rooms to admire, and a smattering of works by van Dyck, Lely, Gainsborough and Reynolds adorn the walls. While Adam beautified Syon House, Capability Brown laid out its **gardens** around an artificial lake, surrounding the water with oaks, beeches, limes and cedars. The gardens' real highlight, however, is the crescent-shaped Great Conservatory.

Kew Gardens

MAP P.154
⊖ Kew Gardens ☎ 020 8332 5655, ⓦ www.kew.org. Daily from 10am, closing time varies (4–7pm). From £16 online.

Established in 1759, Kew's **Royal Botanic Gardens** have grown from their original eight acres into a 300-acre site in which more than 33,000 species are grown in plantations and glasshouses. The display attracts nearly two million visitors every year, who come to

Great Conservatory, Syon Park

enjoy the beautiful landscaped parkland and steamy palmhouses. There's always something to see, whatever the season, but to get the most out of the place, come sometime between spring and autumn, bring a picnic and stay for the day.

The majority of people arrive at Kew Gardens tube and train station, a few minutes' walk east of the Victoria Gate. Immediately opposite the Victoria Gate, the **Palm House** is by far the most celebrated of the glasshouses, a curvaceous mound of glass and wrought-iron designed by Decimus Burton in the 1840s. Its drippingly humid atmosphere nurtures most of the known palm species,

while there's a small but excellent tropical aquarium in the basement. South of here is the largest of the glasshouses, the **Temperate House**, which contains over 1500 plant specimens from every continent. Nearby is the **Treetop Walkway**, which lifts you 60ft off the ground, and gives you a novel view of the tree canopy.

Elsewhere in the park, Kew's origins as an eighteenth-century royal pleasure garden are evident in the diminutive royal residence, **Kew Palace** (April–Sept daily 10am–5.30pm), bought by George II as a nursery for his umpteen children. There are numerous follies dotted about the gardens, the most conspicuous of which is the ten-

River transport

From April to October, **Westminster Passenger Services** (☎ 020 7930 2062, ⓦ wpsa.co.uk) runs a scheduled service from Westminster Pier to Kew, Richmond and Hampton Court. The full trip takes three hours one-way, and costs £19 single, £27 return; cash only. In addition, **Turks** (☎ 020 8546 2434, ⓦ turks.co.uk) runs a regular service from Richmond to Hampton Court (March–Oct Tues–Sun), which costs £9 single or £11 return. For the latest on boat services on the Thames, see ⓦ www.tfl.gov.uk.

Kew and Richmond

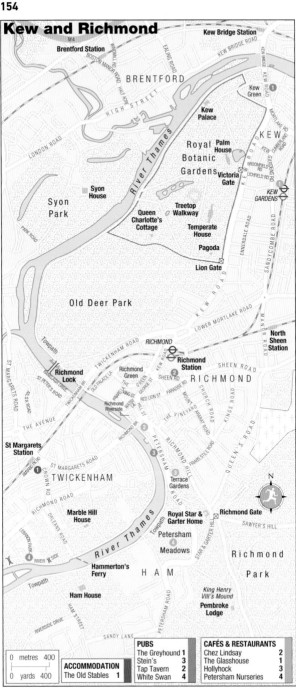

PUBS	
The Greyhound	1
Stein's	3
Tap Tavern	2
White Swan	4

CAFÉS & RESTAURANTS	
Chez Lindsay	2
The Glasshouse	1
Hollyhock	3
Petersham Nurseries	4

ACCOMMODATION	
The Old Stables	1

0 metres 400
0 yards 400

storey, 163ft-high **Pagoda**, visible to the south of the Temperate House. A sure way to lose the crowds is to head for the thickly wooded, southwestern section of the park around **Queen Charlotte's Cottage** (April–Sept Sat & Sun 11am–4pm), a tiny thatched summerhouse built in the 1770s as a royal picnic spot for George III's queen.

Richmond

MAP P.154

Richmond & Richmond train station.
Pedestrianized, terraced and redeveloped in the 1980s, Richmond's **riverside** is a neo-Georgian pastiche for the most part, and a popular one at that. The real joy of the waterfront, though, is **Richmond Bridge**, an elegant span of five arches made from Purbeck stone in 1777 and cleverly widened in the 1930s, thus preserving what is London's oldest extant Thames bridge. From April to October you can rent rowing boats from the nearby jetties, or take a boat trip to Hampton Court or Westminster. Alternatively, simply head south down the towpath, past the terraced gardens which give out great views over the river. On either side are the wooded banks of the Thames: to the left cows graze on Petersham Meadows; beyond lies Ham House.

Ham House

MAP P.154

Ham St. Bus #371 or #65 from
Richmond & Richmond train station
020 8940 1950, www.nationaltrust.org.uk/hamhouse. House daily noon–4pm, Jan–March, Nov & Dec select rooms only. Gardens daily 10am–5pm, Nov–Jan closes 4pm. £11.05.
Expensively furnished in the seventeenth century but little altered since then, Ham House boasts one of the finest Stuart interiors in the country, from the stupendously ornate Great Staircase to the Long Gallery,

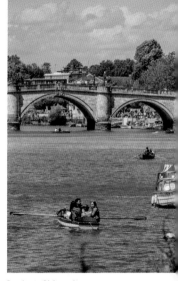

Row boats, Richmond

featuring six "Court Beauties" by Peter Lely. Elsewhere, there are several fine Verrio ceiling paintings, some exquisite parquet flooring, lavish plasterwork and silverwork, and paintings by van Dyck and Reynolds. A bonus is the formal **gardens**, especially the Cherry Garden, with a lavender parterre surrounded by yew hedges and pleached hornbeam arbours. The Orangery, overlooking the original kitchen garden, serves as a tearoom.

Marble Hill House

MAP P.154

Marble Hill Park, Richmond Rd. St Margarets train station from Waterloo
020 8892 5115, www.english-heritage.org.uk. April–Oct Sat & Sun 10am–3.30pm; closed for renovation until April 2019, after which open hours could be extended. £7.40.
This stuccoed Palladian villa, set in rolling green parkland, was built in 1729 for the **Countess of Suffolk**, mistress of George II for some twenty years and, conveniently, also a lady-in-waiting to his wife, Queen Caroline. She was renowned for her wit and intelligence and she entertained

the Twickenham Club of Pope, Gay and Horace Walpole. The few original furnishings are enhanced with reproductions, giving the place something of the feel of an eighteenth-century villa. **The Great Room**, on the piano nobile, is a perfect cube whose coved ceiling carries on up into the top-floor apartments. Copies of van Dycks decorate the walls as they did in Lady Suffolk's day, but the highlight is **Lady Suffolk's Bedchamber**, with its Ionic columned recess – a classic Palladian device – where she died in 1767 at the age of 79. In the grounds, there are occasional **open-air concerts** on summer evenings.

Richmond Park

MAP P.154
Bus #371 or #65 from ⊖ Richmond ☎ 0300 061 2200, ⓦ royalparks.org.uk. Pedestrians daily 24hr, except Feb & Nov daily 7.30am–8pm. Vehicles daily: March–Sept 7am–dusk; Oct–Feb 7.30am–dusk. Free.

Richmond's greatest attraction is its enormous park, at the top of Richmond Hill – 2500 acres of undulating grassland and bracken, dotted with coppiced ancient woodland. Eight miles across at its widest point, this is Europe's largest city park, famed for its red and fallow deer, which roam freely, and for its venerable oaks. For the most part untamed, the park does have a couple of deliberately landscaped areas. The most popular spot is **Isabella Plantation**, a carefully landscaped woodland park, with a little rivulet running through it, two small artificial ponds, and spectacular rhododendrons and azaleas in the spring. For refreshment, head for **Pembroke Lodge**, once the childhood home of the philosopher Bertrand Russell, and now a teahouse at the park's highest point, affording wonderful views up the Thames valley. Tradition has it that Henry VIII waited here for the flare that signalled the execution of his second wife, Anne Boleyn.

Richmond Park

Cafés and restaurants

Chez Lindsay

MAP P.154
11 Hill Rise ⊖ Richmond ☎ 020 8948
7473. Mon–Sat noon–11pm, Sun
noon–10pm.

There's a wide choice of galettes
(from £7) or more formal French
main courses, including lots of
fresh fish and shellfish, at this
bright, authentic Breton *creperie*.
Mains £14–23.

The Glasshouse

MAP P.154,
14 Station Parade ⊖ Kew Gardens ☎ 020
8940 6777. Tues–Sat noon–2.30pm &
6.30–10.30pm, Sun 12.30–4pm.

A swish restaurant for a swish
neighbourhood, serving delicate,
accomplished French/Modern
British dishes. Three courses lunch
£37.50; dinner £57.50.

Hollyhock

MAP P.154
Terrace Gardens ⊖ Richmond ☎ 020 8948
6555. Daily 8.30am–dusk.

Laidback, fair-trade veggie café,
perfect for tea and cakes on the terrace
overlooking the gardens and the river.

Petersham Nurseries

MAP P.154
Off Petersham Rd. Bus #371 or #65 from
Richmond ☎ 020 8332 8665. Restaurant
Tues–Sun noon–5pm. Teahouse Tues–Sun
9am–5pm.

Expect fresh, organic, expensive
food at this lovely restaurant,
hidden away in a posh garden
centre. Mains £20–30. There's a
cheaper self-service tea room too.

Pubs

The Greyhound

MAP P.154
82 Kew Green ⊖ Kew Gardens. Mon–Sat
10am–11pm, Sun 10am–10.30om.

Petersham Nurseries

One of a handful of options on
and around Kew Green, this light,
contemporary pub offers real ales
and a long food menu.

Stein's

MAP P.154
Richmond Towpath ⊖ Richmond ☎ 020
8948 8189. May–mid-Oct daily noon–10pm;
mid-Oct–April Wed–Sun noon–dusk.

An authentic Bavarian beer garden,
serving up wurst and sauerkraut
washed down with *echt* beers (no
beer without food). Outdoor
seating only; the place is closed in
wet weather.

Tap Tavern

MAP P.154
Princes Street ⊖ Richmond. Mon–Wed
noon–11.30pm, Thurs noon–1am, Fri & Sat
noon–1.30am, Sun noon–10.45pm.

Just off Richmond's High Street,
the *Tap* ticks all the boxes for
current drinks trends: dozens of
local and international craft beers,
a dedicated artisan gin menu and
comfort food bar snacks to soak up
the booze, making this a tempting
place to linger.

White Swan

MAP P.154
Riverside. Twickenham train station from
Waterloo. Mon & Sun 11am–10.30pm,
Tues–Sat 11am–11pm.

Filling pub food, draught beer and
a quiet riverside location – except
on rugby match days – make this a
good halt on any towpath ramble.
The riverside terrace is a big draw.

Hampton Court

Hampton Court Palace is the finest of England's royal abodes and well worth the trip out from central London. A wonderfully imposing, sprawling red-brick ensemble on the banks of the Thames, it was built in 1516 by the upwardly mobile Cardinal Wolsey, Henry VIII's Lord Chancellor, only to be purloined by Henry himself after Wolsey fell from favour. Charles II laid out the gardens, inspired by what he had seen at Versailles, while King William III and Queen Mary II had large sections of the palace remodelled by Wren. With so much to see, both inside and outside the palace, you're best off devoting the best part of a day to the place, taking a picnic with you to have in the grounds.

State Apartments

MAP P.159

☎ 020 3166 6000, ⓦ hrp.org.uk. Daily: April–Oct 10am–6pm; Nov–March 10am–4.30pm. From £19.20 online (£22.70 on the gate).

The palace's Tudor west front may no longer be moated but it positively prickles with turrets, castellations, chimneypots and pinnacles. Its impressive **Great Gatehouse** would have been five storeys high in its day. King Henry lavished more money on Hampton Court than any other palace, yet the only major survival from Tudor times in **Henry VIII's Apartments** is his Great Hall, which features a glorious double hammerbeam ceiling. The **Haunted Gallery** is home to the ghost of Henry's fifth wife, 19-year-old Catherine

Hampton Court Palace

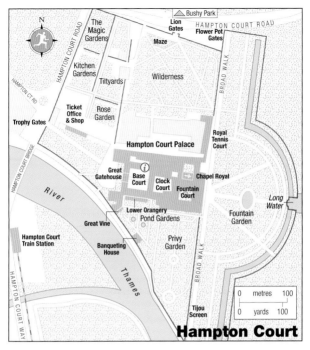

Hampton Court

Howard, who ran down the gallery to plead for the king's mercy – only to be dragged kicking and screaming back to her chambers. Another highlight is the superbly ornate **Chapel Royal**, one of the most memorable sights in the whole palace, with its colourful plasterwork vaulting, heavy with pendants of gilded music-making cherubs.

The **Cumberland Art Gallery**, housed in the Georgian part of the palace, shows some truly remarkable paintings from the royal collection. Artemisia Gentileschi's *Self-portrait as the Allegory of Painting* from 1638–9 is a uniquely powerful depiction of the female artist as worker, and is shown alongside works by Caravaggio, who she was influenced by, Rembrandt and Holbein. **William III's Apartments** are extremely grand, particularly the militaristic trompe-l'oeil paintings on the King's Staircase and the King's Great Bedchamber, which boasts a superb vertical Gibbons frieze and ceiling paintings by Verrio.

Several early Tudor rooms, with striking linenfold panelling and gilded strapwork ceilings, are now used to display **Young Henry VIII's Story**. This is a worthy attempt by the palace to portray Henry in his virile youth, during his happy, twenty-year marriage to his first wife, Catherine of Aragon. Last, but not least, are the earthy and evocative **Henry VIII's Kitchens**, large sections of which have survived to this day and have been restored and embellished with historical reconstructions.

The Gardens and the Maze

MAP P.159

Magic Garden April–Oct daily 10am–6pm. All formal gardens included in palace ticket; Magic Garden and Maze only ticket £7 (kids £5.20); Maze only £4.40.

Getting to and around the palace

Trains from Waterloo take around half an hour to reach Hampton Court train station, which is just across the river from the palace; in summer you can also take the boat from Westminster, Richmond or Kew (see page 152).

Hampton Court is a huge complex – the most rewarding sections are Henry VIII's Apartments, the Cumberland Gallery, William III's Apartments and Henry VIII's Kitchens. And be sure not to miss out on the splendid Maze.

You can pick up **audioguides** (included in ticket price) from the information centre off Base Court. **Historical scenes and tours** take place throughout the State Apartments in summer; all are led by period-costumed historians, who do a fine job of bringing the place to life; ask at the information centre what's on that day when you arrive.

If you're coming from the State Apartments, you'll probably emerge onto the magnificent Broad Walk, which runs along Wren's austere east front and is lined with superbly maintained herbaceous borders. Halfway along is the indoor **Royal Tennis Court**, established here by Henry VIII – if you're lucky, you might catch a game of this arcane precursor of modern tennis (summer only).

Hampton Court Maze

Fanning out from the Broad Walk is the **Fountain Garden**, a grand, semicircular parterre featuring conical, overgrown dwarf yew trees. To the south of the palace is the more formal **Privy Garden**, which features magnificent wrought-iron riverside railings by Jean Tijou. The **Pond Gardens**, originally constructed as ornamental fish ponds stocked with freshwater fish for the kitchens, feature some of the gardens' most spectacularly colourful flowerbeds. Further along, protected by glass, is the palace's celebrated **Great Vine**, grown from a cutting in 1768 by Capability Brown and averaging about seven hundred pounds of Black Hamburg grapes per year (sold at the palace in September).

Close by stands the Wren-built **Lower Orangery**, now home to Andrea Mantegna's luminous richly coloured masterpiece, *The Triumphs of Caesar*, painted around 1486 for the Ducal Palace in Mantua and characterized by an accomplished use of perspective and archeological and historical accuracy.

The most famous feature of the palace gardens, however, is the deceptively tricky trapezoidal yew hedge **Maze**, planted in the 1690s. Mazes, or labyrinths as they were

Bushy Park

called at the time, were originally designed for pilgrims, who used to crawl along on hands and knees reciting prayers as penance for not making a pilgrimage to the Holy Land. They were all the rage among the eighteenth-century nobility, who used them primarily for amusement, secret conversations and flirtation. The maze was originally planted with hornbeam, but with the onset of the tourist boom in the 1960s, the hornbeam took quite a battering and had to be replaced with yew. Nearby, in Henry VIII's former tiltyard, the **Magic Garden** is an imaginative adventure playground, designed around such fairy-tale themes as dragons, beasts and battlements.

Bushy Park

MAP P.159

ⓦ royalparks.org.uk. Daily 24hr for pedestrians, except Sept & Nov Mon–Fri 8am–10.30pm. Free.

Beyond the Lion Gates to the north of the Maze and across Hampton Court Road lies **Bushy Park**, the palace's semi-wild enclosure of over a thousand acres, which sustains copious herds of fallow and red deer. Wren's mile-long royal road, **Chestnut Avenue**, cuts through the park, and is at its best in May when the trees are in blossom. The park's main architectural feature is the **Diana Fountain**, situated a third of the way along to help break the monotony. The statue – which, in fact, depicts Arethusa – was commissioned by Charles II from Francesco Fanelli and originally graced the Privy Garden; stranded in the centre of a vast pond, she looks ill-proportioned and a bit forlorn.

Off to the west, a little further up the avenue, you'll come upon the **Waterhouse Woodland Gardens**, which are at their most colourful each spring when the rhododendrons, azaleas and camellias are in bloom. The crowds are fairly thin even here, but if you really want to escape the visitors make for the park's wilder western section, which is home to abundant wildlife.

ACCOMMODATION

Artist Residence

Accommodation

Accommodation in London is expensive. Compared with most European cities, you pay over the odds in every category. The cheapest option is to go to one of the independent hostels, where in high season dorm beds start at around £20. Going up a notch, even the most basic B&Bs struggle to bring their tariffs below £100 for a double with shared facilities, which is why so many people head for the budget chain hotels – which themselves are not at all cheap. For a really decent hotel room, you shouldn't expect much change out of £140 a night. Most B&Bs and many hotels are housed in former residential properties, which means that rooms tend to be on the small side. That said, even the most basic rooms tend to have TVs, and breakfast is often included in the price. Though hostels normally don't provide breakfast, they do usually have cooking facilities – exceptions are mentioned in the text. The prices quoted are for the cheapest double room or dorm bed in high season, though rates often vary online and according to availability (see box opposite).

Westminster

ARTIST RESIDENCE MAP p.26, POCKET MAP G10. 52 Cambridge St ⊖ Pimlico ☎ 020 3019 8610, ⊕ www.artistresidence. co.uk. Boutique guesthouse offering relaxed luxury and lifestyle magazine cool. The rooms are gorgeous (though the cheapest are quite small), packed with vintage boho trappings. There's a cocktail bar and a Modern British restaurant, too. **£260**

LUNA SIMONE HOTEL MAP p.26, POCKET MAP G10. 47–49 Belgrave Rd ⊖ Victoria ☎ 020 7834 5897, ⊕ www.lunasimonehotel. com. Popular B&B/hotel with very friendly staff and plain, well-maintained en-suite rooms. Big breakfasts. **£159**

ST ERMIN'S HOTEL MAP p.26, POCKET MAP H9. Caxton St ⊖ St James's Park ☎ 020 7222 7888, ⊕ sterminshotel.co.uk. A bit of a sanctuary, set back from the street thanks to its long, leafy courtyard, but convenient for Victoria and Westminster, this is a classy four-star. Beyond the theatrical plaster-work reception and grand stairwell, rooms are more contemporary, with marble bathrooms, while some of the larger ones are suitable for families. Discounts for prepaying. **£250**

SANCTUARY HOUSE MAP p.26, POCKET MAP F19. 33 Tothill St ⊖ St James's Park ☎ 020 7799 4044, ⊕ www. sanctuaryhousehotel.com. A Fuller's hotel above a Fuller's pub, decked out in uncontroversial modern style. Breakfast costs extra, and is served in the pub, but the location by St James's Park is terrific. Rates vary – ask about the special deals. **£180**

St James's

THE STAFFORD MAP p.35, POCKET MAP D17. 16–18 St James's Place ⊖ Green Park ☎ 020 7493 0111, ⊕ www. thestaffordlondon.com. Tucked into a quiet backstreet off St James's Street, *The Stafford* provides high-class rooms in the main building, the unique Carriage House, a luxuriously converted row of eighteenth-century stables, and in the upmarket Mews Suites. The *American Bar* was founded to provide cocktails for American visitors in the 1930s, and its courtyard terrace remains a delight. **£372**

Marylebone

22 YORK STREET MAP p.46, POCKET MAP A13. 22 York St ⊖ Baker Street ☎ 020 7224 2990, ⓦ www.22yorkstreet. co.uk. Centrally located ten-room B&B in a friendly home. The Georgian house itself is elegant, with antiques and cosy, comfortable public spaces where guests can read or play board games. Breakfasts are communal. **£150**

CENTRAL YHA MAP p.46, POCKET MAP D12. 104 Bolsover St ⊖ Great Portland Street ☎ 0345 371 9154, ⓦ www.yha.org. uk. Excellent three-hundred-bed hostel in a quiet West End spot, with a kitchen, a 24hr café and a bar. Dorms are mostly en suite, or with bathrooms near. No groups. Free wi-fi in communal areas. **Dorms £33; doubles £89**

SUMNER HOTEL MAP p.46, POCKET MAP E6. 54 Upper Berkeley St ⊖ Marble Arch ☎ 020 7723 2244, ⓦ www.thesumner.com. A spruce B&B – with the feel of a boutique hotel – in a Georgian townhouse. The twenty rooms vary in size and style – the best are light and modern, some have tiny balconies, those facing the street can be noisy – but all are tasteful and comfortable, and there's a tranquil sitting room. Breakfast is a buffet. Free wi-fi. **£160**

Soho and Covent Garden

DEAN STREET TOWNHOUSE MAP p.54, POCKET MAP F15. 69–71 Dean St ⊖ Tottenham Court Road ☎ 020 7434 1775, ⓦ www.deanstreettownhouse.com. This 1730s beauty, owned by the Soho House club, has rooms ranging from "broom cupboard" and "tiny" right up to "bigger", where you'll have plenty of space. All are luxurious with gorgeous details. **£230**

THE FIELDING HOTEL MAP p.54, POCKET MAP H15. 4 Broad Court, Bow St ⊖ Covent Garden ☎ 020 7836 8305, ⓦ www.thefieldinghotel.co.uk. Quietly situated on a traffic-free court, this

Booking a room

Demand for beds is so great that London doesn't really have a low season. Most hotels vary their prices considerably depending on demand, so it's worth booking online well in advance to get the best price – you may be able to shave £50–100 off room rates at some of the more upmarket hotels – and if you're flexible with dates you can find some good deals.

London's **tourist offices** (see page 182) operate a room-booking service, for which a small fee is levied (they also take the first night's fee in advance).

Meanwhile, you can book accommodation for free **online** at ⓦ www.londontown.com; payment is made directly to the hotel and they offer very good discounts. Other useful websites for last-minute offers include ⓦ www.laterooms. com and ⓦ www.lastminute.com. ⓦ www.londonbb.com sources classy **B&B** options. Apartment rentals, such as ⓦ airbnb.co.uk and ⓦ homeaway.com, can be much better value, though the city has some restrictions on short-term rentals, while the Alastair Sawday's site (ⓦ www.sawdays. co.uk) has a selection of interesting properties in the capital, ranging from B&Bs and hotels to pubs and even apartments and houseboats.

excellent hotel is one of Covent Garden's hidden gems. Its simple en-suite rooms are a favourite with visiting performers, since it's very near the Royal Opera House. No lift and no breakfast, but hot drinks in rooms. **£192**

HAZLITT'S MAP p.54, POCKET MAP F14. 6 Frith St ⊖ Tottenham Court Road ℹ 020 7434 1771, Ⓦ www.hazlittshotel.com. Located off the south side of Soho Square, this early eighteenth-century building is a hotel of real character and discreet charm, offering en-suite rooms exquisitely decorated with period furniture. Breakfast (served in the rooms) is not included in the rates. **£255**

NADLER SOHO MAP p.54, POCKET MAP F14. 10 Carlisle St ⊖ Tottenham Court Road ℹ 020 3697 3697, Ⓦ www.thenadler. com. Modern hotel offering good value. Rooms are comfy and high-tech, if unexciting (the cheapest are pretty small), and each has a microwave, fridge and kettle – and an espresso machine – so you could effectively self-cater. **£215**

OXFORD STREET YHA MAP p.54, POCKET MAP E14. 14 Noel St ⊖ Oxford Circus or

Tottenham Court Road ℹ 0345 371 9133, Ⓦ www.yha.org.uk. The Soho location and relatively modest size mean this hostel tends to fill quickly. The atmosphere is more party central than family-friendly, though kids are welcome. Café and kitchen. Free wi-fi in communal areas. **Dorms £35; doubles £89**

THISTLE PICCADILLY MAP p.54, POCKET MAP F16. Coventry St ⊖ Piccadilly Circus ℹ 0800 330 8395, Ⓦ www.thistle. com. You're in the heart of things here, surrounded by Theatreland – in a no-surprises chain hotel that offers modern, quiet, well-equipped rooms with free (soft drink) minibars, Nespresso machines and rainfall showers. Check for online pay-in-advance discounts. **£240**

Bloomsbury

ALHAMBRA HOTEL MAP p.68, POCKET MAP J3. 17 Argyle St ⊖ King's Cross St Pancras ℹ 020 7837 9575, Ⓦ www. alhambrahotel.com. Clean, friendly, budget hotel a stone's throw from St Pancras. Cheapest rooms have shared facilities and there's no lift, but a generous breakfast is included. **£110**

Budget chain hotels

Chain hotels have pretty much got the budget hotel market sewn up. B&Bs may be able to offer a more personal touch and more character in the decor, but the franchises are often in unbeatable central locations. Although they will never really be more than perfunctory places to stay, on the whole they can be guaranteed to provide clean if anonymous rooms.

Bumping along at the bottom are **easyHotel** (Ⓦ www.easyhotel. com), whose summer prices start at just £55 for an en-suite cubbyhole – if you want a window, wi-fi, TV use or room cleaning, it's extra; there are branches in Victoria, South Ken, Paddington, Barbican and Heathrow. **Travelodge** (Ⓦ travelodge.co.uk) has some very handily situated hotels; rooms are unexciting, but if you book online well in advance, en-suite doubles can cost less than £65. **Premier Inn** is generally considered a cut above Travelodge (and it doesn't have quite the online bargains), with rooms from £80; their "hub" hotels offer small pod rooms from £70, with locations including Covent Garden, while the **point.a** chain offers smart minimal rooms in Lambeth North, Liverpool Street, Paddington, Canary Wharf and King's Cross (Ⓦ pointahotels.com), starting at £80–90.

AROSFA HOTEL MAP p.68, POCKET MAP F12. 83 Gower St ⊖ Goodge Street or Euston Square ☎ 020 7636 2115, ⓦ www.arosfalondon.com. Fifteen en-suite B&B rooms. Some are tiny, but it's clean, comfy and reliable, with contemporary touches. Full breakfast. **£160**

CLINK 261 HOSTEL MAP p.68, POCKET MAP J3. 261–265 Gray's Inn Rd ⊖ King's Cross St Pancras ☎ 020 7183 9400, ⓦ www.clinkhostels.com. A clean and friendly hostel, with dorms ranging from four to eighteen beds in a converted office block near King's Cross station, with laundry, lounge and kitchen – guests can use the bar at *Clink 78*. Breakfast £1. **Dorms from £23; doubles £75**

CLINK 78 HOSTEL MAP p.68, POCKET MAP K3. 78 King's Cross Rd ⊖ King's Cross St Pancras ☎ 020 7183 9400, ⓦ www.clinkhostels.com. This party hostel has funky decor, a lively bar, some pod beds, and plenty of period features from the days when it was a Victorian courthouse – you can even stay in an old cell (bunks for two: £65). Breakfast £1; kitchen facilities from noon; four- to sixteen-bed dorms, some girls-only, some en suite. **Dorms from £24; doubles £77**

GENERATOR MAP p.68, POCKET MAP J4. 37 Tavistock Place ⊖ Russell Square ☎ 020 7388 7666, ⓦ www.generatorhostels.com. A huge party hostel, with over eight hundred beds, in a converted police barracks tucked away down a cobbled street. The decor is colourful and hip, and there's a young, sociable atmosphere with a cool late-night bar and regular movie nights. Laundry, but no kitchen; breakfast and snacks available in the café. Groups welcome. **Dorms £20; doubles £85**

GREAT NORTHERN HOTEL MAP p.68, POCKET MAP J3. Pancras Rd ⊖ King's Cross St Pancras ☎ 020 3388 0800, ⓦ gnhlondon.com. Grand old Victorian railway hotel offering boutique rooms with a luxe, Deco feel. Generous extras include espresso coffee, pastries and fresh fruit on each floor. **£220**

THE HOXTON, HOLBORN MAP p.68, POCKET MAP H13. 199–206 High Holborn ⊖ Holborn ☎ 0207 661 3000, ⓦ thehoxton.com. The hipster industrial aesthetic of the Hoxton (see page 168) is transplanted to the West End, along with the never-ending buzz of the lobby/bar/café. Cleverly designed rooms, with artworks and faux-vintage furniture, make good use of the spaces (some tiny, rooms start with "shoebox" up to "roomy"). **£160**

RIDGEMOUNT HOTEL MAP p.68, POCKET MAP F12. 65–67 Gower St ⊖ Goodge Street ☎ 020 7636 1141, ⓦ www.ridgemounthotel.co.uk. Very friendly, old-fashioned, family-run place, with 33 small rooms (half of them with shared facilities), a garden and free hot drinks machine. Full breakfast. **£100**

ST PANCRAS YHA MAP p.68, POCKET MAP J4. 79–81 Euston Rd ⊖ King's Cross St Pancras ☎ 0345 371 9344, ⓦ www.yha.org.uk. Popular hostel near the Eurostar terminal on the busy Euston Road; rooms are very clean and bright. Family rooms are available. No groups. They don't have a kitchen but there's a café. Free wi-fi in communal areas. **Dorms £29; doubles £90**

The City

APEX CITY OF LONDON HOTEL MAP p.74, POCKET MAP N6. 1 Seething Lane ⊖ Tower Hill ☎ 020 3553 7262, ⓦ www.apexhotels.co.uk. A four-star hotel on a secluded City street, designed for corporate clientele. Rooms are modern and well appointed; the pricier ones enjoy more light and better views. Rates vary enormously according to availability, so book early. On-site gym, restaurant and bar. **£120**

THE ROOKERY MAP p.74, POCKET MAP L5. 12 Peter's Lane, Cowcross St ⊖ Farringdon ☎ 020 7336 0931, ⓦ www.rookeryhotel.com. Rambling Georgian townhouse near Smithfield Market that makes a fantastically discreet little hideaway. It's as charming as can be with its panelled walls, flagstone floors and creaky, timeworn floorboards; rooms offer faded Baroque glam with super bathrooms. **£180**

ST PAUL'S YHA MAP p.74, POCKET MAP L6. 36 Carter Lane ⊖ St Paul's ☏ 0845 371 9012, ⓦ yha.org.uk. Map p., POCKET MAP L6. Large 215-bed hostel in a superb historic building opposite St Paul's Cathedral. There's a lounge and a café for dinner, but no kitchen. Small groups only. Free wi-fi in communal areas. **Dorms £29; doubles £79**

THE ZETTER HOTEL MAP p.74, POCKET MAP L4. 86–88 Clerkenwell Rd ⊖ Farringdon ☏ 020 7324 4567, ⓦ www. thezetter.com. A warehouse converted with real style and a dash of vintage glamour. The 59 rooms are funky and colourful, with Penguin paperbacks in many. Ask for a room at the back, overlooking quiet, cobbled St John's Square. Water for guests is supplied from *The Zetter*'s own well, beneath the building; good offers sometimes available. **£150**

The East End

ACE HOTEL MAP p.90, POCKET MAP 04. 100 Shoreditch High St ⊖ Liverpool Street ☏ 020 7613 9800, ⓦ www. acehotel.com/London. Super-slick hipster accommodation in the London outpost of a trendy USA chain. There's lots going on, with interesting art and music events, DJ nights and pop-ups, and coffee shops, bars, a Modern British restaurant and a club on site. Rooms are quirky and cool, with vintage design touches – the suites include record players and vinyl. **£17**

CULPEPPER MAP p.90, POCKET MAP 05. 40 Commercial St ⊖ Aldgate East or Liverpool Street ☏ 020 7247 5371, ⓦ theculpeper.com. This welcoming gastropub (see page) has five simple but artfully decorated rooms. Cooked or continental breakfast is included and served on the plant-filled roof terrace (weather permitting). It's a good-value choice for those who want a place to stay near the East London scene, but is of course noisy until pub-closing time. **£120**

HOXTON HOTEL MAP p.90, POCKET MAP N4. 81 Great Eastern St ⊖ Old Street ☏ 020 7550 1000, ⓦ www.hoxtonhotels. com. The "Hox" brand – now extended to Holborn and Amsterdam – started here, and though it's not as hip as it once was, it's a popular choice. The facilities are good, with flat-screen TVs and duck-down duvets. A light breakfast is delivered to your room. The DJ bar and brasserie are destinations in themselves. **£150**

QBIC MAP p.90. 42 Adler St ⊖ Aldgate East ☏ 020 3021 3300, ⓦ www.london. qbichotels.com. Bright, colourful flashpacker place with comfy, eye-popping rooms and fab bathrooms; the cheapest are tiny, though, and you'll pay around £15 more for a window. Tea and coffee facilities on each floor. **£100**

SHORDITCH ROOMS MAP p.90, POCKET MAP 04. Shoreditch House, Ebor St ⊖ Shoreditch High Street Overground ☏ 020 7739 5040, ⓦ shoreditchhouse. com/hotel. Hip little place with 26 rooms from "tiny" to "small-plus", and larger rooms in a separate building. Lots of tongue-and-groove and fresh, sunbleached colours, old school desks and vintage tiled bathrooms. **£210**

Tower and Docklands

WOMBAT'S CITY HOSTEL MAP p.100. 7 Dock St ⊖ Tower Hill ☏ 020 7680 7600, ⓦ www.wombats-hostels. com. This big (more than five hundred beds), newish hostel, part of a popular European chain, has light, spacious communal areas, a large kitchen (pasta provided), and a popular, big bar. Dorms – four to eight beds – and doubles are all en suite, and everything is very clean, but very plain. No children. **Dorms £28; doubles £120**

South Bank and around

CAPTAIN BLIGH GUESTHOUSE MAP p.105, POCKET MAP K9. 100 Lambeth Rd ⊖ Lambeth North ⓦ www. captainblighhouse.co.uk. The former home of Captain Bligh (of *Bounty* fame) is now a nautically flavoured Georgian B&B, a short walk from the South Bank, run by a friendly, unobtrusive couple. There are just a handful of rooms and an apartment, all self-contained and with self-catering facilities. Three-night minimum. **£100**

MAD HATTER MAP p.105, POCKET MAP L7. 3–7 Stamford St ⊖ Southwark or Blackfriars ☎ 020 7401 9222, Ⓦ www. madhatterhotel.co.uk. Good-value Fuller's hotel with thirty clean and comfy en-suite rooms, above a Fuller's pub in an old hat factory. This is a great location, a short walk from Tate Modern and the South Bank, and staff are friendly. **£185**

MONDRIAN AT SEA CONTAINERS MAP p.105, POCKET MAP L7. 20 Upper Ground ⊖ Southwark or Blackfriars ☎ 020 3747 1000, Ⓦ morganshotelgroup.com. This incredibly slick, nautically themed hotel occupies a prime spot right on the south bank of the Thames, in what was once a 1970s office building (known as the Sea Containers building). It features its own Curzon cinema, rooftop bar and well-regarded restaurant. **£195**

POINT A WESTMINSTER MAP p.105, POCKET MAP K19. 118–120 Westminster Bridge Rd ⊖ Lambeth North or Waterloo Ⓦ www.pointahotels.com. It's a bit of a stretch to say this smart, no-fuss hotel is in Westminster – it's nearer Waterloo and the South Bank, but still convenient. Rooms are tiny, and £10 more for one with a window. **£85**

SAFESTAY MAP p.105. 144 Walworth Rd ⊖ Elephant and Castle ☎ 020 7703 8000, Ⓦ www.safestay.co.uk. Reliable hostel in a handsome Georgian building – clean and tidy, with good beds (with curtains) and showers, and spacious common areas. Some of the four- to eight-bed dorms are en suite. Groups welcome. There's another branch in Holland Park. **Dorms £21; triple £155**

Bankside and Southwark Borough

IBIS STYLES LONDON MAP p.112, POCKET MAP M7. 43–47 Southwark Bridge Rd ⊖ London Bridge ☎ 020 7015 1480, Ⓦ www.ibis.com. The *Southwark* branch of this chain is a good central, no-fuss option with colourful design touches

that raise the ambience a little above the other bland chain hotels in this area. Rooms are generally comfortable and clean and a buffet breakfast is included in rates, which vary widely depending on availability. **£135**

THAMESIDE YHA MAP p.112. 20 Salter Rd ⊖ Rotherhithe ☎ 0845 371 9756, Ⓦ www.yha.org.uk. London's largest YHA hostel, with 320 beds, is in a quiet spot near the river. It can feel a bit of a trek from the centre, but it often has space and the riverside pubs round here are good. Self-catering is available, and there's a café-bar serving breakfast and dinner. Free wi-fi. **Dorms £18; doubles £55**

Kensington and Chelsea

ASTER HOUSE MAP p.120, POCKET MAP D10. 3 Sumner Place ⊖ South Kensington ☎ 020 7581 5888, Ⓦ www.asterhouse. com. Pleasant, award-winning B&B in a luxurious, white-stuccoed South Ken street with a lovely garden at the back and a large conservatory where breakfast is served. **£240**

B+B BELGRAVIA MAP p.120, POCKET MAP F9. 64–66 Ebury St ⊖ Victoria ☎ 020 7259 8570, Ⓦ www.bb-belgravia. com. Very close to the train and coach station, this place offers small B&B rooms and self-catering studios. The rooms are comfortable, with original features as well as contemporary touches. Communal spaces are light and well designed, and staff welcoming and enthusiastic. Free bike loan; pet friendly. **£140**

CARING HOTEL MAP p.120, POCKET MAP C6. 24 Craven Hill Gardens ⊖ Bayswater, Queensway or Lancaster Gate ☎ 020 7723 0888, Ⓦ www.caringhotel.co.uk. This large guesthouse, in a quiet street, is a popular budget choice. Rooms are clean and functional: some have shared facilities, some showers only, and others are en suite. Free wi-fi in public areas and free continental breakfast. **£85**

COLUMBIA HOTEL MAP p.120, POCKET MAP C7. 95–99 Lancaster Gate ⊖ Lancaster Gate ☎ 020 7402 0021, Ⓦ www.

columbiahotel.co.uk. This large hotel, once five Victorian houses, offers a variety of en suites – singles, doubles, triples and quads, some with views over Hyde Park. It's all a bit dated but it has a certain faded charm. Breakfast included. **£120**

GARDEN COURT HOTEL MAP p.120, POCKET MAP B6. 30–31 Kensington Gardens Square ⊖ Bayswater or Queensway ☎ 020 7229 2553, ⓦ www. gardencourthotel.co.uk. Unfussy hotel close to Portobello Market; rooms are small, but all (except some singles) are en suite. Rates vary considerably. Buffet breakfast. **£120**

THE HALKIN MAP p.120, POCKET MAP B19. 5 Halkin St ⊖ Hyde Park Corner ☎ 020 7333 1000, ⓦ www.comohotels. com. A luxury hotel that spurns the chintzy country-house theme: elegant, East-meets-West minimalism prevails in each of the 41 rooms. The high-end dining options include Michelin-starred Basque restaurant *Amesta*. **£435**

KENSINGTON HOUSE HOTEL MAP p.120, POCKET MAP C8. 15–16 Prince of Wales Terrace ⊖ High Street Kensington ☎ 020 7937 2345, ⓦ www.kenhouse.com. Friendly hotel in a nineteenth-century townhouse. The en-suite rooms are smallish and worn in places, but clean and comfy; one has a tiny balcony. Free continental breakfast. **£160**

THE MAIN HOUSE MAP p.120, POCKET MAP A6. 6 Colville Rd ⊖ Ladbroke Grove or Notting Hill Gate ☎ 020 7221 9691, ⓦ www. themainhouse.co.uk. Three enormous suites that are both homey – thanks to some lovely period furniture – and bohemian. Perfectly placed for Portobello Road, with lots of thoughtful touches. Three-night minimum. No breakfast (but discounts in local deli-café). **£130**

MEININGER MAP p.120, POCKET MAP C9. Baden Powell House, 65–67 Queen's Gate ⊖ Gloucester Road or South Kensington ☎ 020 3318 1407, ⓦ www.meininger-hostels.com. Bright and cheerful modern hostel, part of a German chain, secure and clean and located near the South Ken

museums. Free wi-fi. No kitchen; breakfast available. Dorms (4–12 beds), plus private rooms; rates vary depending on demand. **Dorms £22; doubles £120**

MYHOTEL CHELSEA MAP p.120, POCKET MAP D10. 35 Ixworth Place ⊖ South Kensington ☎ 020 7225 7500, ⓦ www. myhotels.com. Though the decor isn't to everyone's taste, and rooms small, they are well equipped and the atmosphere is peaceful. Good online deals. **£180**

NADLER KENSINGTON MAP p.120, POCKET MAP B10. 25 Courtfield Gardens ⊖ Earl's Court ☎ 020 7244 2255, ⓦ www. thenadler.com. Excellent-value boutique hotel. The 65 rooms range from singles and "luxury bunks" for two to "deluxe"; all are comfortable, clean and quiet, modern and attractive, with mini-kitchens. Good early-bird offers. **£150**

SAFESTAY HOLLAND PARK MAP p.120, POCKET MAP A8. Holland Walk ⊖ Holland Park ☎ 020 7870 9629, ⓦ safestay.com. With its picturesque location in Holland Park itself, this bright hostel is a good budget choice. The dorms, which sleep four to thirty-three, are clean and tidy (with curtains and reading lights) and showers, though you're stacked three-high in the bigger ones; the private twins (some en suite) have TVs. There's a garden, lounge and pool room, a café and laundry facilities, but no self-catering. Families and groups welcome. **Dorms £19; twins £80**

ST DAVID'S HOTELS MAP p.120, POCKET MAP D6. 14–20 Norfolk Square ⊖ Paddington ☎ 020 7723 3856, ⓦ www. stdavidshotels.com. Inexpensive, no-frills guesthouse famed for its English breakfast. Most rooms are en suite, and the large family rooms make it a good option for families on a budget. Free wi-fi in lobby (charge in rooms); no lift. **£100**

VANCOUVER STUDIOS MAP p.120, POCKET MAP B6. 30 Prince's Square ⊖ Bayswater ☎ 020 7243 1270, ⓦ www. vancouverstudios.co.uk. Good-value, luxurious and well-equipped self-catering suites (from singles to quads, some with balconies) in a stately Victorian townhouse with maid service and a pretty walled garden. Also apartments on site and nearby. **£150**

Greenwich

NUMBER 16 MAP p.148. 16 St Alfeges Passage ⊖ Cutty Sark DLR ☎ 020 8853 4337, Ⓦ st-alfeges.co.uk. Stylish three-room B&B – owned by a flamboyant ex-antique dealer/actor – offering a warm welcome and offbeat touches. **£125**

Kew and Richmond

THE OLD STABLES MAP p.154. 1 Bridle Lane, Twickenham. St Margarets train station from Waterloo ☎ 020 8892 4507, Ⓦ oldestables.com. Three bedrooms and one apartment in a house in a quiet street by the train station; walking distance to Richmond and the Thames. No on-site staff, but the manager is a phone call away and breakfast is provided. **£90**

ESSENTIALS

London transport

Arrival

The majority of visitors arrive in London at one of its five airports, all but one of which can involve an expensive trip to the centre. Those arriving by train or bus are dropped right in the middle of the city, with easy access to public transport.

By plane

Flying into London, you'll arrive at Heathrow, Gatwick, Stansted, Luton or City **airport**, each of which is less than an hour from the city centre.

Heathrow

Heathrow Airport (☎ 0844 335 1801, ⊛ heathrowairport.com) lies around fifteen miles west of central London, and is the city's busiest airport, with five terminals and three train/tube stations: one for terminals 1, 2 and 3, and separate ones for terminals 4 and 5. The fastest **train** service into London is the high-speed, non-stop Heathrow Express to Paddington station (daily 5am–11.40pm; journey 15min); tickets cost from £22–25 one-way or £37 return. The Elizabeth Line (Crossrail) runs four trains an hour from terminals 2, 3 and 4 to Paddington (with a service from terminal 5 from December 2019 onwards), with several stops on the way; Oyster pay-as-you-go £10.10 single.

A cheaper alternative is to take the Piccadilly **Underground** line, which connects the airport to numerous tube stations across central London (daily 5am–11pm; Fri & Sat 24hr to terminals 1, 2, 3 & 5; every 5min; journey 50min); tickets cost £5.10 peak times; £3.10 off peak single to zone 1 with an Oyster card (see page 176). A **taxi** from Heathrow will cost in the region of £50–85, depending on traffic and the time of day.

Gatwick

Gatwick Airport (☎ 0344 892 0322, ⊛ www.gatwickairport.com) is around thirty miles south of London, and has a train station at its South Terminal. Non-stop Gatwick Express **trains** run between the airport and London Victoria (daily around 5am–11pm; every 15min; journey 30min); £17.80 one way, £32.70 return, if bought online; group savings and other discounts available; ⊛ gatwickexpress. com. It's cheaper, however, to take a Southern train to Victoria (every 15min; journey 35min), or a First Capital Connect train to various stations within London (every 15–30min; journey 30–45min), including London Bridge and St Pancras; one-way tickets with Oyster: peak £16.20, off-peak £10.70; return ticket £20.50. National Express buses run from Gatwick direct to central London (daily 24hr; 1–2 hourly; 1hr 30min); tickets cost around £8–10 single. A **taxi** will set you back a ludicrous £100 or more, and take at least an hour.

Stansted

Stansted Airport (☎ 0808 169 7031, ⊛ www.stanstedairport.com) is roughly 35 miles northeast of the capital. Stansted Express **trains** run non-stop to Liverpool Street (5.30am–12.30am; every 15–30min; journey 45min), and cost £17 single, £29 return. National Express runs buses 24 hours a day calling at various places in London, including Victoria Coach Station (every 20–30min; journey 1hr 30min), with tickets for around £9–13 single. A **taxi** will set you back £100 or more, and take at least an hour.

Luton

London Luton Airport (☎ 01582 405100, ⊛ www.london-luton.co.uk) is roughly thirty miles north of London and mainly handles low-cost flights. A free shuttle bus takes five minutes to reach Luton Airport Parkway station, which is connected by **train** to King's Cross St Pancras (every 15–30min; journey 45min) and other stations in central London; single tickets cost around £14.70. National Express runs buses to Victoria Coach Station (daily 24hr; every 20min–1hr; journey 1hr 5min–1hr 20min; £6–12 one way). A **taxi** will cost in the region of £70–80 and take at least an hour to central London.

City

London City Airport (☎ 020 7646 0088, �🌐 www.londoncityairport. com), the capital's smallest and used primarily by business folk, is situated in the Royal Albert Docks, ten miles east of central London, and handles almost exclusively European flights. The **Docklands Light Railway** (DLR) takes you straight to Bank in the City (Mon–Sat 5.30am–12.15am, Sun 7am–11.15pm; every 8–15min; journey

20min), where you can change to the tube; use an Oyster card (see page 176). A **taxi** from the airport to the City's financial sector will cost around £20, and take half an hour or so.

By train and coach

Eurostar (☎ 0343 218 6186, �🌐 www. eurostar.com) trains arrive at the beautifully refurbished St Pancras International train station, next door to King's Cross, which is served by several Underground lines. Arriving by **train** from elsewhere in Britain (☎ 0345 748 4950, �🌐 www. nationalrail.co.uk), you'll come into one of London's numerous mainline stations, all of which have nearby Underground stations linking into the city centre's tube network. Coming into London by **coach** (☎ 0871 781 8181, �🌐 www.nationalexpress.com), you're most likely to arrive at Victoria Coach Station, a couple of hundred yards south down Buckingham Palace Road from Victoria train station and tube.

Getting around

London's transport system is generally efficient and comprehensive, though often overcrowded and can be subject to delays because of upgrade work. It is also one of the most expensive transport systems in the world.

   Transport for London (TfL) provides excellent free maps and information on bus and tube services from its **Visitor Information Centres**. Central ones include Euston, King's Cross, Victoria and Liverpool St (all Mon–Sat 8am–6pm, Sun 8.30am–6pm) plus Piccadilly Circus (daily 9.30am–4pm), Heathrow 2 & 3 Underground Station (daily 7.30am–8.30pm) and Gatwick North and South terminals (daily 9.15am–4pm). There's also a **24-hour**

helpline and an excellent website (☎ 0343 222 1234, �🌐 tfl.gov.uk).

   For transport purposes, London is divided into six concentric **zones** (plus a few extra in the northwest), with fares calculated depending on which zones you travel through: the majority of the city's accommodation and sights lie in zones 1 and 2. If you cannot produce a valid ticket for your journey, or travel further than your ticket allows, you will be liable to a **Penalty Fare** of £80, reduced to £40 if you pay within 21 days. Try and avoid travelling during the **rush hour** (Mon–Fri 8–9.30am and 5–7pm) if possible, when tubes can become unbearably crowded and hot, and some buses get so full they literally won't let you on.

Oyster cards, contactless payments and tickets

The cheapest, easiest way to get about London is to use a **Contactless debit or credit card** or **Oyster card**, London's transport smartcard, available from all tube stations and TfL Visitor Centres, and valid on the bus, tube, Docklands Light Railway (DLR), Tramlink, Overground, and almost all suburban rail services, Thames Clipper river boats and the cable car. The simplest way to use an Oyster card is as a pay-as-you-go card – you can top-up your card with credit at all tube stations and most newsagents. As you enter the tube or bus, simply touch in your card at the card reader and the fare will be taken off. If you're using the tube or train, you need to touch out again or up to £8 will be deducted (within London; £19.80 outside). Oyster operates daily price-capping from £6.80 (zones 1 and 2) to £12.50 (zones 1–6; more for outer zones). The system will stop taking money off your card, though you still need to touch in (and out). To obtain an Oyster card you must hand over a £5 refundable deposit or you can purchase a non-refundable Visitor Oyster Card for £5, for pay-as-you go travel, which comes with some tourist discounts. If you have a contactless debit or credit card, it works in the same way, though note not all overseas cards work and you may be charged overseas bank charges; weekly capping applies to contactless cards (£34.10 zone 1–2).

If you don't have an Oyster card, you can buy a paper **Visitor Pass** for two days for £25.40 or three days for £38.10 for zones 1–6, but Oyster is better value. Paper **Travelcards** from machines and booths at all tube and train stations start from £12.70 (zones 1 and 2) so really aren't worth it. Other paper tickets are also roughly double the cost of the Oyster equivalent.

Children under 11 travel for free; children aged 11–15 travel free on all buses and trams and at child-rate on the tube; children aged 16 or 17 can travel at child-rate on all forms of transport. However, all children over 10 must have a Zip Oyster photocard to be eligible for free travel – these should be applied for in advance online and cost £20; alternatively you can get an Oyster for a child that will charge half-price fares; ask at any station or visitor centre; a child's Visitor Pass costs £12.60 for two days.

The tube

Except for very short journeys, the **Underground** – or tube, as it's known to Londoners – is by far the quickest way to get about. Eleven different lines cross the metropolis, each with its own colour and name – all you need to know is which direction you're travelling in: northbound, eastbound, southbound or westbound (this gets tricky when taking the Circle Line). As a precaution, it's also worth checking the final destination displayed on the front of the train, as some lines, such as the District and Northern lines, have several different branches.

Services are frequent (Mon–Sat 5.30am–12.30am, Sun 7.30am–11.30pm), and you rarely have to wait more than five minutes for a train between central stations. A **Night Tube** core service covers five main lines for Fridays and Saturdays (every 10min), plus some of the Overground in East London. **Tickets** must be bought in advance from automatic machines. With an Oyster card most single fares range from £2.40 (zone 1 anytime) to £5.10 (zone 1 to 6 peak; £3.10 off peak). Paper ticket single fares are outrageously expensive – a journey in zone 1 costs an unbelievable £4.90 – so if you're intending to make more than one journey, an Oyster card is by far your best option.

Buses

London's famous double-decker **buses** are fun to ride on, with most running at a frequency of five to ten minutes during the day, and good value. Some stops have live departure information and there are several apps that will do the same for you, like Citymapper. Cash is not accepted on-board buses; you must pay with an Oyster card, Travelcard or contactless payment card. A single fare costs £1.50; you don't tap out on a bus and this fare allows you to change buses for up to an hour (you must tap-in every time you change bus but won't be charged).

A lot of bus stops are **request stops** (easily recognizable by their red sign) – stick your arm out to hail the bus or it will pass you by, and when on board ring the bell to request it to stop. Some buses run a 24-hour service, but most run between 5am and midnight. **Night-**buses (prefixed with the letter "N"), operating outside this period, depart at fifteen- to thirty-minute intervals, more frequently on some routes and on Friday and Saturday nights.

Overground, DLR and trains

The orange **Overground** line is a large network that connects with the tube in an outer loop from Richmond in the west to Stratford in the east. It's particularly useful for East London, where it runs every 5–15min; a night service runs from Highbury & Islington to New Cross Gate on Fridays and Saturdays. There are also **suburban trains**, useful for sights like Hampton Court, Richmond and Greenwich. For enquiries, call ☎ 0345 748 4950 or visit ⊛.nationalrail.co.uk or ⊛tfl.gov.uk. In East London, the **Docklands Light Railway** (DLR) runs driverless trains to Docklands, Greenwich and beyond. Oyster and Travelcards are valid on all suburban, Overground and DLR trains.

Museum tickets and the London Pass

London's big national museums – the British Museum, both Tate galleries, the National Gallery, the South Ken museums and more – are free, though they ask for (voluntary) donations and charge for special exhibits. Others, including the royal palaces, charge an entrance fee, and often ask for an additional donation of £1 or so (which has tax benefits for them). Prices quoted in this guide are the cheapest available. For many sights, it's worth buying tickets online in advance to save a few pounds. If you're thinking of visiting a lot of fee-paying attractions in a short space of time, it's worth considering buying a **London Pass** (⊛www.londonpass.com), which includes entry to a whole host of attractions including Hampton Court Palace, Kensington Palace, Kew Gardens, London Zoo, Westminster Abbey and the Tower of London. The pass costs around £69 for one day (£49 for kids), rising to £154 for six days (£114 for kids), though there are discounts to be had online. It often gives you "fast-track" entry as well. The pass can be bought online or in person from tourist offices and from London's mainline train and principal underground stations.

Cycling

Cycling is increasingly popular in London because – in the centre at least – it's the fastest way to get around. Only folding bikes can be taken on public transport, although conventional bikes can go on certain tube and railway lines at off-peak times – check ⓦtfl.gov.uk for details. London's public bicycle sharing scheme, officially **Santander Cycles**, is perfect for short journeys, with over seven hundred docking stations. It's £2 for access, after which the first 30 minutes are free; every subsequent 30 minutes costs £2. You need a bank card to use the scheme. Bikes can be **rented** from the London Bicycle Tour Company, 1a Gabriel Wharf on the South Bank (ⓞ020 7923 6838, ⓦlondonbicycle. com), costing around £20 a day or £50 a week.

Taxis

Compared to most capital cities, London's metered **black cabs** are an expensive option unless there are three or more of you (take note, they're not always black). The minimum fare is £2.60, and a ride from Euston to Victoria, for example, costs around £16–20 (Mon–Fri 5am–8pm). After 8pm on weekdays and all day during the weekend, a higher tariff applies, and after 10pm, it's higher still; all cabs accept contactless payments. Tipping is customary. An illuminated yellow light tells you if the cab is available – just stick your arm out to hail it. London's cabbies are the best trained in Europe; every one of them knows the shortest route between any two points in the capital, and they won't rip you off by taking another route.

Minicabs look just like regular cars and are considerably cheaper than black cabs, but they cannot be hailed from the street. All minicabs carry a private hire sticker and all drivers should have TfL ID.

The **Uber** app (ⓦwww.uber. com) is ubiquitous in London, and, despite some initial problems with its operating practices, retains its licence in the city. It's handy if you have a smart phone and internet access. The app connects you to the nearest Uber driver, and it normally takes under five minutes to reach you (you can't book ahead on the basic service). You pay through the app rather than paying the driver, so there's no need for cash. Prices for the standard UberX service can be up to fifty percent cheaper than black cabs (under £40 to Heathrow; under £10 across town). Be aware, though, that "surge" pricing operates at peak times (typically pub closing time), when they can be three times as much, but the app will let you know when this is operating.

Boats

Boat trips on the Thames are a fun way of sightseeing. The **Thames Clipper** service (ⓦthamesclippers.com) runs a regular commuter service (every 20–30min; approximately Mon–Fri 6am–9pm, Sat & Sun 8.30/9.30am–9pm, then hourly service until around 10.30/11pm) between the London Eye and Greenwich (including the O2), with some boats going as far as Woolwich. There are piers on both sides of the river, including Embankment, Bankside, Blackfriars, London Bridge and Tower. You can buy tickets at a pier, but there is a discount if you buy online in advance or use an Oyster card. Typical fares are £8.40 single (£6.50 with an Oyster), with an unlimited hop-on, hop-off River Roamer costing £16.30 if bought online, £19.50 from the pier. Other companies run boats upstream from Westminster to Kew, Richmond and Hampton Court from April to October (see page 153).

Congestion charge

All vehicles entering central London on weekdays between 7am and 6pm are liable to a congestion charge of £11.50 (£10.50 online) per vehicle; certain older, more polluting vehicles also have to pay additional emissions charges (£12.50; operating 24hr/day). Drivers can pay the charge online or over the phone (☎ 0343 222 2222), and must do so before midnight the same day; paying the next day costs £14 – 24 hours later, you'll be liable for a £160 **fine** (£80 if you pay within 14 days). Local residents, the disabled, motorcycles, minibuses and some alternative-fuel vehicles are exempt from the charge, but must register in order to qualify. For more details, visit ⊛ www.tfl.gov.uk.

Sightseeing tours and guided walks

Standard **sightseeing tours** are run by several rival bus companies, their open-top double-deckers setting off every thirty minutes from Victoria station, Trafalgar Square, Piccadilly and other conspicuous tourist spots. You can hop on and off several different routes as often as you like with The Original Tour (☎ 020 8877 1722, ⊛ theoriginaltour.com; daily 8.30am till 6 or 9pm, depending on the route; every 15–20min; £30.50 online).

A much cheaper option is to hop on a modern **London double-decker** – the #11 bus from Victoria station, for example, will take you past Westminster Abbey, the Houses of Parliament, up Whitehall, round Trafalgar Square, along the Strand and on to St Paul's Cathedral. Alternatively, you can take an old double-decker **Routemaster**, with open rear platform and roving conductor, on a "heritage" route (daily every 20min 9.30am-6.30pm); #15 from Trafalgar Square to Tower Hill.

Walking tours are infinitely more appealing and informative, mixing solid historical facts with juicy anecdotes in the company of a local specialist. Walks on offer range from a literary pub crawl round Bloomsbury to a roam around the East End. Tours cost approx £10 and take around two hours; normally you can simply show up at the starting point and join. If you want to plan – or book – walks in advance, contact the most reliable and well-established company, Original London Walks (☎ 020 7624 3978, ⊛ www.walks.com). Tours run daily from the City Information Centre by St Paul's (see page 80).

Directory A–Z

Addresses

London addresses come with postcodes at the end. Each street name is followed by a letter or letters giving the geographical location of the street in relation to the City (E for "east", WC for "west central" and so on) and a number that specifies its location more precisely. Unfortunately, this number doesn't correspond to the district's distance from the centre. Full postal addresses end with a digit and two letters, which specify the individual block.

Cricket

Most years three Test matches are played in London each summer: two at **Lord's** (ⓦ lords.org; ⊖ St John's Wood), the home of English cricket; the other at **The Oval** (ⓦ kiaoval.com; ⊖ Oval). There are also numerous one-day internationals and Twenty20 matches, some of which are usually held in London.

Crime

Should you have anything stolen or be involved in an incident that requires reporting, go to the local **police station** (ⓦ met.police.uk) or phone ☎ 101; the ☎ 999 number should only be used in emergencies. Central 24hr police stations include: Charing Cross, Agar St ⊖ Charing Cross; Holborn, 10 Lambs Conduit St ⊖ Holborn; and West End Central, 27 Savile Row ⊖ Oxford Circus. The City of London Police (ⓦ cityoflondon.police.uk) are separate from the Metropolitan Police, and have a police station at 182 Bishopsgate ⊖ Liverpool Street. If there's an incident on public transport, call the British Transport Police on ☎ 0800 405040.

Electricity

Electricity supply in London conforms to the EU standard of approximately 230V. Sockets are designed for British **three-pin plugs**, which are totally different from those in the mainland EU and North America.

Embassies and consulates

Australian High Commission Australia House, Strand ☎ 020 7379 4334, ⓦ uk.embassy. gov.au; ⊖ Temple. **Canadian High Commission** Trafalgar Square ☎ 020 7004 6000, ⓦ unitedkingdom.gc.ca; ⊖ Charing Cross. **Irish Embassy** 17 Grosvenor Place ☎ 020 7235 2171, ⓦ embassyofireland.co.uk; ⊖ Hyde Park Corner. **New Zealand High Commission** New Zealand House, 80 Haymarket ☎ 020 7930 8422, ⓦ nzembassy.com; ⊖ Piccadilly Circus. **South African High Commission** South Africa House, Trafalgar Square ☎ 020 7451 7299, ⓦ southafricahouseuk.com; ⊖ Charing Cross. **US** 33 Nine Elms Lane, Battersea ⊖ Vauxhall ☎ 020 7499 9000, ⓦ uk.usembassy.gov.

Football

Over the decades, London's most successful club by far has been **Arsenal** (☎ 020 7619 5000, ⓦ arsenal.com). However, since the arrival of Russian oil tycoon Roman Abramovich, fellow London club **Chelsea** (☎ 0371 811 1955, ⓦ chelseafc.com) have had a resurgence, winning the league five times since 2004. Chelsea's closest rivals (geographically) are **Fulham** (☎ 0843 208 1222, ⓦ fulhamfc. com), while Arsenal's are **Tottenham Hotspur** (☎ 0344 499 5000, ⓦ www. tottenhamhotspur.com). East London's premier club is **West Ham** (☎ 020 8548 2748, ⓦ whufc.com), based at the Olympic Stadium (see page 92). Tickets for most Premier League games start at £40–50 and are virtually impossible to get hold of on a casual basis, though you may be able to see one of the Cup fixtures. A better bet is to head to one of London's numerous, less illustrious clubs such as **Crystal Palace** (ⓦ cpfc.co.uk), **Millwall** (ⓦ millwallfc.co.uk), **Queens Park Rangers** (ⓦ qpr.co.uk) or **Charlton Athletic** (ⓦ cafc.co.uk).

Emergencies

For **police**, fire and ambulance services, call ☎ 999.

Health

For minor complaints, pharmacists, known as **chemists** in England, can dispense a limited range of drugs without a doctor's prescription. Most pharmacies are open standard shop hours, though some stay open later: Zafash, 233–235 Old Brompton Rd, SW5 (☎020 7373 2798; ⊖Earl's Court), is open 24 hours.

If there's an emergency, you can turn up at the **Accident and Emergency** (A&E) department of your local hospital, or phone for an ambulance (☎999). A&E services are free to all. For non-emergency health concerns you can phone the NHS ☎111 service; they can let you know the nearest place to go, including for dental emergencies.

Internet

Nearly all hotels and hostels in London have internet access. After that, your best bet is a café with **wi-fi**; try the one in Foyles bookshop at 107 Charing Cross Rd (⊖Tottenham Court Road). Alternatively, the Southbank Centre, the British Library, St Pancras station and many museums have free wi-fi.

Left luggage

Luggage storage facilities are available at all airports and major train terminals. The Excess Baggage Company (☎0800 077 4250, ⓦexcess-baggage.com) runs outlets at Heathrow, Gatwick and Luton terminals (generally 5am–11pm); and King's Cross, Liverpool Street, Euston, Charing Cross, Paddington, Victoria and Waterloo stations (generally 7am–11pm). All facilities cost around £20/24hr.
London City (Mon–Fri 5am–10pm, Sat 5am–1pm, Sun 11am–10.20pm; ☎020 7646 0000; £10/24hr).

LGBTQ travellers

Pink News (ⓦpinknews.co.uk) is a useful online news site. London LGBTQ Switchboard (daily 10am–11pm; ☎0300 330 0630, ⓦswitchboard. lgbt) runs a helpline for LGBTQ people, including legal advice and counselling.

Lost property

Airports Gatwick (daily 10am–4pm; ⓦlostproperty.org); Heathrow, terminals 3 and 5 ☎020 3761 1800, ⓦmissingx.com (daily 7am–7pm); London City ☎020 7646 0000; Luton ☎01582 809174; Stansted ☎0330 223 0893. **Eurostar** ☎0344 822 4411. **Transport for London** Lost Property Office, 200 Baker St NW1 ☎0343 222 1234, ⓦ.tfl.gov.uk (Mon–Fri 8.30am–4pm).

Money

The basic unit of **currency** is the pound sterling (£), divided into 100 pence (p). Coins come in denominations of 1p, 2p, 5p, 10p, 20p, 50p, £1 and £2; notes come in denominations of £5, £10, £20 and £50. Many shopkeepers may not accept £50 notes – the best advice is to avoid having to use them. The exchange rate can fluctuate considerably, but at the time of writing, £1 was worth US$1.28, €1.12, Can$1.67, Aus$1.75, NZ$1.94 and ZAR18. For the most up-to-date exchange rates, visit ⓦxe.com.

Credit/debit cards are by far the most convenient way to carry your money, and most hotels, shops and restaurants in London accept the major brand cards – with contactless payment ubiquitous (even in some markets) for small amounts, as well as on public transport. There are ATMs all over the city and every area has a branch of at least one of the big-four high-street **banks** (NatWest, Barclays, Lloyds and HSBC); opening hours are generally Mon–Fri 9.30am–4.30pm. Outside banking hours go to a **bureau**

de change; these can be found at train stations and airports and in most areas of the city centre.

The high **cost** of accommodation, food and drink make London a very expensive place to visit. Staying in a budget hotel and eating takeaways, you'll still need in the region of £85 per person per day (slightly less in a hostel). Add in a restaurant meal and tourist attraction or two, and you are looking at £100–120.

Opening hours

Generally speaking, opening hours are Monday to Saturday 9am or 10am to around 6pm and Sundays noon to 6pm. Some places in central London stay open until 8pm, and later on Thursdays and Fridays (around 9pm).

Phones

Public **payphones** in London are iconic, but are only used for photo opportunities nowadays.

If you're taking your **mobile/cell phone** with you, check with your service provider whether your phone will work abroad and what the call charges will be.

Post

The only (vaguely) late-opening post office is at 24–28 William IV St, WC2N 4DL, near Trafalgar Square (Mon–Fri 8.30am–6.30pm, Tues opens 9.15am, Sat 9am–5.30pm). To find other branches visit: ⓦ postoffice.co.uk.

Smoking

Smoking is banned in all indoor public spaces including all cafés, pubs, restaurants, clubs and public transport. These restrictions often cover e-cigarettes.

Time

Greenwich Mean Time (GMT) is used from the end of October to the end of March; for the rest of the year the country switches to **British Summer Time** (BST), one hour ahead of GMT. GMT is two hours behind South Africa; five hours ahead of the US East Coast; eight ahead of the US West Coast; and nine behind Australia's East Coast.

Tipping

There are no fixed rules for tipping. However, there's a certain expectation in restaurants or cafés that you should leave a tip of ten percent of the total bill – check first, though, that service has not already been included. As a general rule, tip when there is table service, but not when you go to the bar or are served drinks in a pub. Taxi drivers also expect tips – add about 10 to 12.5 percent of the fare – as do traditional barbers. The other occasion when you'll be expected to tip is in upmarket hotels where porters and table waiters rely on being tipped to bump up their often dismal wages.

Toilets

There are surprisingly few public toilets in London. All mainline train and major tube stations have toilets (though you will generally have to pay £0.30). Department stores and free museums and galleries are another good option.

Tourist information

Though there is no large proper, central tourist office in London, TfL Visitor Information Centres (see page 176) can provide information and tickets for attractions. The central **City of London Tourist Information Centre**, on the south side of St Paul's Cathedral (Mon–Sat 9.30am–5.30pm, Sun 10am–4pm; ☏ 020 7332 3456, ⓦ visitthecityco.uk; ⊖ St Paul's) serves the City of London. You can buy tickets to many attractions here, along with Oyster cards, and book guided tours (several walking tours depart from here each day), as well as find information about travel across England. Another useful borough tourist office is in **Greenwich** at the old Royal Naval College (daily 10am–5pm; ⓦvisitgreenwich.org.uk; Cutty Sark DLR).

The weekly **listings magazine** *Time Out* is free and comes out on a Tuesday, but for full listings, you need to visit their website (ⓦtimeout. com). Other useful **listings websites** include ⓦlondonist.com and ⓦ.londonnet.co.uk and the website of the free weekday *Evening Standard* (ⓦstandard.co.uk).

Travellers with disabilities

London is an old city, not well equipped for travellers with disabilities, though all public venues are obliged to make some effort towards accessibility. Public transport is improving, with buses now wheelchair accessible, and up to a quarter of all tube stations – they're marked with a blue symbol on the tube map. A useful source of information is ⓦtourismforall.org.uk.

Travelling with children

London is a great place for children and needn't overly strain the parental pocket. The city boasts lots of excellent parks and gardens, public transport is free for under 11s and many of the major museums can be visited free of charge. For the most part kids are tolerated in cafés and restaurants – and pubs in the daytime.

Festivals and events

London Parade

January 1 ⓦlnydp.com.
At noon, a procession of floats, marching bands, cheerleaders and clowns wends its way from Parliament Square to Green Park. Admission charge for grandstand seats in Piccadilly, otherwise free.

Chinese New Year

late January/early to mid-February ⓦwww.chinatownlondon.org.
Soho's Chinatown, Leicester Square and even Trafalgar Square all erupt in a riot of dancing dragons and firecrackers – expect serious human congestion. Free.

Oxford and Cambridge Boat Race

late March/early April ⓦtheboatrace. org.
Since 1845 rowers from Oxford and Cambridge universities have battled it out over four miles from Putney to Mortlake. The pubs at prime vantage points pack out early. Free.

London Marathon

third or fourth Sunday in April ⓦvirginlondonmarathon.com.
The world's most popular marathon, with around forty thousand masochists sweating the 26.2-mile route. Most of the competitors are running for charity, often in some ludicrous costume. Free.

IWA Canalway Cavalcade

May Bank Holiday weekend ⓦwww. waterways.org.uk.
Lively three-day celebration of the city's inland waterways, held at Little Venice, with scores of decorated narrow boats, Morris dancers and lots of children's activities. Free.

Beating Retreat

early June ⓦhouseholddivision.org.uk
Annual military display on Horse Guards' Parade over two consecutive

evenings, marking the old custom of drumming and piping the troops back to base at dusk. Tickets must be booked in advance.

Trooping the Colour

second Saturday in June
ⓦ householddivision.org.uk
Ticket-only celebration of the Queen's official birthday featuring massed bands, gun salutes and fly-pasts. The royal procession along the Mall allows you a glimpse for free, and there are rehearsals (minus Her Majesty) on the two preceding Saturdays.

Wimbledon Lawn Tennis Championships

first two weeks of July ⓦ www.wimbledon.com.
This Grand Slam tournament (played on grass) is one of the highlights of the sporting and social calendar.

Pride London

late June or early July ⓦ www.prideinlondon.org.
A month of LGBTQ events – performances, film-screenings and so on – culminates in a colourful, whistle-blowing march through the city streets followed by a rally and concert in Trafalgar Square.

Henry Wood Promenade Concerts

mid-July to mid-September ⓦ bbc.co.uk/proms.
Commonly known as the Proms, this series of nightly classical concerts at the Royal Albert Hall (and elsewhere) is a well-loved British institution.

Notting Hill Carnival

last bank holiday weekend in August
ⓦ nottinghillcarnivalguide.com.
World famous two-day street festival established nearly fifty years ago, Carnival is a tumult of imaginatively decorated floats, eye-catching costumes, thumping sound systems, live bands, irresistible food and huge crowds. Free.

Open House

third weekend in September
ⓦ londonopenhouse.org.
A once-a-year opportunity to peek inside over 750 buildings around London, many of which don't normally open their doors to the public. You'll need to book in advance for some of the more popular places. Free.

London Film Festival

late October ⓦ www.bfi.org.uk/lff.
A two-week cinematic season with scores of new international films screened at the BFI Southbank, some West End venues and beyond.

Public holidays

You'll find all banks and offices closed on the following days, while everything else pretty much runs to a Sunday schedule (except on Christmas Day when everything shuts down; museums and sights are often closed Dec 24–26): New Year's Day (January 1); Good Friday (late March/April); Easter Monday (late March/April); Spring Bank Holiday (first Monday in May); May Bank Holiday (last Monday in May); August Bank Holiday (last Monday in Aug); Christmas Day (Dec 25); Boxing Day (Dec 26). Note that if January 1, December 25 or December 26 falls on a Saturday or Sunday, the holiday falls on the following weekday.

Bonfire Night

November 5

In memory of Guy Fawkes – who tried to blow up King James I and the Houses of Parliament in 1605 – effigies are traditionally burned on bonfires. Today, the council-run celebrations tend to stick to fireworks displays. Some free; some are ticketed. Alexandra Palace is a good vantage point.

Lord Mayor's Show

second Saturday in November
Ⓦ lordmayorsshow.london.

Big ceremonial procession from Mansion House to the Law Courts on the Strand and back again. Some 140 floats and military bands followed by the new Mayor in his gilded coach and a whole train of liverymen in carriages. After dark, there's a fireworks display on the Thames. Free.

New Year

New Year's Eve Ⓦ london.gov.uk.
New Year is seen in by a spectacular fireworks display centred on the London Eye. TfL runs free public transport all night. Advance tickets required for access to riverside areas.

Chronology

43 AD Romans invade and establish a permanent military camp by the Thames called Londinium.

c.61 Queen Boudica, leader of the Iceni tribe, burns Londinium to the ground.

c.100 Londinium becomes the capital of the Roman province of Britannia, boasting a vast basilica, a forum and an amphitheatre.

410 The Romans abandon Londinium and leave the place at the mercy of marauding Saxon pirates.

871–1066 The Danes and Norwegians fight it out with the kings of Wessex over who should control London.

1066 Following the defeat of the English King Harold at the Battle of Hastings, William the Conqueror, Duke of Normandy, is crowned king in Westminster Abbey.

1290 King Edward I expels London's Jewish population.

1348 The Black Death wipes out a third of London's population of 75,000.

1381 During the Peasants' Revolt, London is overrun by the rebels who lynch the archbishop, plus countless rich merchants and clerics.

1532–39 The Reformation: King Henry VIII breaks with the Roman Catholic church, establishes the Church of England, dissolves the monasteries and executes religious dissenters.

1553–58 The religious pendulum swings the other way as Elizabeth's fervently Catholic sister, forever known as "Bloody Mary", takes to the throne and it's the Protestants' turn to be martyred.

1558–1603 During the reign of Elizabeth I, London enjoys an economic boom and witnesses the English Renaissance, epitomized by the theatre of William Shakespeare.

1603 James VI of Scotland becomes James I of England, thereby uniting the two crowns and marking the beginning of the Stuart dynasty in England.

1605 The Gunpowder Plot to blow up the Houses of Parliament (and King

James I along with it) is foiled and Guy Fawkes and his Catholic conspirators executed.

1642–49 English Civil War between the Parliamentarians and Royalists ends with the victory of the former under the leadership of Oliver Cromwell. King Charles I (1625–49) is tried and beheaded in Westminster.

1660 The Restoration: Charles I's son, Charles II (1660–1685), returns from exile to restore the monarchy and encourages the development of the arts and sciences.

1665 The Great Plague kills some one hundred thousand Londoners, around a fifth of the population.

1666 The Great Fire rages for four days, kills just seven people but destroys four-fifths of the City.

1714–1830 The Georgian period: from the reign of George I to George IV, London's population doubles to one million, making it Europe's largest city. The period is one of boom and bust, gin drinking, rioting and hanging.

1750 Westminster Bridge opens, the first rival river crossing to London Bridge in over seven centuries.

1836 London gets its first railway line from London Bridge to Greenwich.

1837–1901 During the reign of Queen Victoria, London becomes the capital of an empire that stretches across the globe. Its population increases to nearly seven million, making it the largest city in the world. Industrialization brings pollution, overcrowding and extreme poverty.

1851 The Great Exhibition is held in a giant glasshouse known as the "Crystal Palace", erected in Hyde Park.

1855 The Metropolitan Board of Works is established to organize the rapidly expanding city's infrastructure.

1914–18 During World War I, London experiences its first aerial attacks, with Zeppelin raids leaving some 650 dead – a minor skirmish in the context of a war that takes the lives of millions.

1939–45 During the course of World War II, London suffers a lot of bomb damage, with sixty thousand killed and many thousands more made homeless.

1948 The SS *Windrush* brings the first postwar immigrants to London from the West Indies; over the next two decades, thousands more follow from former colonies.

1951 The Festival of Britain is held on the south bank of the Thames in an attempt to dispel the postwar gloom. The Royal Festival Hall is its one lasting legacy.

1960s Pop music and fashion helps turn London into the centre of the "Swinging Sixties", with King's Road and Carnaby Street the hippest places to be seen.

1980s Under the Conservative Thatcher government, the gap between rich and poor grows. London's elected governing body is abolished.

2000 London gets to vote for its own Mayor (Ken Livingstone) and its elected assembly. London's national museums introduce free entry; the London Eye and Tate Modern open.

2005 A day after London is awarded the 2012 Olympics, on July 7, the city is hit by four suicide bombers who kill themselves and over fifty commuters in four separate explosions.

2008 Conservative candidate Boris Johnson defeats Ken Livingstone and becomes Mayor.

2012 London hosts the Olympic games for the third time.

2016 London elects Labour candidate Sadiq Khan as mayor. Seven weeks later the UK votes to leave the EU (though in London a majority voted to remain).

2017 Three separate terror incidents (Westminster, London Bridge and Finsbury Park) shake the city. In June, the UK votes in a "snap" general election. The Conservatives come first, but without a majority. In London, the Labour Party increases its dominance.

2018 Two key ministers, including Foreign Secretary Boris Johnson, resign in protest at government's plans for a free trade area with the European Union.

SMALL PRINT

Publishing Information
Fifth edition 2019

Distribution
UK, Ireland and Europe
Apa Publications (UK) Ltd; sales@roughguides.com
United States and Canada
Ingram Publisher Services; ips@ingramcontent.com
Australia and New Zealand
Woodslane; info@woodslane.com.au
Southeast Asia
Apa Publications (SN) Pte; sales@roughguides.com
Worldwide
Apa Publications (UK) Ltd; sales@roughguides.com

Special Sales, Content Licensing and CoPublishing
Rough Guides can be purchased in bulk quantities at discounted prices. We can create special editions, personalised jackets and corporate imprints tailored to your needs. sales@roughguides.com.
roughguides.com
Printed in China by RR Donnelley Asia Printing Solutions Limited

A catalogue record for this book is available from the British Library
The publishers and authors have done their best to ensure the accuracy and currency of all the information in **Pocket Rough Guide London**, however, they can accept no responsibility for any loss, injury, or inconvenience sustained by any traveller as a result of information or advice contained in the guide.

Rough Guide Credits
Editors: Helen Fanthorpe, Zara Sekhavati
Cartography: Ed Wright
Managing editor: Rachel Lawrence
Picture editor: Michelle Bhatia
Cover photo research: Tom Smyth
Original design: Richard Czapnik
Senior DTP coordinator: Dan May
Head of DTP and Pre-Press: Rebeka Davies

Acknowledgements
Alice would like to raise a glass to Team Rough Guides.

Author biography
Alice Park is a freelance editor and writer. She has edited numerous guidebooks and co-authored guides to Switzerland, Germany and Austria, as well as her native London. She has worked on previous editions of this guide along with Samantha Cook.

Help us update

We've gone to a lot of effort to ensure that this edition of the **Pocket Rough Guide London** is accurate and up-to-date. However, things change – places get "discovered", opening hours are notoriously fickle, restaurants and rooms raise prices or lower standards. If you feel we've got it wrong or left something out, we'd like to know, and if you can remember the address, the price, the hours, the phone number, so much the better.

Please send your comments with the subject line "**Pocket Rough Guide London Update**" to mail@uk.roughguides.com. We'll credit all contributions and send a copy of the next edition (or any other Rough Guide if you prefer) for the very best emails.

Photo Credits

(Key: T-top; C-centre; B-bottom; L-left; R-right)

Alamy 2T, 14B, 16T, 28, 48, 50, 63, 64, 67, 71, 72, 76, 82, 86, 87, 91, 93, 94, 96, 97, 110, 134, 138, 139, 160, 161
Dreamstime.com 10
Flesh & Buns 62
Getty Images 14T, 16B, 84
iStock 2BL, 2BR, 5, 12T, 15T, 17B, 31, 53, 66, 85, 92, 99, 102, 111, 115, 147, 149, 150, 151, 158, 172/173
Jon Arnold / AWL Images 22/23
Mandarin Oriental Hotel Group 131
Mark Thomas/Rough Guides 17T, 18MC, 19T, 45, 59, 60, 98, 104, 107, 144
Museum of Brands, Packaging and Advertising 127
Natascha Sturny/Rough Guides 12B, 18T, 19C, 19B, 146, 152
Patricia Niven/Anchor & Hope 108

Paul Massey 162-163
Shutterstock 2MC, 4, 6, 11T, 11B, 13C, 12/13B, 15B 20TC, 20MC, 20MC, 21TC, 21MC, 21MC, 24, 27, 30, 32, 33, 34, 36, 37, 39, 40, 42, 44, 46, 47, 49, 51, 52, 56, 57, 61, 65, 69, 70, 73, 77, 78, 80, 83, 89, 103, 106, 109, 114, 116, 117, 118, 119, 122, 123, 124, 125, 126, 128, 129, 130, 132, 133, 137, 140, 141, 155, 156, 157
Spencer House, London 38
Suzanne Porter/Rough Guides 43, 153
The National Gallery, London 25
Travel Pix Collection / AWL Images 1
Trustees of the Geffrye Museum, London 88
Vivi Pham/Pidgin 95
ZSL 136

Cover: Houses of Parliament **Maurizio Rellini /4Corners Images**

Index

NOTES

NOTES